REDFERN

LIANG CH'I-CH'AO
AND THE MIND OF MODERN CHINA

Liang Ch'i-ch'ao

AND THE MIND OF MODERN CHINA

by

Joseph R. Levenson

UNIVERSITY OF CALIFORNIA PRESS

BERKELEY AND LOS ANGELES 1967

University of California Press
Berkeley and Los Angeles

Cambridge University Press
London, England

PUBLISHED BY ARRANGEMENT WITH HARVARD UNIVERSITY PRESS AND
WITH THAMES AND HUDSON LTD., LONDON

LIBRARY OF CONGRESS CATALOG CARD NUMBER: 53-5069

PRINTED IN THE UNITED STATES OF AMERICA

TO MY FATHER AND MOTHER

PREFACE

Liang Ch'i-ch'ao, a brilliant scholar, journalist, and political figure, contributed heavily to modern Chinese history and helped unwittingly to reveal its meaning. Both his "visible" career and the inner history of his thoughts fall naturally into three consecutive stages. I have tried in the three parts of this study to be first a chronicler, to recount his contribution, and next a historian, to comprehend it.

In Chapters I, III, and V, I describe what meets the eye, the top of the iceberg, the public record. Liang, whose life is thus chronicled, could have done that much himself. He knew what he did. But only others could know what he was. Self-knowledge is a remarkably elusive thing, for the self is transformed in the knowing, and Liang, trapped like any man in his own present, could hardly reveal himself and remain himself. He could not have written the even-numbered chapters, Chapters II, IV, and VI. Had Liang been able to write them, he could never have been their subject; if a man had the key to his own prison, he would not stay fixed where he was.

Liang's prison was a mind laced with necessary inconsistencies, incompatible ideas which he had to believe—not for their logical coherence but because of his personal need. My effort as historian, after giving the record of what he did, is to find out what wracked him as he did it. But this work is not, in its ends, a psychological study of Liang. One should see in it rather a search for news about the "mind of modern China," about history as well as biography, about the way a culture and a society, not just a personality, change and develop. For all the steady concentration on Liang, my intent is to establish what his milieu expected of him and could offer him. When we find Liang using European ideas which in Europe agitated people in a different way, or when we find him putting a different construction on Chinese ideas from that which earlier Chinese had put on them, we learn something not only about Liang but about

societies, how and why China differs from Europe and the Ch'ing
Dynasty from the Han. I have tried throughout the book to maintain an interplay between history and individual, bringing historical analysis to bear on Liang's writings and returning with what
Liang's writings reveal to throw more light upon history.

To write historically of Liang Ch'i-ch'ao is to recognize the rela-
tivities of his situation. The very last impression I would like to
leave is that I want to make debating points and cut down a magnificent reputation. When I speak of "inconsistencies," I mean to show
not that Liang was ridicuolus to think as he did—which would be
odiously presumptuous, false, and in any case historically irrelevant
—but that it was *reasonable* for him to think as he did. And this is
what gives him a specifically historical significance. A philosopher
may test thought for an essentially timeless rationality. But an intellectual historian is particularly concerned with *thinking,* to probe
beneath it for a time's questions by divining how it is reasonable—
perhaps in spite of or precisely because of imperfect rationality.

This approach, and the main conclusions of the work, are found
principally in the analytic chapters, the second chapters in the three
parts. The reader may feel upset shuttling back and forth between
these speculative chapters, with their intuitive treatment of the
material and their broadly significant hero, and the earthbound,
declarative chapters, following a narrow individual like a thin red
line through Chinese history. But perhaps it is helpful to back and
fill. We must be reminded periodically that Liang thought of himself as a force, not as a symbol. He did not mean to live that we
might deduce. We want to generalize about history from the individual and see him as in some way representative, but the person we
see had a single, particular life, and we need to know it. It is a difficult task to discover modern China in a man's mind. A knowledge
of his career, of the possibilities which China afforded to the owner
of the mind, is a check on our discovery.

Like so many students of Chinese history, I am deeply indebted
to John K. Fairbank for great kindness, information, keen criticism,
and stimulating ideas. Francis Cleaves and Lien-sheng Yang have

read portions of the manuscript and have assisted me generously, especially in connection with textual and translation problems. I am grateful, also, to A. Kaiming Chiu, Chase J. Duffy, Marius Jansen, Thomas C. Smith, Arthur Wright, and Mary Wright for their useful suggestions, and to David Aberle, Marion Levy, and Rhoads Murphey for our conversations, over a period of years, which helped me in writing this book, but which were important to me on more serious grounds than that.

The book is largely a product of my years as a Junior Fellow of the Society of Fellows at Harvard. I can hardly express my gratitude to the Society for the intellectual stimulation and material support it has afforded me.

I thank Faber and Faber, Ltd., and Harcourt, Brace and Co. for permission to quote several lines from "The Dry Salvages," by T. S. Eliot. A considerable portion of Chapters I and II has appeared in the *Journal of the History of Ideas.*

Chinese characters have not been inserted in the body of the text. They will be found in the end, in a glossary of transliterated names, titles, terms, and phrases.

J. R. L.

February 1959

Postscript

Unfortunately, it has not been possible for me to make a serious revision of the original 1953 text. Some slight changes in wording could be included in the 1959 edition, which must remain the basis of the present reprint. A considerable amount of new material bearing on Liang's career has been published in recent years, beginning with the documentary collection, *Wu-hsü pien-fa* (The Reform of 1898) (Shanghai, 1953). Most important, of course, is Ting Wen-chiang, *Liang Jen-kung hsien-sheng nien-p'u ch'ang-pien ch'u-kao* (First draft of a chronological biography of Liang Ch'i-ch'ao) (Taipei, 1959). This has contributed markedly to the composition of recent monographs, notably Chang Peng-yuan, *Liang Ch'i-ch'ao yü Ch'ing-chi ko-ming* (Liang Ch'i-ch'ao and the revolution at the end of the Ch'ing period) (Nan-kang, Taiwan, 1964). As a biography, then, *Liang Ch'i-ch'ao and the Mind of Modern China* is very far from "definitive." I hope, however, that it will still seem to offer at least a serviceable biographical context to its real subject: the evocation of history from the writings of a lifetime.

J. R. L.

July 1966

CONTENTS

Introduction: INTELLECTUAL HISTORY AND THE INDIVIDUAL
THINKER, I

Part One 1873-1898: METAMORPHOSIS

 I LIANG AND THE REFORM MOVEMENT, 15
Youth and Education. Reform Activity in Peking. The
Shih-wu pao. Liang at Changsha. The "Hundred Days."

 II THE BREAKDOWN OF THE CONFUCIAN WORLD, 34
Revision of Tradition and Social Change. Syncretism: West-
ern "Idea of Progress" in a Chinese Context. Analogy of
Patterns of Culture-Growth and Analogy of Cultural Values.
Inflationary Distortion. Obscurantism and Self-Effacement.
Rejection of Tradition.

Part Two 1898-1912: BRAVE NEW WORLD

 III EXILE IN JAPAN AND THE WEST, 55
The Escape to Japan. Relations between Revolutionaries
and Reformers. Liang's Work in Japan, 1898-1899. Hawaiian Journey. The Hankow Rising. Liang Overseas and
in Japan, 1900-1903. Liang in America. The Last Years of
Exile. Liang's Influence in His Japanese Years.

 IV THE SUBSTITUTE FOR TRADITION, 84
The Bankruptcy of the Chinese Tradition. The Last Stage
of Liang's Confucian Traditionalism. The Break with Tra-
dition. More Blows against the Historical Culture as the
Basis of Comparison. Culturalism and Nationalism. The
Chinese Nation Confronts the West. The Logical Contra-
dictions in Liang's Second Position: The Role of the In-
dividual in History, The Aims of the Historian, "Patriotic
Schizophrenia." Off-Stage Trumpets: First Heralds of a
New Synthesis. Liang and the Revolutionaries.

xi

Part Three   1912-1929: REMEMBRANCE OF THINGS PAST

V   FROM POLITICS TO SCHOLARSHIP, 173
>   Politics. Liang in Office. The Monarchical Plans of Yuan
>   Shih-k'ai. The Yunnan Revolt. Return to the Peking Politi-
>   cal Arena. The Last Decade.

VI   BACK TO CHINA—THE LAST DEFENSE, 193
>   Liang's Recapitulation. The Decline of the West. The New
>   Syncretism. Persistence of Earlier Rationalizations. Liang's
>   Hostility to Communism. The Area of Agreement between
>   Liang and the Communists. Liang and the Pro-Western
>   Liberals. Conclusion.

Appendix: THE CONTROVERSY OVER THE AUTHENTICITY
>   OF THE CONFUCIAN CLASSICS, 221

Bibliography, 224

Glossary, 230

Index, 249

LIANG CH'I-CH'AO AND THE MIND
OF MODERN CHINA

ABBREVIATIONS USED IN THE NOTES

China-Archiv (Archiv für den Fernen Osten)	CA
Chinese Recorder and Missionary Journal	CR
Chinese Students' Monthly	CSM
Ch'ing-shih kao [Draft history of the Ch'ing Dynasty]	CSK
Hsüeh-heng [Critical Review]	HH
I-chiao ts'ung-pien [Compilation of miscellaneous papers in support of orthodox doctrine]	ICTP
Kuang-hsü cheng-yao [Important political events of the Kuang-hsü reign]	KHCY
Kuang-hsü tung-hua hsü-lu [Kuang-hsü supplement to the archival records]	THL
Millard's Review of the Far East	MR
Mitteilungen des Seminars für Orientalische Sprachen	MSOS
National Review	NR
North China Herald and Supreme Court and Consular Gazette	NCH
Pei-chuan chi pu [Supplement to the *Pei-chuan chi*]	PCCP
Peking Gazette	PG
Shih-hsüeh nien-pao [Historical annual]	SHNP
Shirin [Forest of history]	SR
Ta-feng [The typhoon magazine]	TF
T'ien Hsia Monthly	THM
T'oung pao	TP
T'u-shu-kuan-hsüeh chi-k'an [Library science quarterly]	TSKHCK
Yenching hsüeh-pao [Yenching journal of Chinese studies]	YCHP
Yin-ping-shih ho-chi [Collected works and essays of the Ice-Drinkers' Studio]:	
ch'üan-chi (Collected works)	YPSHC-CC
Wen-chi (Collected essays)	YPSHC-WC
This most recent and complete collection of Liang's writings has been referred to for works not included in the following:	
Yin-ping-shih wen-chi [Collected essays of the Ice-Drinkers' Studio]	YPSWC

INTELLECTUAL HISTORY AND THE INDIVIDUAL THINKER

THERE IS more to biography than the life of an individual. A life-story is not just a "brick for the structure," one of an infinite number of possible monographs which add up to history. A historian who thinks so merely accumulates, and never understands.

But if a man's life is not just a piece of history, neither is it a model-to-scale. We must not think that Liang Ch'i-ch'ao, for example, is a microcosm, with all of modern China locked in his archetypical mind. Many Chinese disagreed with him, at one or all of his life's stages. His opponents, however, no less than his followers, can be comprehended in Liang's story. For a historian can do more than list antagonistic ideas; he can link them. History can be deduced from biography, society derived from the individual.

First, the biography: Every man has an emotional commitment to history and an intellectual commitment to value, and he tries to make these commitments coincide. A stable society is one whose members would choose, on universal principles, the particular culture which they inherit. In its great ages, the Chinese Empire had been such a society. Chinese had loved their civilization not only because they were born into it but because they thought it good. In the nineteenth century, however, history and value were torn apart in many Chinese minds. Liang Ch'i-ch'ao (1873–1929) began writing, in the 1890's, as one who was straining against his tradition intellectually, seeing value elsewhere, but still emotionally tied to it, held by his history.

A man who feels such a tension will seek to ease it, and Liang tried to smother the conflict between history and value. His device was to rethink Chinese tradition so that Confucianism, to which

1

he was predisposed as a product of the history of his own society, should include what he valued in the West. As a disciple of K'ang Yu-wei and, ultimately, of the scholars of the "Han Learning" (seventeenth and eighteenth centuries), he persuaded himself that the authentic teachings of Confucius had been obscured by textual falsifiers and by ignorant or dishonest commentators. If the genuine classics were properly understood, so that Confucius' real intentions were known (and surely every Chinese tradition-alist must reverence the Sage's intentions), it would be clear that the classics foretold and insisted upon the eventual triumph of science, democracy, prosperity, and peace. Now, in the claims of European optimists, these were the promised fruits of Western civilization. And Liang was a westernizer, appealing to the Chi-nese to emulate Western achievements. But it is a striking fact that almost always he cloaked his appeal in the authority of the classics. A good Confucianist must long to see railroads through mountains, representative government, and educated women with unbound feet.

In short, he tried to preserve China from the imputation of failure even as he acknowledged what appeared to be Western success; and he did this in the nineties by arguing, in effect, that Western and Chinese ideals were really the same. This was one way to contemplate the westernization of China and still to assert the equivalence of China and the West. There were other ways, and Liang tried two of them in succession.

First, roughly from 1899 to 1919, he dispensed with the Con-fucian sugar-coating and covered his Westernism with a new non-culturalistic Chinese nationalism. Tradition could be flouted to strengthen the nation, for nation, not culture, was the unit of equivalence; it was not between Chinese and Western civiliza-tions that the issue lay, but between China and Western nation-states. The complexities of this defense forbid our discussing it here. Suffice it to say that it contained historically necessary logical inconsistencies. They came from his nationalistic need both to disparage the Chinese past and to prize it, to admire the West and to grudge the admiration. These inconsistencies represented pressure on the future. They made him destined to move to a new position whenever he should be able to think that Western civilization was discredited; and the First World War gave him that opportunity.

In the last decade of his life, in his third phase, Liang cheerfully argued that Western and Chinese ideals were really opposed. The West was materialistic, the East was spiritual. Previously, like any philistine nineteenth-century European optimist, Liang had believed in the inevitability of progress and had respected Europe for its progressive achievements. But now the progressive Europeans had marched themselves, onward and upward, into rats' alley. The advancement of science, the conquest of the material, had been their only progress, and science had left them spiritually bankrupt. The non-scientific tradition of China had once been the despair of Chinese like Liang, but now the reputation of their "unprogressive" civilization could be rehabilitated. It was Europe's turn for defeatism.

Liang, however, was not a Gandhi. Matter had its place in spiritual China. The fruits of science could be used. When the West worshiped science and proclaimed the faith of science that all was matter, the West had chosen death. But China had always known that not everything was matter, and China, secure in this knowledge, was spiritual and alive. Because the living can safely manipulate things, China could borrow things from the West. And when China borrowed now, it condescended.

Liang's formula in this third phase is no longer what it was in the nineties, in his first phase. Then he had said, in effect, "Science is good, and we can accept it because our traditions provide for it"; now he said, "Science is bad, unless padded by spirituality, which we have and the West has not." Respect for the Chinese past is authorized just for its lack of concern with machines. China stands straight, claiming, now, not to be *gifted* with the scientific spirit as the West is gifted, but to be *untainted* by it as the West is not.

Let us pause here to recapitulate the stages in Liang's way.

First, he tried to smuggle Western values into Chinese history. Second, he denied that "West" and "China" were the really significant terms for comparison. Loyalty was due the nation, not the culture, and besides, the issue in culture-change, as he represented it, was between "the new" and "the old," not between the West and China. The nations of the West had not "westernized" but had modernized themselves, and China could do the same and yet be free of the specter of debt. Third, he reintroduced "West" and "China" as meaningful abstractions and arranged them in a dichotomy of "matter" and "spirit."

We see, then, how Liang changes his mind. But the fact that his mind, one mind, encompasses all these changes assures us that a unity persists beneath them. Alfred North Whitehead, adapting from Plato, has written of something called personal identity or personal unity, which pervades our life-thread of occasions. Personal identity, writes Whitehead, is a locus which persists, an emplacement for all the occasions of experience.[1]

What this means for Liang Ch'i-ch'ao, and for his biographer, is this: Liang's changing ideas are a continuous adjustment of changing outer perceptions to a fixed inner need. This need is the need of a satisfying answer to a persisting question. When we know this question, we come as close as we can to glimpsing his personal identity, to piercing through to persisting, continuous Liang, who binds together, by *his* thinking them, ideas which seem outwardly disconnected. It is the question which imposes unity on all the perceptions which are his food for thought.

The question must be found by hypothesis. What question, we must ask, is the one question to which each of Liang's successive ideas can be construed as an answer? When we find this question, we find the unifying principle which works in his ideas. And this principle, deduced from biography, is a key to the intellectual history in which the individual plays his part.

For there are two unities imposed upon ideas in history, and knowledge of one means knowledge of the other. First, as we

[1] Alfred North Whitehead, *Adventures of Ideas* (New York, 1933), 240-241.

have suggested, the personal identity of a single individual gives a unity to different ideas thought "vertically," in passing time. Second, contemporaneity, the horizontal in time, gives a unity, in one society, to different ideas thought by many individuals. And if the lines intersect, if the single individual of the first instance is one of the many individuals of the second, the unifying principle in his case and in the case of them all will be the same. There is one question to which each of society's simultaneous ideas can be construed as an answer, and it is the same question as the one behind the successive ideas of the individual. Now we can read from the individual to the society. When we recognize Liang's question, we grasp the meaning of anti-Liang ideas. For the thought of Liang's antagonists is as much an answer to his question as his own thought is.

Let us consider, for example, Chinese Communism, spreading in the 1920's and harshly critical of traditional Chinese civilization. This was the period in which Liang was celebrating that civilization as spiritual rather than material. The question to which this was Liang's last answer has already been suggested in our sketch of his intellectual life. This is the question: how can a Chinese be reconciled to the observable dissipation of his cultural inheritance—or how can a China in full process of westernization feel itself equivalent to the West? This question is the inner link between Liang and the Communists, that link which *is* contemporaneity. For a Communist answer was entirely compatible with Liang's question.

If a need for conviction of China's equivalence to the West is buried in Liang's ideas, it is somewhere buried in every modern Chinese theory of Chinese culture, from the most traditionalist to the most radically iconoclastic. Intellectuals who were alienated from their own tradition could yet never rest easy with a westernization which seemed to enjoin on China a spirit of humility; for them, the existence in the West of revolutionary ideas, critical of the very civilization which had impinged on China, offered one way out. No longer had China either to cling to a moribund system or to defer respectfully to a West of unchallengeable prestige. Association with Russia in Communism would seem to put China at the head of the queue, even while it rejected its own traditional culture. Now it could be something more than equivalent to that once-superior West which had forced this rejection on it.

Thus, we see how Liang's life story gives a clue to a history outside it. The question which is extracted from beneath his changing answers is a question which is asked by his contemporaries. This knowledge, however, brings us only half the distance from biography to history. For history involves a society in time. From a study of Liang, an individual in time, we have made our way to society. But we see it as a cluster of contemporaries, society at a moment. How can we grasp what the passage of time means to it?

What can, indeed, the passage of time mean to it? If Liang's thoughts, throughout his life, are threaded on a single question, and if his contemporaries, young and old, must share this question with him, then *their* contemporaries, young and old, and so on throughout eternity, would seem to be drawn to the same question and men's minds stand still forever. Yet, paradoxically enough, the question which does persist in passing time does also, somehow, change in it. It is the kind of change—toward anachronism, encroaching death in persisting life—which only history makes. Contemporaries are yoked in the question, but this change in the question, its becoming anachronistic, redeems them from the treadmill.

How? As an individual thinker can lead us to discover the question, so he can lead us to comprehend the change. Let us consider again Liang's last idea, the Western matter–Chinese spirit dichotomy.

In the nineties, the great Viceroy Chang Chih-tung had advocated Chinese learning for the essence of Chinese civilization and Western learning for practical use. Thus, still loyal to tradition, he sponsored innovation.[2] When Liang, several decades later,

[2] Chang Chih-tung, *Ch'üan-hsüeh p'ien*, translated by Samuel I. Woodbridge, under the title, *China's Only Hope* (New York, 1900), 63: "In order to render

looked to China for spirit and the West for matter, he was stating what would have been the same idea if the significance of time could be denied. But every idea is transformed by time, and not because its positive content changes but just because it fails to change as time passes. For an idea can be grasped only in its relation to contemporary alternatives. Every affirmation includes within itself a rejection of something else possible. A man's convictions are a choice among alternatives, and alternatives change in time.

And so the matter-spirit idea, having acquired something new to deny, had changed. The idea which Chang thought among Confucianists was a different idea when Liang thought it among Communists. Chang begged the literati to get their noses out of the classics and see that Western matter could be used; Liang begged student youth to go back to the classics and see that Chinese spirit existed. An idea which began as a challenge to immovable traditionalists became a challenge to impatient iconoclasts.[3] History had given it new alternatives and had drawn it

China powerful, and at the same time preserve our own institutions, it is absolutely necessary that we should utilize Western knowledge. But unless Chinese learning is made the basis of education, and a Chinese direction given to thought, the strong will become anarchists, and the weak, slaves."

Ibid., 137-138: "To sum up: Chinese learning is moral, Western learning is practical. Chinese learning concerns itself with moral conduct, Western learning, with the affairs of the world. . . If the Chinese heart throbs in unison with the heart of the sages, expressing the truth in irreprovable conduct, in filial piety, brotherly love, honesty, integrity, virtue; if government make use of foreign machinery and the railway from morning to night, and nothing untowards will befall the disciples of Confucius."

[3] Chang: "But if the ruling classes conclude to remain befuddled, indolent, aimless, braggart, useless, ignorant, and not *t'ung;* if they elect to continue hopelessly proud, overbearing, sitting complacently in their places whilst the country is going to pieces and the Holy Religion is being eradicated; although they may adorn themselves in the regalia of Confucius and quote long and elegantly from the Classics, although they may compose extended essays on ancient subjects and talk learnedly about Moral Philosophy, the whole world will forever reproach and revile them, saying, 'Behold the scapegraces of Mencius and Confucius!'" (*ibid.*, 138).

Liang: (*a*) "Not only do others hold China and India cheap, China and India

from sun to shadow, from vitality to exhaustion, from the point where Chang tries to break new ground for China, as someone must, to the point where Liang tries to hold old Chinese ground, as no one can.

For the Western impact, which had moved both Chang and Liang to theorize, was inexorably changing the face of China, and is changing it still. Liang's matter-spirit distinction between the Western and Chinese cultures, regardless of its justice or injustice at the moment he made it, becomes always less applicable to the actual scene; as China industrializes, any distinction between its own culture and the West's, matter-spirit or whatever it may be, must become more and more blurred.[4] The change which worked in Chang's idea by the time Liang came to think it was its procession toward anachronism.

An anachronistic idea is one which is an answer to no living question. When we recognize anachronism in the answer, we recognize change in the question; and the change is a growing irrelevance to the facts of life. This change is the process of intellectual history. The successive different ideas of the individual thinker yield the question which links his contemporaries. And the successive "same" ideas of the individual thinker and his predecessors yield the secret of its change.

Since the history of ideas is not exhausted in one anachronism, and since ideas demand some question behind them, this change in the question, this gathering irrelevance, has a corollary: the

---

hold themselves cheap" (Liang, "Yin-tu yü Chung-kuo wen-hua chih ch'in-shu ti kuan-hsi," YPSWC 62:50b [The family relationship of Indian and Chinese cultures]). (b) "Present-day Chinese students will not admit that China formerly had any worth-while thought" (Liang, "Yen-Li hsüeh-p'ai yü hsien-tai chiao-yü ssu-hu," YPSWC 64.25 [The Yen-Li school and contemporary educational thought-tides]). (c) "Whether or not the Classics should be read in the schools has been indeed a pressing question in educational circles for a decade" (Liang, "Hsüeh-chiao tu-ching wen-t'i," YPSHC-WC 15:43.80 [The question of reading the Classics in the schools]).

[4] For a study of industrialization as an agent in ultimately transforming traditional Chinese society into an approximation of modern western society, see Marion J. Levy, The Family Revolution in Modern China (Cambridge, 1949).

gradual emergence of a new and relevant question. That is why alignments of ideas in contemporaneity are always dissolving. As the question which they share becomes more and more irrelevant, the idea which answers that question alone loses currency, while the idea which has reference to the new question as well persists. Liang, in the twenties, had an answer to a dying question; but the Communists, his contemporaries, linked with him in that question, had an answer compatible also with some new question living. Liang faced the cultural problem in the bringing of industrialism to China. The Communists looked at the cultural problem and the economic problem as well.

Who are the ones that come to hold this versatile idea, this answer to both a fading question and a relevant, newly emerging one? They are, for the most part, of the younger generation (perpetually renewed), the younger contemporaries of the old thinker, who live with him and survive him. The individual thinker, who has discovered to us his contemporaries' question and revealed to us the nature of its change, can show us, too, how his generation comes to be superseded.

We have seen that because ideas must be defined in terms of their contemporary alternatives, men in series, like Chang and Liang, may hold apparently identical ideas which are not the same in fact. We must realize equally that men simultaneously may hold apparently identical ideas which are not the same in fact. Liang Ch'i-ch'ao, in his anti-Confucianist second phase, from 1899 to 1919, justified theoretically the iconoclasm of student youth. But the famous periodical *Hsin ch'ing-nien* (The New Youth), published in Peking 1915-1919, and agitating, like Liang, for a new culture, virtually ignored him.[5] And youth, by and

[5] I have found but two references to Liang in the pages of *Hsin ch'ing-nien*: Kao I-han, "Tu Liang Jen-kung ko-ming hsiang-hsü chih yüan li-lun," *Hsin ch'ing-nien* I, 4 (December 15, 1915) [On reading Liang Ch'i-ch'ao's basic theory of the propensity of revolution to perpetuate itself], which criticizes an article of Liang's, and "Kuo-nei ta-shih.chi," *Hsin ch'ing-nien* III, 4 (June 1917) [Record of national affairs], a regular news column which mentions Liang's contribution to the current pro-war press campaign.

large, deserted him in his postwar matter-spirit phase. The same war proved not the same solvent of the "same" ideas.

For just as no idea is, as it were, an isolated point in space, definable alone, without reference to simultaneous existences, so no idea is an isolated point in time. There are no such isolated points; there are only potentialities working themselves out in process. Immediate fact is more than what the senses can prehend. Just as its contemporary alternatives are immanent in it, immanent in it also are its past and future. The anti-culturalism of a younger generation had a different past from Liang's, and their present potentialities were pointing to different futures.

Liang had been born into the Chinese tradition. If he could have adhered to it unquestioningly, it would have guaranteed the dignity of his Chinese personality. Any new credo had to do the same and to seem besides (else why should he ever change?) intellectually more respectable. When, in his second phase, he abandoned Chinese tradition, he did so not in hatred of it, but in despair of its defense. And when the First World War raised that despair from him, it was wholly natural that he should rediscover China. In his beginning was his end.

But as Liang was taking the long way home, he met youth midway on his journey. That state of anti-culturalism which he had almost broken his heart to reach, they accepted from him as a natural state and a free gift and a starting point. That idea which for him was only the visible part of the iceberg, beneath which lay buried his devotion to the old culture, was for them their base. They followed him for a while, but they were not constrained to follow him forever. That is why the "new youth" of the *Hsin ch'ing-nien,* when they seemed to speak the same language as Liang, spoke so little of it with him. For the language was not

---

Of the books which I have examined on modern Chinese intellectual history, only Wang Feng-yüan, *Chung-kuo hsin-wen-hsüeh yün-tung shu-p'ing* [A critical account of the new literature movement in China] (Peiping, 1935), 56-57, seems to note the real affinity between *Hsin ch'ing-nien* and Liang's writings in Japan, in the early years of the twentieth century.

really the same, "identical" ideas were not identical. When the First World War changed the environment in which these ideas were thought, he, by his origins, was committed to anachronism. They, by his development, were enabled to choose. And in large part they chose Communism, which dealt with his question and dealt with a fresher one.

Thus, from our analysis of Liang's ideas, we see how the Chinese Communists were contemporaries of his. And from our analysis of his ideas, we see why he, or his intellectual heirs, cannot for long be contemporaries of the Chinese Communists. For beyond irrelevance in a question lies silence; the question ceases to be asked. Beyond anachronism in an answer (and all ideas are answers), beyond the death-in-life, lies death, where the links are broken.

PART ONE

1873-1898: METAMORPHOSIS

CHAPTER I

LIANG AND THE REFORM MOVEMENT

Youth and Education

LIANG CH'I-CH'AO was born near Canton on February 23, 1873. Liang himself has identified the date more fully: ". . . ten years after the T'aip'ing regime perished at Nanking, one year after the Grand Secretary Tseng Kuo-fan died, three years after the Franco-Prussian war, and the year in which Italy rounded out its nationhood with the acquisition of Rome."[1] (The last date is wrong.)

It is characteristic of Liang that he should fix the date of his birth in terms of the larger events in world history. Implicit here is the main burden of his early thought: that Chinese tradition and history have an autonomous but not an isolated or a uniquely valuable existence; that East and West must influence each other reciprocally; and that an eclectic philosophy is right for modern China and for a whole world which, on the material plane, is being unified by science.

His father, Liang Pao-ying, was a farmer with a considerable training in the classics, and his grandfather had earned the "bachelor's" degree (*hsiu-ts'ai*).[2] The old man, with an eye for talent, preferred Liang Ch'i-ch'ao to his other seven grandsons. In his fourth or fifth year, the boy began to take instruction from his grandfather in the *Four Books, Ch'un-ch'iu* [Spring and Autumn Annals], and *Shih-ching* [Book of Poetry]. Liang recalled years later the impression made by the grandfather's stories of the great men of antiquity and, particularly, of the evils met by China in the days of Sung and Ming.

[1] Liang Ch'i-ch'ao, "San-shih tzu-shu," YPSWC 44.25 [Autobiography at the age of thirty].

[2] Under the old examination system, the term most commonly used for "bachelor of arts" or graduate of the first degree.

When Liang was six years old, his father took over his education and launched him on a curriculum of the classics, history of China, and belles lettres, all with a leavening of manual labor, upon which Liang Pao-ying, departing from the literati pattern, insisted. The boy cultivated a great taste for the T'ang poets, especially Li Po. At first he owned only the *Shih-chi* [Historical Annals of Ssu-ma Ch'ien] and the *Kang-chien i-chih lu* (a second-degree condensation of a great Sung history of China), both of which he learned thoroughly. (In 1908 he maintained that he could still recite from memory eight- or nine-tenths of the *Shih-chi*.) At the age of nine, Liang was writing thousand-word essays, and his father, delighted with the boy's intelligence, made him a gift of the *Han-shu* [History of the Former Han Dynasty] and the *Ku-wen-tz'u lei-tsuan* (an eighteenth-century anthology of prose literature).[3]

In 1884, Liang became a district-school student. His father sternly supervised his activities and tried to make him believe that he was destined for extraordinary intellectual accomplishment.[4] The next year, he entered the *Hsüeh-hai t'ang* in Canton. This school had been founded in 1801 by the governor general Jüan Yüan for the study of philology and literature. About his education here Liang later remarked, "One might not know there was anything in the universe but commentaries and fine style."[5]

In 1889, just sixteen years old (seventeen, by Chinese reckoning), he received the second academic degree (*chü-jen*). Of the hundred successful candidates in the provincial examination he was the youngest and stood fifth on the list. The examiner, delighted with this performance, arranged for Liang to marry his

[3] This account of Liang's early youth is drawn from Liang, "San-shih tzu-shu," 24b-25; Liu Hsi-sui, "Liang Jen-kung hsien-sheng chuan," TSKHCK 4 (1929), 135 [Liang Ch'i-ch'ao, a biographical sketch]; A. Forke, *Geschichte der Neueren Chinesischen Philosophie* (Hamburg, 1938), 598; P. M. d'Elia, "Un Maître de la jeune Chine: Liang K'i Tch'ao," TP 18 (1917), 250-251. Forke and d'Elia for the most part follow Liang's autobiography.

[4] Liu, 135.

[5] Liang, "San-shih tzu-shu," 25b. The phrase *hsün-ku tz'u-chang* (commentaries and fine style) recurs constantly in Liang's writings as an epithet derogative of the old education.

younger sister.[6] The marriage took place in Peking near the end of 1891. Clearly, some purpose was still served by commentaries and fine style.

Liang never earned a higher degree. In 1890 he failed in the metropolitan examinations in Peking. Whether this failure fed his discontent with the narrow Chinese scholarship is not known, but now for certain the great world began to speak to him. Returning south from Peking, he purchased in Shanghai a copy of the *Ying-huan chih-lüeh,* an outline of world geography compiled in the 1840's by Hsü Chi-yü. On this visit, too, he was able to examine, though not rich enough to buy, European books translated into Chinese by the translation department of the Kiangnan Arsenal of Shanghai.[7] In an article written six years later, he revealed what a watershed this year of 1890 had been in his life. "Since my seventeenth year," he wrote, "I have known much anxiety over the signs of strength and the signs of weakness among foreigners and Chinese."[8]

That year, in the autumn, he became a close friend of Ch'en T'ung-fu, who had been a schoolmate at the *Hsüeh-hai t'ang.* Ch'en spoke enthusiastically about K'ang Yu-wei, whose first reform project had just been rejected by the Throne.[9] In the eighth month (August 26–September 24) the two students, seeking instruction, presented themselves to K'ang, who was then living in the "Study of Scholarly Eminence" (*Yun-ch'ü shu-chü*), in Canton;[10] and at their instance, K'ang in 1891, in a Canton lane called *Ch'ang-hsing li,* set up his famous school, the *Wan-mu-ts'ao t'ang.*[11]

[6] Tseng Yu-hao, *Modern Chinese Legal and Political Philosophy* (Shanghai, 1930), 113.

[7] d'Elia, 253. The arsenal was founded in 1867 by Ting Jih-ch'ang and was sponsored by Tseng Kuo-fan, at that time the Nanking Governor General.

[8] Liang, "Shih-k'o-chai chi-yen chi-hsing hsü," YPSWC 3.46 [Preface to jottings on the talk and doings in the *Shih-k'o-chai*].

[9] d'Elia, 252.

[10] Chao Feng-t'ien, "K'ang Ch'ang-su hsien-sheng nien-p'u kao" SHNP 2 (1934), 187 [A draft chronological sketch of the life of K'ang Yu-wei].

[11] *Ibid.,* 188. In 1892 the location of the school was changed twice; it remained, however, in Canton.

According to Liang's account, there were seven categories of lessons: *tu-shu* (reading books), *yang-hsin* (cultivation of the mind), *chih-shen* (controlling the body), *chih-shih* ("grasping things"; i.e., management), *chieh-jen* (human relations), *shih-shih* (current events), and *i-wu* (barbarian affairs—K'ang still used the traditional term for foreign affairs rather than the modern and unprovocative term, *wai-wu*). K'ang ranged widely, in comparative method, over ancient and modern Chinese and foreign thought.[12] In the Chinese field, although his first concern was Confucian tradition, K'ang and his students made a broad and generally sympathetic study of Buddhism. This intellectual catholicity (which we shall study in the next chapter) has an important bearing on the process of culture-change.

In 1893 Liang and Ch'en, acting as heads of departments of study, took some of the teaching burden from K'ang. Early the next year, the latter closed his school and traveled to Peking with Liang for the metropolitan examination. Both failed. In the fifth month (June 14-July 12) K'ang hurt his leg in a fall and soon thereafter returned to Canton for a rest, but his pupil stayed on in the capital.[13] This, in the next two years, would be the scene of Liang's first serious labor for reform.

Reform Activity in Peking

For a time in those years, Liang acted as Chinese secretary to Dr. Timothy Richard, an English missionary who had a considerable influence in Chinese reform circles. In 1894, soon after the Sino-Japanese War began, Richard published his Chinese translation of Robert Mackenzie's *Nineteenth Century—A History,* a book which painted in strong colors the achievements of science and which, in Richard's version, had a tremendous circulation.[14]

12 Liang, "Nan-hai K'ang hsien-sheng chuan," YPSWC 39.61-61b [Biography of K'ang Yu-wei]. On pp. 63-64 there is an exhaustive outline and diagram of the school's organization and courses of study.

13 Chao Feng-t'ien, 189.

14 For an analysis of the original work, see R. G. Collingwood, *The Idea of*

In his introduction he asked, "What is the cause of the foreign wars, indemnities, and repeated humiliations suffered by China during the last sixty years?" He pointed out that, as he put it, "God was breaking down the barriers between all nations by railways, steamers, and telegraphs, in order that all should live in peace and happiness as brethren of one family"; but the Manchus, by continual obstruction, had been determined from the first to prevent this intercourse.[15] Although Liang never, in print, discussed the dynasty before his escape to Japan in 1898, Richard's vision of the unification of the world was a major theme of Liang's essays in the early years.

China's display of helplessness in the Japanese war had a profound influence on the reformist temper, intensifying both patriotism and exasperation. In this spirit, K'ang and Liang led 1,300 candidates for the *chin-shih* degree[16] in sending to the Censorate a protest against the Shimonoseki peace terms. Liang, representing 190 Kwangtung literati in Peking, memorialized the Emperor on the immediate necessities of China, and he was one of 3,000 students who soon after, under the leadership of K'ang, asked reforms of the Throne.[17] This, the so-called *kung-chü* memorial, was later termed by Liang "the first step in the movement for popular government."[18]

It was to be several years, however, before K'ang or Liang could hope to effect changes by petition. For the time being their task

---

History (Oxford, 1946), 145-146: "In order to realize the lengths to which this dogma of progress was pushed, it is necessary to go slumming among the most unsavoury relics of third-rate historical work. A certain Robert Mackenzie published in 1880 a book called 'The Nineteenth Century—A History'. . ."

[15] W. E. Soothill, *Timothy Richard of China* (London, 1924), 183.

[16] The degree offered to *chü-jen* who pass the metropolitan examinations in Peking.

[17] Liang, "San-shih tzu-shu," 26-26b.

[18] Liang, "Ch'ing-tai hsüeh-shu kai-lun," YPSHC-CC 9:34.60 [A summary of Ch'ing scholarship]. *Kung-chü* (public carriage) is a term for *chü-jen* who have come to Peking for the metropolitan examinations. The name derives from the fact that aspirants were entitled to transportation to the capital by public conveyance.

C

was to educate, to propagandize for *tzu-ch'iang* (self-strengthening), and their first forum was the *Ch'iang hsüeh-hui,* called by Europeans the "Reform Club"[19] or "Mutual Improvement Society" or "Society for the Diffusion of Enlightenment."[20] It was organized in Peking, in the seventh month (August 20–September 18) of 1895, through the efforts chiefly of Wen T'ing-shih, a member of the *Hanlin* Academy.[21] Huang Shao-chi, Wang K'ang-nien, Huang Tsun-hsien, and Ch'en San-li were among the first members.[22]

Prior to the founding of the *Ch'iang hsüeh-hui,* K'ang, Liang, Hsü Ch'in, T'ang Chüeh-tun, and others had organized in the South the *Kuei hsüeh-hui,* (Kwangsi Study Society), whose manifesto declared that without reform and self-strengthening the country could not be saved. When K'ang heard of the Peking group, he immediately went north by sea, joined the society, and soon made it his instrument.[23] Affiliated societies were established at Shanghai, Hankow, Nanking, Wuchang, and Tientsin.[24] The British Minister, Sir Nicholas O'Connor, gave great encouragement.[25] Aid was forthcoming from Yüan Shih-k'ai, Chang Chih-tung donated Tls. 5000 (about $7500), and Sun Chia-nai, the second of the imperial tutors, contributed a house, rent free, for headquarters.[26]

Liang became chief secretary of the Peking organization and took charge of its journalistic activities. In August 1895 publica-

---

[19] M. E. Cameron, *The Reform Movement in China 1898-1912* (Stanford University, 1931), 28.

[20] NCH 55 (Nov. 22, 1895), 851.

[21] Cameron, using non-Chinese sources, spells this name "Weng Ting-shih," and states further that he is a member of the family of Weng Tung-ho. This conclusion is false. Her reference is to Weng T'ung-ho, an imperial tutor and patron of the *Ch'iang hsüeh-hui,* and, as the difference between the characters in the two surnames indicates, not necessarily a relative of Wen.

[22] Ko Kung-chen, *Chung-kuo pao-hsüeh shih* [A history of Chinese journalism] (Shanghai, 1928), 123.

[23] *Ibid.,* 123.

[24] Cameron, 28.

[25] Timothy Richard, *Forty-five Years in China* (New York, 1916), 255.

[26] NCH 45 (November 22, 1895), 851.

tion began of a daily devoted to the spread of constitutional and democratic ideas. It appeared first as the *Wan-kuo kung-pao* [The International Journal], a title borrowed from a foreign-controlled popular magazine dedicated to Christian interests.[27] The society's publication reprinted many articles from its namesake,[28] but Timothy Richard strongly advised the group to launch a completely independent periodical. The derivative effort was abandoned, and Liang's *Chung-wai chi-wen* [The Chinese and Foreign Record], a new paper with a new character came onto the scene.[29]

The society was unable to buy a printing press, but the official *Ching-pao* (called the *Peking Gazette* by the *North China Herald*, which for a time made monthly translations from it) lent the new daily a set of rough wooden blocks, and the format of the *Chung-wai chi-wen* was designed to resemble that of the *Ching-pao*.[30] Generally consisting of four leaves, the paper was distributed free to persons drawn from a list of Gazette subscribers. Varying estimates of circulation set figures ranging from 1000 to 3000.[31]

Liang printed domestic and foreign news and a daily short reformist essay of his own. With three principal aides, he published for more than a month. Liang has written that in spite of makeshift printing facilities, other technical difficulties, and the pressure of daily publication, he derived an intense pleasure from the venture.[32] Hostility in high places put an end to it. In the

[27] The original *Wan-kuo kung-pao* was a monthly started at the Chinese New Year, 1889. It was edited by an American, Dr. Young J. Allen. Cf. Richard, 218.
[28] *Ibid.*, 232.
[29] R. S. Britton, *The Chinese Periodical Press, 1800-1912* (Shanghai, 1933), 91. Ma Te-chih, *Le Mouvement réformiste et les événements de la cour de Pékin en 1898* (Lyon, 1934), 28, calls this paper *Chung-wai shih-wen*. Wu Ch'i-ch'ang, *Liang Ch'i-ch'ao* (Chungking, 1945), 64, calls it *Chung-wai kung-pao*. Chiang Fu-lin, "Chang T'ai-yen yü Liang Jen-kung," TF 79 (1940), 2652 (Chang Ping-lin and Liang Ch'i-ch'ao), calls it *Chung-wai kung-lun*. However, Ko, 124, agrees with Britton. Ko is considered authoritative.
[30] Ko, 124.
[31] Britton, 91, gives 1000; Ko, 124, gives 2000-3000; Wu, 64, gives 3000.
[32] Wu, 64.

tenth month (November 17–December 15), the censor Yang Ch'ung-i, acting, as Liang suggests darkly, on the instigation of a certain minister, investigated the *Ch'iang hsüeh-hui*.[33] This culminated in a denunciation of the newspaper (January 22, 1896) and its subsequent closing, and in a memorial condemning the actions of Wen T'ing-shih. In response to Yang's memorial, an imperial decree, March 29, dismissed Wen from office and banished him to his native town.[34] This meant the end of the *Ch'iang hsüeh-hui*.

Liang continued to occupy the society's premises for study. Cut off for the time being from a mass public, he was still able to persuade in conversation. Here is his account of the illumination of T'an Ssu-t'ung. The young philosopher T'an had come to Peking some months before to see K'ang Yu-wei, but the latter had already returned to Canton. "I was in the capital," writes Liang, "as archivist for the *Ch'iang hsüeh-hui,* and we met for the first time. I told him the methods of developing the land according to the principles which K'ang Yu-wei expounded. Then T'an was moved to great joy and styled himself his disciple, though they were yet strangers to one another."[35]

The Shih-wu pao

By this time, however, no force on earth could long keep Liang Ch'i-ch'ao from rushing into print. When the *Ch'iang hsüeh-hui* in Peking was dissolved, it meant the eclipse of the Shanghai branch and its daily organ, the *Ch'iang hsüeh-pao*.[36] But, though the Peking body died, there was metempsychosis in Shanghai;

[33] "Yang Jui chuan," PCCP 12.10 [Biography of Yang Jui].

[34] THL 132.19b-20. An English translation appears in PG (1896), 38-39, which gives March 30 as the date of the decree.

[35] "T'an Ssu-t'ung chuan," PCCP 12.18 [Biography of T'an Ssu-t'ung].

[36] The *Ch'iang hsüeh-pao*, its first issue appearing January 12, 1896, had been published in the reformers' office, the *Ch'iang hsüeh-hui shu-chü*, located by the Race Course off the Nanking Road in the International Settlement. Tls. 1500 were contributed by Chang Chih-tung and others. The *Ch'iang hsüeh-pao* bore a double dating: first "K'ung-tzu chiang-sheng . . ." (the number of years since the birth of Confucius) and then "Ta-Ch'ing Kuang-hsü . . ." (the reign year)—a significant fusion of Chinese substance and Western form.

personnel, funds, and the ardent spirit made a fast transmigration into the *Shih-wu pao kuan* and its periodical which Liang made famous, the *Shih-wu pao*.

Liang came to Shanghai in the third month (April 13–May 12) upon the invitation of Huang Tsun-hsien, who had been active in the Shanghai *Ch'iang hsüeh-hui* and favored its continuance, in some form, with a paper.[37] Liang, with no modest demurrers, agreed to be editor, and Wang K'ang-nien became director of the society. Wang, Huang, Mai Meng-hua, and Hsü Ch'in were the principal editorial assistants.[38] A few months of promotion ensued; then, August 9, 1896, and every tenth day thereafter, more or less regularly, for two years, the *Shih-wu pao* (often called "The Chinese Progress") made its appearance.

The style of writing was a compromise between high *wen-yen* and the colloquial. The magazine was lithographed with twenty or thirty leaves per issue and numerous sections. It published in extenso decrees promulgated by the Emperor, memorials addressed to the Throne by censors or mandarins, news of the arts and sciences, and commentaries on the domestic and foreign political and social situations.[39] Liang pleaded for industrialization, widespread education in new schools with Sino-Western curricula, translation of books, constitutional government, and so on. He offered such varied fare as a biography of George Washington and an account of British railway history and laws pertaining to railways. Each number contained translations from one or more of the following languages: English, French, Russian, and Japanese.[40] One of the *Shih-wu pao's* most popular features was a serialized version of *The Adventures of Sherlock Holmes*.[41]

This newspaper started the vogue for use of the term *"hsüeh-pao"* in titles of reform periodicals (e.g., *T'ung ——*, Shanghai, 1896; *Nung ——*, Shanghai, 1897; *Shih ——*, Shanghai, 1897; *Kung-shang ——*, Shanghai, 1898, etc.). See Britton, 91, and Wu, 65.

[37] Liang, "San-shih tzu-shu," 26b.

[38] Wu, 65.

[39] Ma Te-chih, 30.

[40] Wen Ching, *The Chinese Crisis from Within* (London, 1901), 43-44.

[41] Lyon Sharman, *Sun Yat-sen, His Life and Its Meaning* (New York, 1934), 53.

The journal was very well received. The Nanking Governor General Liu K'un-i recommended it to subordinates and scholars in areas under his jurisdiction,[42] and in the fourth month (May 13–June 10) memorials on its behalf were submitted by Wuchang Governor General Chang Chih-tung, Chihli Governor General Wang Wen-shao, and Sheng Hsüan-huai of the Court of Judicature and Revision (Ta-li ssu).[43] The Shih-wu pao had a tremendous influence in stimulating the intelligentsia into organizational and subsequent publishing activities. In several provinces societies were founded for purposes of general or technical study and for campaigns against social evils like foot-binding and opium-smoking. Each society had an organ for its opinions.[44]

Liang at Changsha

Changsha came to be the principal center of this activity. Huang Tsun-hsien, whose reformist leanings we have already noted, in 1897 became the Salt Intendant of Hunan and an acting provincial judge. Ch'en Pao-chen, the Governor of Hunan, strongly influenced by his eldest son, was also committed to the principles of reform.[45] Under his auspices a newspaper called Hsiang hsüeh hsin-pao, edited by T'an Ssu-t'ung, was first issued April 22, 1897,[46] and the Shih-wu hsüeh-t'ang (Academy of Current Events) was established at Changsha by T'an, Huang, and Hsiung Hsi-ling.[47] Liang Ch'i-ch'ao was invited to be chief lecturer.

Liang was ready to leave Shanghai. The Shih-wu pao had received heavy financial aid from Chang Chih-tung, who therefore felt free to interfere with editorial policy. After a few months his interference became serious because of what he considered an ex-

[42] Britton, 93.
[43] Liang, "San-shih tzu-shu," 26b.
[44] Ko, 125.
[45] H. H. Hu, "Ch'en San-li, the Poet," THM VI; 2 (February 1938), 134-137. Ch'en San-li recommended Liang to his father.
[46] A. W. Hummel (ed.), Eminent Chinese of the Ch'ing Period, 2 (Washington, 1944), 703.
[47] Liang, "Ch'ing-tai hsüeh-shu kai-lun," 62.

cessive emphasis on the concept of *min-ch'üan*, the people's rights. Liang became increasingly restless under this pressure and came to consider his status vis-à-vis Chang to be that of laborer in relation to capitalist.[48] In the tenth month (October 26–November 23), 1897, he relinquished his editorial post to Wang K'ang-nien and left for Changsha.[49]

Once there, in collaboration with T'ang Ts'ai-ch'ang and others, he organized the *Nan hsüeh-hui*, which endeavored to coördinate the political science studies of scholars in the southern provinces.[50] The newspaper also claimed his attention, and here again he felt, or was meant to feel, the restraining hand of Chang Chih-tung.[51] A letter dated May 11, 1898 (after Liang had left Changsha), from Chang to Ch'en Pao-chen and Huang Tsun-hsien, first pays tribute to the talent and intellect flourishing in Hunan, its leadership over other provinces. But every now and then corrupt practices spread, writes Chang, as witness the *Hsiang hsüeh-pao*, publishing some completely erroneous material, with prejudice and partiality extreme. People are startled and angry, Chang continues, and he requests an investigation.[52]

Liang's main efforts, however, were concentrated on the *Shih-wu hsüeh-t'ang*, where Chinese and Western studies were combined. He lectured in the classroom four hours a day and spent his evenings writing. There were only forty students in his first class, but of these several were extremely talented—Liang, in one account, singles out Li Ping-huan, Lin Kuei, and Ts'ai Ao (with whom he was later to associate in the Yunnan Revolt against Yüan Shih-k'ai).[53] Eight of the students became ardent revolutionaries;

[48] Wu, 65. Liang, "Ch'u kuei-kuo yen-shuo-tz'u," YPSWC 57.1b-2 [Addresses made upon first returning to China].

[49] Liang, "San-shih tzu-shu," 27.

[50] "T'an Ssu-t'ung chuan," PCCP, 12.24.

[51] Ch'en Ch'iu, "Wu-hsü cheng-pien shih fan-pien-fa jen-wu chih cheng-chih ssu-hsiang," YCHP 25 (June, 1939), 62 [The political thought of the anti-reformists during the "Hundred Days of Reform"].

[52] *Chang Wen-hsiang kung ch'üan-chi* [The collected works of Chang Chih-tung] (Peking, 1928), 155.20.

[53] Liang, "Ch'ing-tai hsüeh-shu kai-lun," 62.

some followed T'ang Ts'ai-ch'ang in the Hankow rising against the Empress Dowager Tz'u-hsi (1900) and some figured prominently in the founding of the Republic. Liang considered the school a nerve center in the struggle for change. "The war cries of the new and the old rose at the Hsiang River," he wrote, "and the waves moved in the capital."[54]

The "Hundred Days"

The reform tide was indeed flowing in 1898 and Liang himself was in the capital when it reached its height. He left for Peking in the early spring, after a near-fatal illness.[55] In April, he took once more the triennial examination for the *chin-shih* degree. It was his last quest for the blue-bird.

Even as he tried to meet the classical system on its own terms, he was trying to remake it on his. He used the convocation of scholars as an occasion for a blast against the "eight-legged essay," that feature of the examination which had called such rigidity into the old educational scheme; but hardly a hundred of the thousands of candidates were won over when Liang tried to get signatures for a mass petition.[56] K'ang Yu-wei, representing Liang and the other signatories, presented a memorial on this subject in the fourth month (May 20-June 18).[57]

This particular memorial elicited no response, but K'ang and Liang were drawing near to their moment of power. The Hundred Days of Reform were ushered in by the imperial decree of June 11, a sweeping statement in favor of military and educational reform and the nurture of talent for an effective diplomatic service.[58] Weng T'ung-ho, one of the imperial tutors, had voiced

[54] Wu, 54.

[55] Liang, "San-shih tzu-shu," 27.

[56] O. Franke, *Ostasiatische Neubildungen* (Hamburg, 1911), 76.

[57] Mai Chung-hua (ed.), *Nan-hai hsien-sheng wu-hsü tsou-kao* [K'ang Yu-wei's memorials in 1898] (probably Shanghai, 1911), 3b-8; hereafter referred to as *Tsou-kao*. Chao Feng-t'ien, 197, says this memorial was submitted in the third month (April 21-May 19).

[58] PG (1898), 32-34. THL 144.16b-17.

the opinion that the K'ang–Liang–T'an group had ten times the ability of the ministers.[59] It was inevitable that, under the new dispensation, the reformers would find their way into the inner circle.

The decree of June 11 had many repercussions. One of the first was a memorial from the Hanlin recorder Hsü Chih-ching, commending the example of Japan, whose Emperor Meiji, it was suggested, in order to implement his plans for reform, had taken men of talent where he found them, regardless of their station; the Emperor of China, said the memorialist, if he would take the Japanese example to heart, would raise K'ang, Liang, and T'an, among others, to high positions.[60]

Chang Yin-huan, ex-minister to the United States and a member of the *Tsungli-yamen* (the Chinese foreign office, 1861-1901), exerted himself to win imperial favor for the reformers.[61] The June 13 decree in response to Hsü Chih-ching's memorial offered imperial audience to K'ang Yu-wei and Chang Yüan-chi, ordered Huang Tsun-hsien and T'an Ssu-t'ung summoned to Peking, and concluded, "As for Liang Ch'i-ch'ao, let the *Tsungli-yamen* examine him and memorialize."[62]

Liang was on the inside. He had been eloquent for years on the necessity of translation of foreign books;[63] now, by a decree of

[59] Wu, 78.

[60] KHCY 24.12b-13.

[61] Wen, 55.

[62] THL 144, 18b; also KHCY 24.13. The decree is translated in PG (1898), 34. Concerning Liang Ch'i-ch'ao, the translation concludes, the Tsungli-yamen should "find out where he is at present and report to us." This is a faulty rendering of the last phrase, *"ch'a-k'an chü-tsou."*

[63] For examples, see the following works by Liang. (*a*) "Hsi-hsüeh shu-mu-piao hsü-li," YPSWC 3.54 [Preface to an index of Western scholarly books]: "Therefore, if the nation desires to strengthen itself, let it make large-scale translation of western books the basis." (*b*) "Ta-t'ung i-shu-chü hsü-li," YPSWC 4.3 [Remarks on the Ta-t'ung Translation Bureau]: Liang pleads for translation of Western books to make innovations possible; he complains that the *T'ung-wen kuan* (foreign language college in Peking), the *Shui-shih hsüeh-t'ang* (Naval Academy at Tientsin), and the *Chih-tsao chü* (Arsenal of Shanghai) have been translating for thirty years, have published only 100 books in that time, and

July 3, he was made director of a translation bureau,[64] with a budget of Tls. 1000 per month. He soon found that his agency was seriously embarrassed by a paucity of competent translators. In July, through the Minister of France, he asked Monsignor Garnier (the Vicar Apostolic of Ching-nan) to authorize Father Joseph Ma Hsiang-pei to direct a "college of translators" to be founded at Peking. Mgr. Garnier acceded to the request and authorized the participation of Ma, who, however, laid down the conditions that the college be established at Shanghai and that the Jesuits of Zicawei should take part. These conditions were accepted,[65] and the proposition cleared official channels with a memorial by Sun Chia-nai, who reported Liang's desire to found such a school, and with the decree of August 26, which granted Liang permission and promised tax exemption for materials used.[66]

---

have recently all suspended activities. (c) "Hsi-shu t'i-yao nung-hsüeh tsung-hsü," YPSWC 4.5 [General preface to Western books elucidating agronomy]: Liang avers that the key point in reference to China's agricultural ills is the fact that only one Western book outlining new agricultural techniques is available in Chinese. (d) "Tu Jih-pen shu-mu-chih shu-hou," YPSWC 4.8b-11 [Postscript to a reading of a Japanese bibliography]: A threnody of "translate" runs all through the text; on 9: "The strength of the West lies not in its soldiers or its guns but in the study by its sons of books about new methods."

[64] CSK, *Pen-chi* section, 24.7b. THL 145.8: "The *chü-jen* Liang Ch'i-ch'ao is granted brevet rank of the sixth class and will manage the affairs of the translation bureau." Liu, 135, says that Liang was put in charge of the Peking University as well as of the translation bureau. Actually, Sun Chia-nai was chosen to administer the University. Liu perhaps was led astray by the fact that both appointments were made on the same day and are recorded together in CSK, *Pen-chi* section. Ma Te-chih, 54, gives July 26 as the date of Liang's appointment. He seems to have used carelessly a memorial and imperial decree of July 26 which refer to the fact that Liang by *previous decree* had been designated head of a translation bureau; see THL 146. 5b-6 and KHCY 34.31b-32. H. F. MacNair, *China in Revolution* (Chicago, 1935), 14-15, gives August 16 as the date of Liang's appointment. He appears to have misread the decree of August 16 which urges speedy action by Liang's translation bureau to supply Western books for the Imperial University; see THL 146. 16b-17 and PG (1898), 54.

[65] d'Elia, 254.

[66] THL 147.5b; PG (1898), 61. Yano Jinichi, "Bojutsu no hempō oyobi seihen," SR 8 (1923), 449 [The reform and political change of 1898], attributes the memorial directly to Liang, but the imperial decree mentions only Sun Chia-nai as the initiator.

Liang's absorption in the affairs of the translating bureau kept him from reverting to his old role as editor of the *Shih-wu pao*. On July 17, the Censor Sung Po-lu memorialized suggesting that the *Shih-wu pao* of Shanghai be transformed into an official organ. The Emperor, on the same day, sent a decree to the Nei Ko (Grand Secretariat) directing that Sun Chia-nai should "take the matter into consideration and memorialize the throne upon his deciding satisfactorily how to manage the affair."[67] Sung Po-lu had recommended Liang as editor, but Sun Chia-nai, in his memorial, noted that Liang, by the decree of July 3, had been designated head of the translation bureau and was too pressed to undertake the *Shih-wu pao* project. K'ang was suggested instead, and it was so ordered by decree on July 26.[68]

[67] THL 145.29; PG (1898), 44.

[68] THL 146.6; also KHCY, 34-31b-32. This conversion of the *Shih-wu pao* into an official newspaper was not accomplished without bitterness. Wang K'ang-nien keenly resented his expropriation. He turned to publication of a counter-reformist newspaper called *Ch'ang-yen pao* [Straight-talk journal], with Liang Ting-fen as editor, and fought a pen-war with the new *Shih-wu pao* (Ko, 126). Liang entered the polemical controversy with a biting article, "Ch'uang-pan Shih-wu pao yüan-wei chi" [An account of the circumstances of the founding of the *Shih-wu pao*], written to controvert the implication of a notice published by Wang and beginning, "K'ang-nien, in autumn, 1896, founded and managed the *Shih-wu pao* in Shanghai and extended an invitation to the *chü-jen* of Hsin-hui Liang Chuo-ju to be editor-in-chief. . ." Liang goes into detail about the origins of the *Shih-wu pao* to blot out the impression that the *Shih-wu pao* had been founded solely by Wang and had then been taken over by a K'ang-Liang cabal. Liang's article, which is reprinted in Ko, 137-141, presents the facts as follows: In the ninth month, 1896, K'ang Yu-wei was in Shanghai as director of the branch *Ch'iang hsüeh-hui*. Because of the sickness of his aged mother in Kwangtung, K'ang was forced to leave Shanghai. Wang K'ang-nien was summoned from Hupei to take over the directorship. By the time of his arrival in Shanghai, the society had been closed. Tls. 700 remained in the *Ch'iang hsüeh-hui* treasury and Tls. 500 were realized from the sale of books and office fixtures. The *Shih-wu pao kuan* thought it politic to conceal the origin of its finances. Therefore, Wang took it upon himself to enter the funds in the books as "contributions of Wang K'ang-nien *et al.*" Huang Tsun-hsien changed this to read "Wang K'ang-nien and Liang Ch'i-ch'ao *et al.*" (*ibid.*, 137).

Britton, 92, has an account of these financial manipulations. He generally follows Liang's article but simplifies, so that the implication of subterfuge by Wang is lost. Liang gives the credit for the *Shih-wu pao* groundwork to Huang Tsun-hsien, Wu Chi-ch'ing, Chou Chang-shu, and himself; he refers to Wang contemptuously as a "self-styled founder" (Ko, 138).

One may suspect that Sun Chia-nai was motivated less by consideration for Liang than by a desire to shunt K'ang Yu-wei to Shanghai, away from the center of power. Reactionary sentiment was crystallizing, and even in circles supposedly favorable to reform, K'ang's influence on the Emperor was decried. The undercurrent was clearly discernible in the battle to set up a constitutional bureau.

This was one of the most cherished aims of the reformers. K'ang had submitted his first memorial on this subject in the first month (January 22–February 20), 1898. His plea for the establishment of a constitutional or a policy bureau (*Chih-tu chü*) drew heavily on the reformers' arsenal of shining models and awful examples—Emperor Meiji, Peter the Great, Poland, Annam, India. "Reform and be strengthened," he wrote, "guard the old and die." Japan had been strengthened, and one of Japan's first and basic moves had been the establishment of a constitutional bureau.[69]

In the seventh month (August 17–September 15) he tried again, with the same emphasis on the Japanese precedent.[70] Other memorials were submitted by Sung Po-lu and Yang Shen-hsiu; Liang made the last attempt. Speaking through his father-in-law, Li Tuan-fen, the president of the Board of Ceremonies, he submitted a memorial which sought, among other things, to spur the ministers into creating some kind of central planning body. The memorial asked that a *mou-ch'in tien* (energetic labor pavilion) be established to determine policy; that the regulations of the Six Boards be revised; and that court officials be sent to supervise the provincial schools. Sun Chia-nai obstructed action on this memorial, and K'ang's enemies charged that his aim was to ruin the Six Boards, the Grand Secretariat, and the provincial governments.[71]

On September 11, Tseng Lien of the Hunan Conservative Party

---

[69] KHCY, 24.4-7.
[70] *Tsou-kao*, 46-48b.
[71] Chao Feng-t'ien, 203-204.

(*Hunan shou-chiu tang*) submitted a memorial asking death for K'ang and Liang.[72] The Emperor still resisted such pressure; his decree of September 12 was a eulogy of Western civilization.[73] For some weeks now K'ang had been in secret meeting with the Emperor every night at the Palace. Liang and others had often accompanied him. They sat on lounges by the Emperor's side. All reserve and ceremony were thrown off as they planned real reforms which would attack not only the prejudices but the material interests of the official class.[74] The bold decrees of August 30–September 16 abolished sinecures, reformed the army, and introduced a budget system; but reaction was swift.

A scholar who saw these dramatic September days in Peking in the next month wrote the following note in his diary: "In the design of K'ang and Liang, the new and the old, Manchu and Chinese, England and Russia were set at odds, and so, truly, were mother and son."[75] For in the palace counterrevolution of September 21, the Empress Dowager reasserted her authority, the Emperor, her son by adoption, was put into the shadows, and new decrees revoked the abolitions, the reforms, and the introductions.[76]

On September 22, the Empress Dowager struck at K'ang and Liang with an order for their arrest.[77] The former was absent from Peking in these days, but Liang was still within the city walls and in imminent danger of capture and certain death. Nevertheless, before seeking refuge for himself, he joined T'an

<hr>

[72] "Liu Kuang-t'i chuan," PCCP 12.86 [Biography of Liu Kuang-t'i].

[73] THL 147.22-22b; PG (1898), 74-75.

[74] PG (1898), 78-79.

[75] Yeh Ch'ang-ch'ih, *Yüan-tu lu jih-chi* [Yüan-tu lu diary] (Shanghai, 1933), 7.73-73b (Entry of October 23, 1898).

[76] Yeh's reference to England and Russia is explained by his entry of October 21, *ibid.*, 7.73. He mentions here the rumor brought from Tientsin to the effect that the K'ang–Liang reform ideas had been sponsored by England and Japan for their own purposes and that the Empress Dowager's regency was the fruit of a Russian scheme. Therefore, when the startling coup broke, England and Japan did not dare to intervene.

[77] CSK, *Pen-chi*, 24.9b.

Ssu-t'ung in a private conference with Timothy Richard about the threat to the Emperor. They decided that Yung Wing, being an American citizen,[78] should see the United States minister, Liang should see the Japanese, and Richard the British to induce them to move for the Emperor's protection. But the United States minister was away in the hills and the British minister was at a water resort.[79]

The Japanese minister was in town. For the Emperor he could not intercede, but Liang was granted refuge in the legation, where he had his last conversation with T'an Ssu-t'ung, the young man whom he had met so short a time ago and set on the road to martyrdom. T'an had waited in his lodgings all day and night, until he could slip past the cordon of men waiting to seize him. He made his way to the legation to say good-by to his friend. Liang begged him to come east with him to Japan. T'an said that there would never be a new China until men had died for it. He left Liang and stepped back into the open, for capture, condemnation, and death.[80]

The city gates were closed to prevent the escape of the proscribed reformers, but Liang managed to reach Tientsin. The Japanese consul in Tientsin escorted him to Taku, and in the Japanese gunboat Ōshima he sailed into exile.[81]

The Empress Dowager followed him with decrees designed to make his life harder and a little shorter. On September 22, October 1, and December 5, she reiterated her demands for his capture, ordered his property confiscated, and offered a reward for his apprehension.[82] But it was the decree of September 29 which told Liang most succinctly how fondly he was regarded by the powers in Peking: "There is also the M. A. Liang Ch'i-ch'ao, a devoted follower and fellow-conspirator with K'ang Yu-wei. Liang's writ-

[78] Yung Wing had been the first Chinese to be educated in the United States.
[79] Richard, 266.
[80] "T'an Ssu-t'ung chuan," PCCP 12. 20b-21; "T'an Ssu-t'ung chuan," CSK, *Lieh-chuan* section, 470.5b.
[81] For a further discussion of Liang's escape see below, Chapter III.
[82] CSK, *Pen-chi*, 24.9b; 24.9b; 24.10b.

ings have always been treacherous and extravagant boastings, and he is also to be arrested and decapitated when caught."[83]

This *Peking Gazette* translation does not indicate precisely what the reactionaries thought of Liang. He was only to be beheaded, K'ang was to be sliced; and a more literal rendition would describe him as "the *chü-jen* Liang Ch'i-ch'ao, helplessly dependent on K'ang Yu-wei."[84] "Helplessly dependent" is "lang-pei," a little animal with short legs, riding on the back of a wolf. It is not a heroic image and not fully exact. Liang said many things that his teacher said, but even in the nineties one can detect the germ of later divergence. K'ang Yu-wei finished the classical tradition. Liang Ch'i-ch'ao finished it and took the next step into the dark.

[83] PG (1898), 85.
[84] THL 148.8.

CHAPTER II

THE BREAKDOWN OF THE CONFUCIAN WORLD

LIANG'S WRITINGS are documents of acculturation, the process of displacement or modification of the techniques, institutions, values, and attitudes of one culture by those of another. There are four conditions to acculturation: need for change, example of change, means of change, and justification of change. Liang tried to point out the existence of the first three conditions and to fulfill the last. I suggested in the Introduction that almost every time he urged reform, he looked to the classics for justification. He was faithful, in this, to the old intellectual outlook; for it was in the nature of Chinese thought, historically oriented, to sanctify practice in terms of precedent.[1] Yet, his traditional intellectual procedure swept Liang to nontraditional conclusions. What was this process? How did Confucian sanctions cover the disintegration of Confucianism?

Revision of Tradition and Social Change

In an article written in 1896 Liang describes the historic experience of the West with class stratification enforced by a hereditary governing nobility. Elimination of the hereditary principle, which the West desires and has yet to achieve, was proclaimed some thousands of years ago by Confucius. Liang insists that he has real grounds for eulogizing Confucius and proclaiming the utility of the classics. But Chinese thought has been overgrown with stylistic embellishment and arid semanticism, and if we compare that phase of it with modern thought, how can the Chinese help but seem weak?

There is a way out. Read the classics, Liang enjoins, and the

---

[1] The Chinese term for this operation is *t'o-ku kai-chih*—"finding in antiquity the sanction for present-day changes."

philosophers, and the histories, but with certain points in mind. If traditional Chinese thought, he says, is to be a vehicle for moderns, they must believe that Confucius' teaching is primary; that the Six Classics were all written by Confucius; that prior to Confucius there existed an older teaching; that the Six Classics were all books which changed the system of government; that after the Ch'in and Han periods all philosophers followed the heretical Hsün-tzu, who made of Confucianism a belief in the evil nature of man; that Confucius' oral sayings are all in the commentaries; that the "Ancient-character [*ku-wen*] classics" of the Eastern Han are forgeries by Liu Hsin; that, to a large extent, the corrupt texts of the ancient teachings have been restored by collators.[2]

Some interesting notes are struck here. There are echoes of K'ang Yu-wei's critical study of the authenticity of the orthodox classics, the *Hsin-hsüeh wei-ching k'ao* (1891),[3] and anticipations of K'ang's analysis of Confucius as a Reformer, the *K'ung-tzu kai-chih k'ao* (1897). The significance of this combination of motifs, iconoclasm and reform, is brought home by further reading in Liang's work, which reveals the prominence he assigns to the *Kung-yang* commentary on the *Ch'un-ch'iu,* the Spring and Autumn Annals.

The *Ch'un-ch'iu,* a chronicle of events from 721 to 481 B.C., was traditionally accepted as the work of Confucius himself, and his most important achievement. K'ang and Liang by no means disputed this. What they did dispute was the acceptance of a text called the *Tso-chuan* as an authentic commentary on the *Ch'un-ch'iu;* for the *Tso-chuan* was one of those *ku-wen* texts which K'ang and Liang called forgeries. They advanced the claim of another commentary, the *Kung-yang chuan,* to be the only genuine Confucian interpretation of the *Ch'un-ch'iu.* Now, the striking

[2] Liang, "Hsi-hsüeh shu-mu-piao hou-hsü," YPSWC 4.2-2b [Colophon to an index of books of Western learning].

[3] Liang and Ch'en T'ung-fu helped K'ang publish this work. See Chao Feng-t'ien, 188.

D

fact about the *Kung-yang chuan* is this: on the one hand, its claims on Confucian attention as a key to the *Ch'un-ch'iu* had been smothered for centuries by the reverently accepted *Tso-chuan;* on the other hand, it supplied texts which might seem to order drastic social change.

Here, in the linked textual and social unorthodoxies of the *Kung-yang* school, we have the confluence of two streams of history, streams mingling to dissolve the traditional Chinese ethnocentrism. Sacred texts are stripped of their canonical character and alien institutions come in. Western innovation and the subversion of Chinese doctrine—these work together, necessarily together, in the Chinese acculturation. If one element of a culture hitherto thought eternal (for example, the classical canon) comes to be seen as temporal, the mind may open to accept a change in every element. Liang asks for changes, changes dictated by modern Western encroachment and modern Western example.[4] But the foreign promise feeds on the native doubt, and Liang, becoming a westernizer, deserts a Chinese orthodoxy. For decades of Western incursion could not turn him by themselves; centuries of Chinese textual criticism had first flowed into them, and made him ready.

K'ang Yu-wei, says Liang, settled the "classics controversy."[5] K'ang was the man who surveyed the whole field of these classics whose authenticity had been questioned, first in Han times and again in Ch'ing, and he made the definitive findings.[6] His work on the false classics (*Hsin-hsüeh wei-ching k'ao*) which linked Liu Hsin's forgeries to Wang Mang's usurpation (A.D. 8-23—the "New [*Hsin*] Dynasty"), made a great stir in the philosophical

---

[4] For a clear exposition of the sense of urgency about China's future engendered by the Sino-Japanese War and the European menace, see Liang, "Nan hsüeh-hui hsü," YPSWC 4.15b-18 [Introductory remarks on the *Nan hsüeh-hui*].

[5] See the Appendix for the history of this controversy, which was the intellectual point of departure for K'ang and Liang.

[6] Liang, "Ch'ing-tai hsüeh-shu kai-lun," 54-55. Actually, K'ang's findings were far from definitive; his more radical conclusions are untenable. For a refutation of K'ang's thesis on the authorship of the classics, see Ch'ien Mu, "Liu Hsiang Hsin fu-tzu nien-p'u," YCHP 7 (June 1930), 1189-1318 [Chronological lives of Liu Hsiang and Liu Hsin, father and son].

world. His work on "Confucius as a Reformer" and his *Ta-t'ung shu* [Book of the Great Harmony] aroused even more excitement. "If the 'Study of the False Classics of the Hsin Learning' may be likened to a typhoon," wrote Liang, "then these two books were one a volcanic eruption and one a mighty earthquake."[7]

Syncretism: Western "Idea of Progress" in a Chinese Context

With these two works, most germinal for Liang's thought, K'ang achieved the wedding of the Chinese critical tradition to the impulse to introduce reforms from the West. In the first, by insisting that Confucius *invented* the Golden Age of Yao and Shun and did not really look back to it, he reoriented Confucianism toward the future. The Western idea of progress comes in, and that idea, in the nineteenth-century West, was linked with the scientific and social achievements which the reformers wished to borrow.

The second work, on the "Great Harmony," even more explicitly rivets the idea of progress to Confucianism. From the *Kung-yang* commentary on the *Ch'un-ch'iu,* he takes the concept of the *san-shih,* the three ages, and the last of the three is K'ang's world of the Great Harmony, in which there is internationalism, popular election, emancipation of women, general education, hospitalization of the sick, and institutional care of the aged.[8] The sequence of the three ages became by far the most recurrent symbol in the writings of Liang Ch'i-ch'ao.

The three ages, which in Liang's writings undergo multiple

[7] Liang, "Ch'ing-tai hsüeh-shu kai-lun," 57. The *Hsin-hsüeh wei-ching k'ao* was burned by imperial decree. In 1894 the censor Yü Chin-san and others memorialized accusing K'ang of "deceiving mankind and oppressing the masses" (*huo-shin wu-min*), of blasphemy and lawlessness (*fei-sheng wu-fa*), and asked for the burning of the book. The censor An Hsiao-fen also memorialized for its destruction (See ICTP, 2.1-1b). An edict to Li Han-chang (a brother of Li Hung-chang), the Governor General at Canton, ordered him to have the book examined (see *ibid.,* 2.1b-2b). The blocks were destroyed. Liang, in Peking, tried to assist K'ang during this episode, but to no effect. See Chao Feng-t'ien, 189.

[8] Liang, "Ch'ing-tai hsüeh-shu kai-lun," 58-59.

definition, are the *chü-luan shih* (Chaos), the *sheng-p'ing shih* (Peace), and the *t'ai-p'ing shih,* (Great Peace).[9] In "Tu Meng-tzu chieh-shuo" [An explanation of Mencius], 1898, Liang associates three concepts of the nature o. man with the three ages.

In the words of Confucius, character too has three interpretations. The character of the people of the *chü-luan shih* is evil; the character of the people of the *sheng-p'ing shih* is good and evil, has potentialities for both; the character of the people of the *t'ai-p'ing shih* is good. Hsün-tzu teaches the words of the *chü-luan shih;* Mi-tzu, Ch'i T'iao-tzu, and Shih-tzu teach the words of the *sheng-p'ing shih;* Mencius teaches the words of the *t'ai-p'ing shih.*[10]

It is important here to recall that the concept of human perfectibility was fundamental to the Western idea of progress in its eighteenth-century flowering and that it was indispensable to men like Timothy Richard and his favorite historian, Mackenzie, who from an appreciation of the advances of science distill an unqualified optimism about the destiny of man. If human nature were not fundamentally good, scientific techniques might only magnify man's power to tear society apart. It is not surprising, then, that Liang, who believed in the beneficence of science, should stand with Mencius on human nature. And the circle is closed completely when, as we shall see below, Mencius becomes Liang's principal Chinese repository of the humanitarian ideas which the reformers associated with western technological civilization.

[9] Liang. "Tu Jih-pen shu-mu-chih shu-hou," 8b, calls the first age *po-lan* (widespread confusion). K'ang, weaving his own work in with the classics in an elaborate network, says that the *Kung-yang*'s *sheng-p'ing shih* (Peaceful Age) is equivalent to the *hsiao-k'ang* (Peaceful Era) of the *Li-yün,* a chapter of the *Li-chi,* and that the *Kung-yang*'s *t'ai-p'ing shih* (Age of the Great Peace) is equivalent to the *Li-yün*'s *ta-t'ung* (Great Harmony). K'ang states that China for the past 2000 years has been in the *hsiao-k'ang* state. If China does not seek change but clings to the past, it will be controverting Confucius' idea. This was K'ang's theory before the 1898 reform. After the failure of the reform he decided that China had not reached the second stage, but was still in the first. See Kuo Chan-po, *Chin wu-shih nien Chung-kuo ssu-hsiang shih* [A history of Chinese thought in the last fifty years) (Peking, 1926), 8-9.

[10] Liang, "Tu Meng-tzu chieh-shuo," YPSWC 1.14b-15.

Liang used this ethical interpretation of the three ages in his blasts against the practice of foot-binding. He appealed to "the principles of the *Annals*"—oppression by force is the regime of the *chü-luan* age, the Age of Chaos, but not of the two succeeding ages. The world today has already moved into the second age, and therefore the evil custom of oppression is gradually passing away.[11] In another essay he elaborates on this sequential pattern of moral progress. In the *chü-luan* age, he wrote, one triumphed by force; in the *sheng-p'ing* age, by force and wisdom; in the *t'ai-p'ing* age, by wisdom. "In the transition of the world from chaos to peace, the sources of success pass from force into wisdom."[12]

Liang also interpreted the three ages in economic and political terms. In discussing the problem of fostering national prosperity, he states that the practice of financial speculation (*kuan shih-pien che*) exists in the first two ages but not in the Age of the Great Peace. What is the reason for this?

So-called "fluctuation" (*shih-pien*) comes from differences in market value; differences in market value come from inequities and uneven-ness, and these come from lack of commercial intercourse. Either the transportation routes are difficult or customs barriers mutually breed separation. . .[13]

But Liang has already, in this article, coupled "speculation" with "utilization of resources" (*chin ti-li che*) as the two forms of economic activity and the latter process is defined as "agricultural, extractive, and industrial work."[14] This is exactly what the re-formers wish to further, and this is the type of economic activity left to the *t'ai-p'ing* age, in which speculation will no longer be

[11] Liang, "Chieh ch'an-tsu hui hsü," YPSWC 4.23b [Statement for the anti-footbinding society].

[12] Liang, "Pien-fa t'ung-i," YPSWC 1.28-28b [The general principles of reform].

[13] Liang, "Shih-chi huo-chih lieh-chuan chin-i," YPSWC 1.10 [Modern prin-ciples derived from the *Shih-chi* biographies of those who were successful in the increase of their wealth].

[14] *Ibid.*, 9b.

operative because "fluctuation" cannot occur. We see here the tortured reasoning whereby "progress" is tied to a quasi-Confucian philosophy of utopia.

Financial speculation is impossible in the *t'ai-p'ing* age because the national barriers which foster it by interfering with the natural free market will be leveled. Liang comes to this conclusion by a political application of the *Kung-yang's* three-age formula. The first age is that of many sovereigns, the second is that of one sovereign, the third is that of the people. Using this framework, Liang courses through a generalized account of Chinese, Japanese, Russian, English, and French histories. In the West, he writes, the multi-sovereign phase was long, the single-sovereign phase was short. In China it operated the other way.

Here Liang comes to the crux of his argument about barriers. He asks whether the United States and France may be said to be in their *t'ai-p'ing* age. It might appear so, says Liang, but actually no nation, whatever the extent of popular rule within its borders, is living in the *t'ai-p'ing* age as long as it claims the attributes of sovereignty. From a world viewpoint, we are all in the *chü-luan* age of the many sovereigns.[15]

This great system of Liang's, despite its fanciful character, has a certain coherence. All roads lead from the *Kung-yang* doctrine of the three ages to science, democracy, prosperity, and peace, the same goods Timothy Richard offered without benefit of Confucius.[16] But that is only one facet of Liang's syncretism. The

[15] Liang, "Lun chün-cheng min-cheng hsiang-shan chih li," YPSWC 3.1-4b [A discussion of the principle of the succession of monarchical government and popular government]. See also Liang, "Shuo-ch'ün hsü," YPSWC 3.45b [Preface to *Shuo-ch'ün*]: "There are the people of a nation and the people of the world. Western government is by the people of the nation; we have not yet attained to government by the people of the world. . . In the age of the Great Peace, far and near, great and small in the world will be one."

[16] It may be remarked here that Hsü Chih-ching, in his memorial recommending Liang and others for office (see above, page 27), said that he was acting on the principle of "evolution from impoverishment to eternal peace." This phrase, *ch'iung pien t'ung chiu* (from *I-ching*), is part of the terminology which Liang borrowed from the classics and used to describe the trend of history. Cf. Liang, "Tu Jih-pen shu-mu-chih shu-hou," 8b, where he gives *ch'iung tse pien, pien tse t'ung* as a statement of Confucius' world-view.

evolutionary doctrine has two great characteristics, very revealing symbols of the corrosion of Confucian tradition. The first characteristic is its inconsistency with certain other of Liang's writings. The second is the theory which it implies of the universal application of Confucianism. Discussion of each of these points will lead us far afield.

Analogy of Patterns of Culture-Growth and Analogy of Cultural Values

The inner inconsistency in Liang's reasoning stems from the equivocal manner in which he relates innovation to Chinese tradition. Liang's constant concern is to protect Chinese culture from the imputation of failure. Therefore, borrowings must be converted into natural elements of the native tradition. Using the evolutionary *san-shih,* three-age formula, Liang locates these elements in the future—an authentic Chinese future which Confucius counted on. This rationalization we shall call "analogy of patterns of culture-growth." Chinese history, following its own native, Confucian course, points to the goals which the West has reached.

But at other times, using an "analogy of cultural values," Liang's apologia for China is of quite a different kind: he finds not parallel courses of history but identical essential ideals, and he holds that the desired innovations are not really new, for they had existed in China in the olden times. Using almost a golden-age legend of his own, he speaks of divergence from a past that must be recaptured. We have already glimpsed this idea in the first article cited in this chapter, "Hsi-hsüeh shu-mu-piao hou-hsü" [Colophon to an index of books of Western learning]; the reader will recall its remarks about China's ancient rejection of the hereditary principle and about the effectiveness of traditional modes of thought before bad scholarship had choked them off.

What this represents is Liang's crack-up in his effort to reconcile history and value. I shall cite two texts which together illustrate the intellectual weakness thrust on Liang by the demands of his time. The argument of one of these texts explicitly contradicts the argument of the other, but given Liang's historical situation, his illogicality might logically be expected.

In 1896 Liang discussed the theory that democracy had existed in the ancient world in the West.

> . . . Liang Ch'i-ch'ao emphatically does not agree. Western histories say that the democratic conception arose in Greece and Rome. Liang Ch'i-ch'ao considers that age to have been non-democratic. If that is called democracy, then our China, too, in ancient times could be said to have democracy.

He then undertakes his *san-shih* analysis and affirms that all the world must proceed from the first age to the Great Peace, when democracy at last will be real.[17]

In an article written the same year, Liang did say that ancient China had democracy. He wrote that the secret of Western strength was parliamentary democracy, the hallmark of which is the precedence of law over king. Ancient China, although it lacked the institution, had the idea. He cites, in abridged form, a passage from Mencius to the effect that a king should hearken not to his great officers, not to those about him, but to the voice of the people:

> When all those about you say, "This man deserves death," don't listen to them. When all your great officers say, "This man deserves death," don't listen to them. When the people all say, "This man deserves death," put him to death. . . You must act in this way in order to be the parent of the people.[18]

[17] Liang, "Yü Yen Yu-ling hsien-sheng shu," YPSWC 4.27 [Letter to Yen Fu]. See also Liang, "Lun chün-cheng min-cheng hsiang-shan chih li," 3-3b, where he rules out the claim that ancient .Greek representative institutions were equivalent to modern parliamentarianism. He skeptically believes them to have been manipulated by great families like those of the ancient Chinese feudal states. The alleged parliamentarianisms of Greece and Rome were still specimens of the multi-sovereign government.

[18] Translation of Mencius is from J. Legge, *The Chinese Classics*, 2 (Oxford, 1895), 165-166.

He quoted also from the *I-ching* and the *Shu-ching* to bolster his contention that once China had recognized the ideal of democracy. "Therefore," he wrote, "although there was not the name of representative government, there was yet the fact of it."[19]

It is obvious that between the respective premises in these two articles there is a logical chasm. In both he is concerned with history and value, but his two arguments proceed from opposite assumptions. In the first article, he ascribes value to parliamentarianism because it is considered to be in the stream of Chinese history. Confucius said it was coming, and good Confucianists should therefore wish it to come. In the second article, he locates parliamentarianism in the stream of Chinese history because he considers it to have value. Western experience has shown that it is a good thing, but Chinese must not believe that they were incapable of thinking it up for themselves.

And so Liang Ch'i-ch'ao is setting off simultaneously in two directions. On the one hand, he is a determinist, but not a convinced or convincing one, for his determinism is compounded of disparate beliefs: that change occurs because an end (the Great Peace) has been appointed to history, and that change occurs because effective natural causes of mutation exist in life itself.[20]

[19] Liang, "Ku i-yüan k'ao," YPSWC 1.1-1b [Researches into ancient parliaments].

[20] Biological illustrations are not uncommon in Liang's work, viz.: (*a*) "As all nature is in continual development, so is the life of society in the state. The history of China, in conformity with nature, shows also thoroughgoing transformations in the state—it would be absurd now to want to barricade oneself artificially against innovations" ("Pien-fa t'ung-i," quoted in O. Franke, "Die wichtigsten chinesischen Reformschriften vom Ende des neunzehnten Jahrhunderts," *Bulletin de l'Académie Impériale des Sciences de St. Pétersbourg*, fifth series, 17 [1902], 050). (*b*) Social Darwinist coloration of this quote from K'ang Yu-wei: "The late-comers on earth triumphed over the ones who came first; in the human realm, the later men exceed their predecessors. Reforms in the West came slowly. It is five hundred years since it turned its back on its beginnings, and the art of government in the West is in a developmental stage. Japan's march in the footsteps of the West was quick. It is thirty years since the restoration, and the Japanese art of government has reached its fine flowering" ("Tu Jih-pen shu-mu-chih shu-hou," 10).

For evidence of a tinge of the racism associated in Europe with Social Dar-

This is the association of a pseudo-Confucian teleology and a pseudo-Darwinian science, two of the most uneasy bedfellows in the philosophical roster. On the other hand, he is a voluntarist. He cannot believe that Chinese history has been rigidly determined, because that would rule Mencius, for example, out of court as a witness to the basic soundness of Chinese culture. The question he must answer is, "Why, at some point in Chinese history, did these ancient values disappear from Chinese society?" For Liang never romanticizes about modern China—he knows that the values have been lost: "Mencius says that the people are to be held in honor, the people's affairs may not be neglected. The governments of present-day Western states come near to conformity with this principle, but China alas, is cut off from the teachings of Mencius."[21]

If the inflexible course of Chinese history blotted out the ideals of Mencius, then the society which is the culmination of that history certainly cannot use Mencius as one of its showpieces. If, given its premises, Chinese history could have come into its modern phase only as it did, then the observed differences between the two civilizations and the higher valuation set on Western ways would leave the Chinese with only dust and ashes for his culture. The only possible explanation for the apologist is a moral one. Blame it on corruption, blame it on stupidity, on anything humanly remediable, but never say that Chinese culture, by the eternal law of its being, could not encompass literacy, democracy, or science.

Thus we find Liang saying that the parliamentary effort was abortive in China "because parliamentarians are what self-serving leaders in high places have least use for."[22] Again, he writes that

---

winism, see Liang, "Lun Chung-kuo chih chiang-ch'iang," YPSWC 3.8 [A discussion of the strengthening of China): Liang holds that the calibre of man is related to race and that the black and brown races are stupid, lazy, irresponsible, and unhappy.

[21] Liang, "Tu Meng-tzu chieh-shuo," 14.

[22] Liang, "Ku i-yüan k'ao," 2.

the roots of Chinese weakness lie in the progressive enhancement of the power of the monarch and the sapping of the people's rights. The blame for this lies heaviest, some say, on Ch'in Shih Huang-ti; on Yüan T'ai-tsu, on Ming T'ai-tsu, say others.[23] Elsewhere Liang says that Western inventions often came accidentally from a common or simple event. "We Chinese are not less clever than they and yet we have not invented anything. The reason lies in the lack of thought."[24] And in the same article, originally delivered as an address to the scholars at the Changsha school, he made his point of view crystal clear: "Now you gentlemen, who wear the scholar's robes and read the writings of the sages, must find out whose fault it is that our country has become so crippled, our race so weak, our religion so feeble."[25]

Liang, then, puts the emphasis on corruption, which ruins the system, rather than on the system, which begs for corruption. Thus, for example, he can plead eloquently for education of women, with the force of moral exhortation, and from the same premises, argue for industrialization without seeing any connection between the two except a common identification with the *t'ai-p'ing* age. He never sees that female education might be causally linked to an antecedent industrialism which would do it the preliminary service of shattering the Confucian family system. Liang could not admit that it was the system which deprived women of educational opportunity. Thus, in one article, urging this education, he implies that it was an authentic part of the tradition; his remarks begin with a statement of Mencius which likens the person of no learning to the birds and beasts.[26]

---

23 Liang, "Hsi-hsüeh shu-mu-piao hou-hsü," 3.

24 Liang, "Hu-nan Shih-wu hsüeh-t'ang hsüeh-yüeh," YPSWC 4.41b-46 [The Aims of the Hunan Modern School]; text and translation in E. Morgan, *Wenli Styles and Chinese Ideals* (Shanghai, 1931), 228-229.

25 *Ibid.*, 214.

26 Liang, "Pien-fa t'ung-i," 1. 17b-34. The same emphasis may be found in Liang, "Ch'ang she nü-hsüeh-t'ang ch'i," YPSWC 4.48-49 [Statement advocating the establishment of schools for women].

Inflationary Distortion

Liang's necessary emphasis on human failings was one of the elements involved in his theory of the universal application of Confucianism, that second characteristic of the *san-shih* doctrine which we mentioned above. Confucianism was in decay, he wrote, because scholars were ignorant of its true aims; Confucianism should be saved.[27] An observer who could think in institutional rather than moral terms might conclude from the same data that Confucianism was in decay not because the Chinese no longer served it, but because it had ceased to serve the Chinese; Confucianism should be scrapped. Decay of Confucianism, in either case, was apparent, and Liang, with the best will in the world, was helping to scrap it.

His idea of its true aim was that it was meant to conquer the world. "The Spring and Autumn Annals were not for one country but for the world," he wrote, "not for one time but for eternity."[28] "Now is the time to reveal the sentiments, teachings, rules, and essence of the Six Classics and test each with the new learning; then Confucius will be once more regarded as the example and model of ten thousand ages and the pattern of the world."[29] Students should vow to spread the Confucian religion of peace and brotherhood among all nations. He quoted the *Analects* to justify this: "The master was wishing to go and live among the nine wild tribes of the east," and "My doctrines make no way, I will get upon a raft and float about on the sea."[30] The formula of the three ages, which served the dual purpose of making world history fit a Confucian pattern and fitting a Confucian China into world history, was a striking application of this universalism.

Of course, universalism was a little more than Confucianism

[27] Liang, "The Aims of the Modern Hunan School," in Morgan, 234-236.

[28] Liang, "Ch'un-ch'iu Chung-kuo i-ti pien hsü," YPSWC 3.49b [Preface to the Ch'un-ch'iu's distinction between the natures of Chinese and barbarians].

[29] Liang, in Morgan, 234-236.

[30] *Ibid.*, 234-236.

could bear. The particular appeal of Confucianism which made it worth saving to a Chinese came from its particular association with China. Liang is the perfect symbol of the transitional age, adapting Confucianism to modern life and adapting it into the ground.

When Confucianism is being called upon to join all kinds of synthetic alloys the world over, it is not to be expected that the little parochial barriers in the Chinese world should stand. The very sentence in which Liang describes to the Hunan scholars their Confucian obligations is phrased in Buddhist terminology: "It is only the courage that dares face hell or the spirit that dares risk life, in governing, that will encompass success."[31] It is not surprising that the lines are blurred. Eclecticism is natural when a tradition is dying. A society which, when self-sufficient, could enjoy the luxury of supporting mutually exclusive creeds must pool its resources when the foreign onslaught comes.

Obscurantism and Self-Effacement

There were two varieties of reaction to this onslaught which Liang wished to avoid. The first was obscurantist refusal to consider change; the second was Chinese self-effacement which might be corollary to acceptance of foreign values. Obscurantism he fought by an appeal for realism.[32] He fought self-effacement,

[31] *Ibid.,* 218. Buddha must go to hell to be a savior.

[32] The argument is twofold: (*a*) inevitability of change and (*b*) need for action against palpable weaknesses. Examples: (*a*) "Pien-fa t'ung-i" 1.18: "From beginning to end, for thousands of years, there has been no time without change, nothing which has not changed. . . Those who speak against change say 'maintain the old, maintain the old unaltered.' How surprising is it that they certainly do not know the infinite number of changes from extreme antiquity . . . to the present. What are today regarded as old laws and so preserved—what departures they are from the ideas of the ancients!" (*b*) Liang begins "Po-lan mieh-wang chi," YPSWC 1. 16-17b [The record of the destruction of Poland], with an account of Poland's degradation under the Russian regime. He traces its history from the seventeenth century when, he remarks, it was one of Europe's virile, strong nations. Cause of its collapse: an unreformed government. In "Shen-shih yin-shu hsü," YPSWC 3.46b [Preface to Mr. Shen's phonetic writing], Liang expresses

first, by the efforts we have seen to smuggle Western values into Chinese tradition, and second, by conjuring up an equal and opposite reaction, a Chinese institution which would be saleable and could restore the balance of trade. Liang believed in the universality of science. He could believe no less of Confucius.

In the doctrine of Confucian universality we see the beginnings of the matter-spirit dichotomy, that simplifying formula by which the ethos of Europe and the ethos of China may be differentiated, to the implied advantage of the latter. It is not yet fully articulated, because Liang in this period never applied the term "materialism" in its derogatory sense to Western culture and still believed in the possibility of synthesis.[33] But, as the whole emphasis of this chapter has indicated, he was extremely concerned that it be a synthesis, that Chinese culture should not wither,

---

his concern about Chinese illiteracy. Germans and Americans are 96 to 97 per cent literate, Japanese more than 80 per cent literate. "China, trumpeting its civilization to the five continents, has yet not attained to 20% literacy."

In the last essay, Liang anticipates the *pai-hua* movement. He traces the growth of illiteracy from the composition of the Confucian canon. Scholars read this in their own spoken language—Liang compares this to translation of the Western classics into English, French, Russian, and German. Later generations of scholars abandoned contemporary speech and would not condescend to use it. Liang holds that the cleavage between the spoken and written languages is a source of injury. The gap grew ever wider after the third century of the Christian era (end of the first empire-period), the study of the written language gradually becoming more difficult (47-47b). Note the suggestion of moral responsibility for illiteracy.

[33] Liang frequently urged that action be based on a correlation of Chinese and Western experience. Examples: (*a*) In "The Aims of the Hunan Modern School" Liang insists that to discover the principles of government, one must understand the classics and compare them with the works of the Chou and Ch'in scholars and with western books about international politics and law. He urges comparison of the dynastic histories with the histories of Greece and Rome, etc. (Morgan, 232-234). The same emphasis may be found in Liang, "Yü Lin Ti-ch'en t'ai-shou shu," YPSWC 4.33b [Letter to the prefect Lin Ti-ch'en] and in Liang, "Fu Liu Ku-yu shan-ch'ang shu," YPSWC 4.39-41b [Letter in reply to the educator Liu Ku-yu]. (*b*) In a discussion of Chinese foreign policy, Liang cites Mencius' injunction that attainment of success or failure rests on one's own efforts—if one relies on others he courts disaster. Therefore, says Liang, when he hears someone advise China to join Russia in order to ward off England, he points to Poland; if someone advises joining England to ward off Russia, he points to India ("Lun chia-shui," YPSWC 3.20 [On extra taxes]).

should not simply be displaced by the culture of the modern West. To that end, he meant to be selective.

He wanted selected values from the West, but he realized that, in any civilization, many institutions are preserved purely through inheritance and have no intrinsic value. In a mood of self-efface-ment a culture will take from another these worthless accretions with the good, and that is the mark of complete decay. Thus, though both Tseng Kuo-fan and Liang favored selectivity, Liang was moved by a more extreme sense of urgency, and the difference in tone between Liang's plea for selectivity and Tseng's is the gauge of Confucianism's failure of nerve in the space of one gen-eration. Tseng was sure he could pick and choose. Liang had no such confidence. Both feared the material danger of foreign con-quest, but only Liang saw the specter of inner collapse.

> If there is no moral culture in the schools, no teaching of patriotism, students will as a result only become infected with the evil ways of the lower order of Westerners and will no longer know that they have their own country. . . . The virtuous man, then, will become an employee of the foreigners in order to seek his livelihood; the de-generate man will become, further, a traitorous Chinese in order to subvert the foundations of his country.[34]

A hundred times more than Western soldiers, Western commerce weakens China. In the state of disrepair of Chinese armaments, we see one road to weakness; in the stagnation of culture, a hundred roads.[35]

Liang of course by no means implies that China should desire isolation. On the contrary, he goes on to castigate the Chinese failure to see that in the beginning Westerners desired neither to acquire lands nor destroy the country. They sought only trade, says Liang, and trade profits the home country twice as much as it does the country which comes in quest of it. But China with-drew into a "dry well' and closed its eyes to foreign things.[36]

[34] Liang, "Cheng-p'ien yüan-yin ta k'o-nan," YPSWC 3.23 [Answers to a friend's questions about the causes of the *coup d'état*].

[35] Liang, "Shih-k'o-chai chi-yen chi-hsing hsü," 45b-46.

[36] *Ibid.*, 46.

Rejection of Tradition

Japan, as the nation which had climbed out of its own dry well, was the beau ideal of the reformers.[37] The fact that Liang was able to reconcile political opposition to Japan with cultural admiration is another index of the inroads of westernization. Such an attitude would have been impossible for the early official westernizers, to whom it was inconceivable that there be a Chinese national interest severed from pride in the Chinese culture. Until ethnocentrism has broken down, a nation cannot disentangle itself intellectually from its way of life, for the way of life completely dominates the mind which would examine it. Not until a culture has been stripped of its dogmatic sanctions can one of its participants stand back and examine it, and only then does it compete in the open with possible alternatives.

Once a people and its traditional culture have been put asunder, they may possibly be thought of as mutually opposed. That view, associated today with the Chinese revolutionaries, was not possible for the young Liang Ch'i-ch'ao, whose great effort was to paste

[37] Examples of this Japanophilism have already appeared in the text. I include here a few of Liang's expressions of this feeling: In "Cheng-p'ien yüan-yin ta k'o-nan," 24b, he cites Japanese reform as model for China, but thinks the accumulated corruptions in China much more serious than those of Japan in the *Bakumatsu* period. In "Jih-pen kuo-chih hou-hsü," YPSWC 3.52b [Colophon to *Annals of Japan*], he tells of lessons learned from Huang Tsun-hsien's history of Japan (completed 1887); on page 53, Liang emphasizes Japan's rise to strength in period of mere thirty years. In "Shang Nan-p'i Chang shang-shu shu," YPSWC 4.25 [Letter to Board President Chang of Nan-p'i] he lauds Japan for its successful fusion of East and West. "The Japanese reform made schools its first concern, and Japanese schools considered government the most important thing. Japan took western legal principles and adapted them to Japanese circumstances." In "Chih-ch'ih hsüeh-hui hsü," YPSWC 4.18-19b [Remarks on the *Chih-ch'ih* study society]—the name of which society is taken from the reformers' slogan, "Know the shame (*chih-ch'ih*) of not being like Japan"—Liang cites causes of shame for China: lag in material development, shocking degree of illiteracy, etc. He ends rhetorically, "That the lustre of Confucianism is dimmed and no stop put to corruption in high places; that the dominion of the Great Peace makes no headway and that no sign is there of the Great Harmony—that is Liang Ch'i-ch'ao's shame."

together philosophically what he and his fellow Reformers were blowing apart. The disharmonies set up in such an effort have already been remarked, and, in the last analysis, they could never be resolved. When Liang Ch'i-ch'ao linked reform to the authority of the classics, the sands were shifting under his feet, for the reforms he urged would finally destroy the one society which could do the classics reverence.

PART TWO

1898-1911: BRAVE NEW WORLD

EXILE IN JAPAN AND THE WEST

OCTOBER 1898:

A Shanghai dispatch of the 1st inst. says that Ryo Kei-cho, a leader of the Reform party, is still at large. He is believed to be under the protection of a certain Power.[1]

The search of the boat of the Japanese Consul at Tientsin by a Chinese man-of-war would, apart from Treaty considerations, appear to have had some warrant, for it is now reported that the Oshima, which recently returned from Taku, has a foreigner, presumably a Chinese, on board. Many rumours have been in circulation on this matter, and there appears to be no doubt that a Chinese of position has been assisted to escape by the Japanese authorities, but who it is has not at present been disclosed. One telegram a few days ago announced that the Oshima was bringing a "very valuable present" to Japan.[2]

Two distinguished Chinese refugees have now reached Tokyo. . .[3]

The Escape to Japan

When the Empress Dowager turned suddenly on the partisans of reform, Count Itō Hirobumi, then in Peking, received secret Japanese orders to facilitate the escape of K'ang Yu-wei and Liang Ch'i-ch'ao.[4] K'ang was away from the capital when the troubles

[1] *Kobe Chronicle*, October 8, 1898, 301. "Ryo Kei-cho" is the Japanese reading of the characters in Liang's name.

[2] *Ibid.*, October 22, 1898, 338.

[3] *Ibid.*, October 29, 1898, 369.

[4] Kuzū Yoshihisa, *Tōa senkaku shishi kiden* [Historical records of East Asian pioneer adventurers] (Tokyo, 1933-1936), I, 624. This publication is drawn from the archives of the Kokuryūkai (Black Dragon Society) and is an important source.

Shumbō Kō tsuijōkai (Prince Shumbō eulogy society), *Itō Hirobumi den* [Biography of Itō Hirobumi] (Tokyo, 1942), the standard Japanese biography of Itō, III, 394-401, reports his presence in Peking from September 14 to September 29,

began, and after many vicissitudes he reached Hong Kong, where a Japanese named Miyazaki Torazō (Tōten) met him and designated himself escort for the trip to Japan.[5] In Peking, the task of spiriting Liang out of the country was handled by one Hirayama Shū. He visited Liang and his associate Wang Chao in their refuge in the Japanese legation, had them change into Japanese clothes, and got them to Tientsin, Taku, and the Ōshima.[6] When the gunboat put in at Miyajima, on the Inland Sea, Takahashi Kichitaro of the Japanese Foreign Ministry was there to welcome them. Escorted to Tokyo, they were installed in lodgings already prepared. A few days later, Miyazaki ushered K'ang to the same address.[7]

Who were these good fairies, Miyazaki and Hirayama? They were Japanese pan-Asiatics, and in 1897 they had become the personal agents of Inukai Takeshi, the lieutenant of Count Ōkuma. The latter was then foreign minister in the Matsukata cabinet (popularly known as the "Matsukuma" cabinet, in recognition of Ōkuma's great political stature).[8] In June 1898, after an interlude of private life, Ōkuma became foreign minister again. This time the cabinet included Inukai, whom an old revolutionary partisan of Sun Yat-sen has called the Japanese leader most interested at that time in seeing a new government in China.[9]

That summer, when Sun Yat-sen returned to Japan after several years of conspiratorial, anti-Manchu travels, Inukai sent Miyazaki and Hirayama to Yokohama to welcome him. They took Sun to

1898, but it states that his trip to China was taken on his own initiative, and there is no mention of instructions, from whatever source, concerning K'ang and Liang. Itō did, however, according to this account, intercede with Li Hung-chang for the life of one of the reformers, Chang Yin-huan.

[5] Miyazaki Torazō, *San-ju-san nen no yume* [Thirty-three years' dream] (Tokyo, 1926), 155.

[6] Feng Tzu-yu, *Ko-ming i-shih* [Historical reminiscences of the revolution] (Chungking, 1943), I, 48.

[7] Kuzū, I, 624.

[8] *Ibid.*, I, 612.

[9] Feng Tzu-yu, *Chung-hua min-kuo k'ai-kuo-ch'ien ko-ming shih* [History of the revolution prior to the establishment of the Chinese Republic] (Chungking, 1944), II, 110.

Tokyo for a conference with Inukai, their first meeting and an extremely cordial one. Inukai introduced him to Ōkuma, and Sun's relations with Japanese political circles were at last established.[10]

Sun chose Yokohama as his headquarters, and Miyazaki writes that, after seeing Sun settled there, he and Hirayama set out for Shanghai.[11] What was the purpose of their journey? According to the Kokuryūkai publication, they were anxious to help Sun keep up his contacts in China and further the revolutionary cause.[12] Feng Tzu-yu suggests a different motive: Sun, hearing of the plight of K'ang and Liang, had urged the two Japanese to go to China and get them out of danger.[13] But Miyazaki's account justifies no such conclusion. At the time of his departure, K'ang and Liang were having no discernible trouble. When he left Sun, he writes, the Emperor Kuang-hsü was under the influence of K'ang and planning reforms.[14] Miyazaki passes through Canton and mentions that K'ang is in Peking.[15] Later he writes of hearing rumors, then the facts of the *coup d'état,* but nowhere does he mention consultation with Sun even by telegram, much less by conversation, about the course of action to be taken.[16] Feng is evidently embroidering the truth, and a plausible reason for this is easy to find. He is trying to put K'ang and Liang in a false moral position with regard to Sun Yat-sen; for though Sun sought eagerly, at first, to unite their forces, the reformers, who opposed the Empress Dowager but supported the dynasty, contemptuously rejected the idea of coalition, and from then on the two parties struck at each other in bitter conflict, throughout the one period of both their exiles.

[10] Sun Yat-sen, "Tzu-chuan" [Autobiography], in *Chung-shan ch'üan-shu* [Collected works of Sun Yat-sen] (Shanghai, 1926), I, 19. "Chung-shan," in Japanese reading "Nakayama," was the name which Sun assumed in Japan.

[11] Miyazaki, 133.

[12] Kuzū, I, 622-623.

[13] Feng, *Ko-ming i-shih,* I, 48.

[14] Miyazaki, 133.

[15] *Ibid.,* 135.

[16] *Ibid.,* 138.

Relations between Revolutionaries and Reformers

Liang for a considerable time felt no burning need to make an enemy of Sun. Some sort of liaison between the two groups had been established well before the Hundred Days of Reform, and it was K'ang who precipitated the final break. There is a story that in 1894, when both were in Canton, Sun sent word to K'ang that he was anxious to meet him. K'ang is supposed to have replied that, if the young man wished to meet him, he should formally apply as a pupil in K'ang's school and send in one of the written applications.[17]

By 1896 we are definitely out of the age of fable in this matter of contact between reformers and revolutionaries. In that year, Kuang Ju-p'an, Feng Ching-ju, and others organized a school for the children of Chinese in Yokohama, which was Sun's headquarters at that time. They deliberated with Sun about inviting teachers from China. Sun, feeling that K'ang and Liang had aspirations for China similar to his own and being well aware of K'ang's experience and success as a teacher, drafted a letter of invitation to K'ang. Kuang Ju-p'an took it to Shanghai and there met with the "modern sage," who declined the post himself but recommended several others. One of these, Hsü Ch'in, went to Japan, conferred with Sun, and appeared to the latter acceptable. However, when Hsü took charge of the school, he gradually subverted Sun's position and drew many Chinese into the reformist camp.[18]

Also in 1896, Sun tried to affiliate with K'ang for less contemplative ends than education. Sun's man Hsieh Tsan-t'ai, in Hong Kong, broached the subject of joint action to K'ang Kuang-jen. He repeated the suggestion in the following year, but the younger K'ang reported that his brother was definitely committed to peaceful change and would have no relations with the revolutionaries, for he was counting on the support of officials like

17 Carl Glick and Hong Sheng-Hwa, *Swords of Silence: Chinese Secret Societies —Past and Present* (New York, 1947), 113.

18 Li Chien-nung, *Tsui-chin san-shih nien Chung-kuo cheng-chih shih* [Political history of China in the last thirty years] (Shanghai, 1930), 68-69.

Chang Chih-tung. However, in 1898, Hsieh wrote a letter on the same subject to K'ang and Liang, and even this letter, which remained unanswered, would not be his final attempt.[19]

Sun made his first personal bid for a *rapprochement* almost immediately after the refugees reached Tokyo in 1898. A conference was arranged between Sun, his friend Ch'en Shao-pai, K'ang, and Liang. At the appointed time, no K'ang appeared. He had been unavoidably kept away, explained Liang, and had commissioned him spokesman. The three conferees aired their views until dawn.

Several days later, Ch'en and Hirayama were sent by Sun to call on K'ang. This time the latter put in an appearance, together with Wang Chao, Hsü Ch'in, Liang T'ieh-chün, and Liang Ch'i-ch'ao. Ch'en spoke of the rotten corruption of the Ch'ing dynasty, the futility of hoping to change it or to save China by its agency. He pleaded with K'ang to become a revolutionary; K'ang replied that his views would not change. Suddenly, Wang Chao burst out in bitter protest against the restraints on his movements put upon him, he alleged, by K'ang since their coming to Tokyo. Black rage was K'ang's reaction. Liang T'ieh-chün pushed the gesticulating Wang out of the room at a word from K'ang, who was shocked and angry at this defection, the forerunner of many in the years to come.[20]

For a few seasons he had reason to wonder whether even Liang Ch'i-ch'ao was safe and sound. In the spring of 1899, Liang, in his old capacity as newspaper editor, printed "The Strange Adventures of a Beautiful Woman" (*Chia-jen ch'i-yü chi*), a translation of a Japanese article with an anti-Manchu tone. When K'ang saw this, he banned reprinting and delivered stern admonitions to Liang.[21] But it was only with K'ang's departure on a world tour, very soon after this newspaper episode, that Liang's nervous flirtation with the rival coterie assumed any real proportions.

Renewed blandishments came from the Sun party, but Liang

[19] Feng, *Chung-hua min-kuo*, I, 38.
[20] Feng, *Ko-ming i-shih*, I, 49.
[21] *Ibid.*, I, 63.

at first, uncertain and hard to please, backing and filling, inspired no confidence. On June 6, 1898, Yang Ch'ü-yün, a close associate of Sun's old liaison man, Hsieh Tsan-t'ai, was introduced to Liang by Feng Ching-ju, who was then nominally editor-in-chief (Liang did most of the work) of the reformers' Yokohama newspaper, the *Ch'ing-i pao*. After this meeting, held in Yokohama, Yang wrote to Hsieh that Liang did not desire early coalition; he felt rather that each party ought to attend first to its own movement and await some future, undefined opportunity for union. Yang noted a sense of exaggerated self-importance on the part of the K'ang party and advised abandonment of the idea of fusion, which would do more harm, he thought, than good. Hsieh, formerly so eager for amalgamation, lost the spirit for it.[22]

Sun, however, was not yet reconciled to the breach and undertook direct discussion with Liang. A plan of union was actually conceived. Sun was to be president of a new society, Liang to be vice-president. What position would K'ang have under the new dispensation? Sun is said to have answered this question of Liang's with another—"when the disciple is the leader, is not the teacher's position then one to be respected?"[23] Liang seems to have been satisfied, but he was greatly mistaken if he imagined that K'ang would abdicate leadership and sit quietly with his old scrolls and his memories, cherishing the cryptic and hypocritical implication that Sun Yat-sen regarded him as his master.

Liang drafted a letter which was to try delicately to win K'ang over to this arrangement. The signatories were thirteen of K'ang's disciples. Soon Liang took another step toward implementing the plan. Visiting Sun's aide Ch'en Shao-pai in Hong Kong, he recommended that Ch'en for the revolutionaries and Hsü Ch'in for the reformers draft articles of union. But Hsü's enthusiasm, such as it was, rapidly chilled, and, together with another of the old reformers, Mai Meng-hua, he wrote K'ang, then in Singapore, that Liang was falling into the snare.[24]

[22] Feng, *Chung-hua min-kuo*, I, 38.
[23] Feng, *Ko-ming i-shih*, I, 64-65.
[24] *Ibid.*, II, 31-32; Li, 69.

K'ang had by this time received the letter from the thirteen
and was already unrestrainedly angry. The letters of Hsü and Mai
brought another turn of the screw. Far from retiring gracefully,
he asserted his position as commander by ordering Liang to put
Sun behind him, leave Japan, and strictly in the reformers' interests, get to Honolulu, that great city, wherein were many
Chinese and also much money.[25]

Liang went to Honolulu, but nowhere in his papers is there
indication that this trip was the upshot of a somewhat shady
backstairs intrigue. Rather he explains it, twice, as a response to
an invitation from America, where, owing to K'ang's initiative,
sympathizers in American-Chinese business circles had established the Chinese Reform Society (*Chung-kuo wei-hsin hui*)
and would appreciate a visit from a prominent reformer; circumstances, however, prevented his getting beyond the Hawaiian
Islands.[26] Yet, the facts as stated in Feng Tzu-yu's recollections of
those days, which he lived in company with the principals of the
story, are as plausible as would be Liang's motives in overlooking
them. There was indisputably a close rapport between Liang and
Sun at this time. Sun gave Liang a letter of introduction to his
elder brother in Hawaii, Sun Te-chang, a letter which would give
him entree into a milieu where Sun's ideas, with his society, the
Hsing-Chung hui (Revive China Society), were well established.[27]
That Sun could have such confidence in Liang Ch'i-ch'ao (though
not, of course, that it would take this form) would not have remained unknown to K'ang, and there were only two gestures he
could have made: either excommunication and an abandonment
of Liang to the contagion, or injunction to a prophylactic and
penitential mission. So on December 20, 1899, Liang left on his
first travels outside the Far East, after something more than a
year in Japan, during which, really, his efforts had not been
confined to futile conversation alone.

[25] Feng, *Ko-ming i-shih*, II, 32; Li, 69.
[26] Liang, "San-shih tzu-shu," 27b; Liang, "Hsin-ta-lu yu-chi chieh-lu," YPSWC
38.2 [Travels in the New World].
[27] Li, 69.

Liang's Work in Japan, 1898-1899

The *Ch'ing-i pao* [Pure Criticism Journal][28] was first in the series of journals which Liang Ch'i-ch'ao published in Japan and which wielded tremendous influence among Chinese overseas and those many Chinese at home who broke the law and read the word. Liang writes in his autobiography that he founded the *Ch'ing-i pao* in the tenth month (November 14-December 12), 1898, with the financial backing of Chinese merchants in Yokohama.[29] The paper's great theme was restoration of the Kuang-hsü Emperor to power. The Empress Dowager, Jung Lu, and Yüan Shih-k'ai were targets of attack. Along with these articles of sarcasm and invective directed against the conservatives in Peking, Liang published pages in bulk of political and social philosophy. Mai Meng-hua took charge of the paper when Liang left for Hawaii.[30] A fire in the printing plant in Yokohama, in the winter of 1900, put an end to publication of the *Ch'ing-i pao*.[31]

Liang's other main concern was formal education. In September 1899, having collected $3000 (Mex.) from various Chinese of Yokohama, he founded the *Kao-teng ta-t'ung hsüeh-hsiao* (Great Harmony Secondary School) in Tokyo. Liang was headmaster and one of Inukai's assistants, Kashiwara Buntarō, was the executive secretary. The curriculum was in large part concerned vith English and French political philosophy. Of the students, eleven had once studied at Liang's old headquarters, the *Hunan shih-wu hsüeh-t'ang*, and seven were products of another *Ta-t'ung hsüeh-hsiao* which had been established in Yokohama in late spring, 1898.[32] After Liang went to Honolulu, the school passed through a series of changes in name. By 1902 it was called *Ch'ing-hua*

[28] The title derives from the "pure-criticism" movement conducted by scholars in the second century of the Christian era.

[29] Liang, *San-shih tzu-shu*, 27.

[30] Feng, *Ko-ming i-shih*, I, 63.

[31] Britton, 119.

[32] Feng, *Ko-ming i-shih*, I, 72; Feng, *Chung-hua min-kuo*, II, 110. For the Yokohama *Ta-t'ung hsüeh-hsiao*, see *Kobe Chronicle*, October 15, 1898, 305, where it is called *Daido-Gakko*, after the Japanese readings of the characters.

hsüeh-hsiao[33] and was ready also for a change in spirit; its last phase was as a school of orthodox principles under the direction of, Ts'ai Chün, the Chinese minister to Japan.[34]

The Chinese government was well aware of these labors of Liang and the other reformers. An imperial edict issued December 20, 1899, was a plain incitement to assassination—a reward was promised for seizure of K'ang and Liang or for proof of their deaths. As previously in a censor's memorial of 1894 (see note 7 of Chapter II), K'ang was charged with "deceiving mankind and oppressing the masses" (*huo-shih wu-min*). The Emperor, so ran the edict, had asked the Empress Dowager to instruct the government to take the rebels prisoner and "bring tranquillity out of danger" (*chuan wei wei an*). But K'ang Yu-wei and his sworn confederate Liang Ch'i-ch'ao had already fled examination and death, and beyond the seas, they still were recklessly making mischief. "The hearts of the rebellious wolves have not changed. . ."[35]

Their heads, however, grew more valuable. The continental circulation of the *Ch'ing-i pao* terrified the Chinese government, and an edict of February 14, 1900, offered a new grand prize of Tls. 100,000 (or official preferment) for delivery of their persons or for the good news of their deaths.[36] Two weeks later, the newspapers noted a rumor that assassins dispatched by the Empress Dowager were on their way to K'ang and Liang.[37]

All things considered, Liang was no hero to the mandarins. Japanese officialdom liked him better. As long as Ōkuma's Progressive Party (Shimpotō) was in power, K'ang and Liang were given Japanese government funds.[38] K'ang, as a matter of fact,

[33] Liang, "San-shih tzu-shu," 27b.

[34] Feng, *Ko-ming i-shih*, I, 72.

[35] THL 157.5-5b.

[36] THL 158.3b. This edict is summarized in Britton, 119, and a portion of it is translated in Lin Yutang, *A History of the Press and Public Opinion in China* (Chicago, 1936), 98. Lin unaccountably gives its date as January 15. Chao Feng-t'ien, 215, mentions the edict, but he, too, dates it wrongly—fifth month (May 28–June 26), 1900.

[37] *Kobe Chronicle*, March 1, 1899, 156.

[38] Feng, *Ko-ming i-shih*, I, 48.

lodged with Ōkuma for a time; then for a half-year, until he left on his travels in 1899, he lived at Waseda University, of which Ōkuma was president.[39] When he left Waseda for the trip to America and Europe, Ōkuma provided him with Tls. 7000 for expenses.[40] In June 1899 we see Liang planning a reception for the Marquis in the Chinese Chamber of Commerce in Kobe.[41] There is no doubt but that Ōkuma was a friend.

Liang had many friends in Japan. He took the Japanese name Yoshida Shin. On December 19, 1899, the day before he sailed from Yokohama, Liang wrote in his diary, "Truly, in Japan, I have the feeling that here is my second home."[42]

Hawaiian Journey

Liang's vessel, the *Hong Kong Maru*, ran immediately into rough water, and Liang has left us a thoroughly conventional account of the voyage: heavy seas—mal de mer—heavier seas—waves like thunder—like snow-capped mountains. When Liang was on his feet, he had long conversations with two Catholic priests, veteran missionaries in Kansu.[43] On the last day of the year, the *Hong Kong Maru* put in at Honolulu. Bubonic plague was reported on the island, and transient passengers were forbidden to land, but Liang came ashore and was met by a colleague who had arranged for his temporary lodging at the Arlington Hotel. Liang's first concern seems to have been to register at the Japanese Consulate.[44]

[39] *Ōkuma Kō hachi-ju-go nen shi hensan kai* [Collected papers on the life of Marquis Ōkuma] (Tokyo, 1926), II, 536.

[40] TP, X, 328.

[41] *Kobe Chronicle*, June 7, 1899, 446. In 1904, Liang translated into Chinese an important Ōkuma speech, *Tōyō no heiwa wo ronzu* [On peace in the Far East]. This speech, delivered in October 1904, reinforced his May address, *Nichirō sensō to sekai no heiwa* [The Russo-Japanese War and world peace], which had been published abroad as the "Ōkuma Doctrine." The speech translated by Liang pleads the basic affinity of China and Japan in race and culture and maintains that only Japan can lead a sick China to health. (See *Ōkuma Kō hachi-ju-go-nen shi hensan kai*, II, 436-438.)

[42] Liang, "Hsia-wei-i yu-chi," YPSWC 37.58 [Hawaiian travel record].

[43] *Ibid.*, 59b-62b.

[44] *Ibid.*, 62b-63.

The reform movement already had a considerable bloc of sympathizers in Honolulu, and several of them met Liang in the hotel that evening. On New Year's Day came more visitors, but on January 2 Liang could recollect that not all Chinese were well-wishers. Consider the Chinese consul. He wrote a letter to the American authorities asking that Liang be deported. It was Saitō, the Japanese consul, who helped Liang get his status settled. Liang pays tribute to the freedom guaranteed by United States law, which protected him from the Chinese government's designs.[45]

On January 7, the local government, in a drive against the plague, began to condemn and burn many Chinese dwellings and shops. Also, large gatherings were forbidden, so that Liang could not speak in public.[46] However, despite this handicap, Liang seems to have made a great impression on the Chinese community. Chinese nationalism was fed by the American action in burning out the dock area, with its attendant serious loss to Chinese, and Liang was able to persuade many that, if Kuang-hsü were only restored to power, China could make a start toward greatness. A huge fund was subscribed, and members began to flock into the reformers' organization, the *Pao-huang hui* (Protect the Emperor Society), which had been founded in Yokohama by K'ang and Liang.[47]

Serious inroads were made on Sun's organization. Liang was received with great kindness by Sun's brother and uncle on Maui (so Feng tells us—Liang is silent on this subject), and *Hsing-*

---

[45] *Ibid.*, 63.

[46] *Ibid.*, 64b.

[47] Feng, *Ko-ming i-shih*, I, 16; Li, 69. Li says that Liang personally organized the *Pao-huang hui* in Honolulu and represented it in a false light, as a revolutionary society, its name notwithstanding. Liang, on the other hand, in "Hsia-wei-i yu-chi," 64b, writes of a meeting at the house of a local *Pao-huang hui* leader, a meeting which occurred only a week after Liang's arrival and seemingly indicates the prior existence of the *Pao-huang hui*. Still, there is the puzzling statement in Liang's "San-shih tzu-shu," 27b, that while he was in the Hawaiian Islands he founded the *Hsia-wei-i wei-hsin hui* (Hawaiian reform society). If this society was not actually the *Pao-huang hui* in another name, it certainly must have duplicated its functions.

Chung hui circles welcomed him at first, since he bore Sun's letter of introduction.[48] Before long the ranks of the *Hsing-Chung hui* became depleted and the *Pao-huang hui* rose to a commanding position in the Hawaiian Chinese world. When Sun realized what was happening, he sent a virulent letter to Liang, upbraiding him for breach of faith.[49] There was no answer. It was a hopeless gulf between them now, and not until 1915, when Liang turned against Sun's enemy Yüan Shih-k'ai, was there ever again a chance that they might work together.

Liang remained in Hawaii for half a year. He insists that he wanted to go on to the United States, but summer, 1900 brought the rising of the Boxers and the intervention of the great powers. Something new might be in the offing for China. All kinds of rumors were current, and letters and telegrams from Japan urged him to return.[50] On July 13, he received an especially important telegram from Shanghai. On July 16, he sailed for that city.[51] T'ang Ts'ai-ch'ang's Hankow revolt was impending, the first and last militant effort of the *Pao-huang hui,* and Liang meant to be on the scene, waiting in south China for a possible call to power.

The Hankow Rising

Liang in his days at the *Hunan shih-wu hsüeh-t'ang* had known T'ang Ts'ai-ch'ang and Lin Kuei. In Changsha, T'ang had become a particularly close friend of T'an Ssu-t'ung and of Pi Yung-nien. When T'an was killed as one of the Six Martyrs of September 1898, those victims of the Empress Dowager's vengeance at the end of the Hundred Days, T'ang sank into a state of desperate depression and began to dwell on the idea of insurrection. At this time Pi was already in Japan and in close touch with Sun, Miyazaki, and Hirayama. When T'ang, early in 1899, came to Japan to discuss plans for an uprising with K'ang and Liang, Pi intro-

[48] Feng, *Ko-ming i-shih,* I, 15-16.
[49] Li, 70.
[50] Liang, "San-shih tzu-shu," 27b.
[51] Liang, "Hsin-ta-lu yu-chi chieh-lu," 38.2.

duced him to Sun, who hoped to win him over. K'ang and Liang tried to hold his allegiance. T'ang wavered.

Lin Kuei also came to Japan in 1899 and studied in the *Ta-t'ung hsüeh-hsiao*. When winter came, some twenty Chinese students under the leadership of T'ang and Lin returned to China with plans for a rising in Hunan, Hupei, and the Yangtze area. Liang and others gave them a great farewell feast.

T'ang and Lin, in Shanghai, secretly organized the *Cheng-ch'i hui* (Uprightness Society)—later called the *Tzu-li hui* (Independence Society)—as an instrument for their conspiracy. Lin Kuei then went to Hankow. Pi Yung-nien, at this time working for Sun in the Hong Kong–Canton area, considered T'ang's tactics and manifestos bad, only ameliorative, not basically revolutionary, and exhorted him to cut off relations with K'ang and Liang. By this time, however, T'ang not only shared their point of view but relied entirely for his funds on K'ang's and Liang's solicitations among overseas Chinese. This money—Liang's work in Hawaii was an important source—kept T'ang in the fold and even won away several of the agents whom Pi sent to Hong Kong.

The Boxer disturbances gave both Sun's party (at Huichow) and T'ang Ts'ai-ch'ang the opportunity to strike. The latter's plan called for simultaneous risings on August 9 in Hankow (the key point, where T'ang and Lin would lead), Tatung (Anhui), Anking (Anhui), Changteh (Hunan), and Hsinti (Hupei). Because remittances failed to come from K'ang and Liang, they extended their deadline two or three times. But on August 7 a government investigation was begun in the Tatung area. The Tatung plotters tried to rise independently on the ninth and naturally failed. This fiasco doomed the main body at Hankow; their plot became known to Chang Chih-tung, who smashed the ring and executed T'ang Ts'ai-ch'ang and nineteen accomplices. Liang was left stranded in Shanghai. There was no one to call him back into China after all.[52]

[52] Li, 70-72.

F

Liang Overseas and in Japan, 1900-1903

He took the long way back to his "second home": south to Hong Kong, Singapore, and Ceylon; then Australia, at the invitation of its *Chung wei-hsin hui* (Chinese Reform Society), for six months of circling the continent; the Philippines; and in late spring, 1901, Japan.[53] For the next two years he was prodigiously active as a journalist and writer.

In the summer of 1901, Liang raised money among Chinese in Japan to found the *Kuang-chih shu-chü* (Wisdom-Extension Bookshop), which invited Chinese students to translate Western literature for publication.[54] Next winter, he and some friends launched a literary magazine, *Hsin hsiao-shuo* [New novels], which emphasized the importance of writing novels and gave further encouragement to the work of translation.[55] His own writings began to appear in more permanent form; in 1902-1903, to facilitate distribution in China, Liang made a selection of articles and lessons written for the *Ch'ing-i pao* and *Ta-t'ung hsüeh-hsiao* and published them in Tokyo under the title *Yin-ping shih ch'üan-chi* [Complete works of the Ice-Drinkers' Studio].[56]

Liang's first concern in these years was his new fortnightly journal, the *Hsin-min ts'ung-pao* [New-people periodical] published in Yokohama. Each number contained about forty pages of creative writing, commentary on current events, and dissertations on many facets of the problem of Chinese culture, its past and its future. All Western thought seemed to be Liang's province, and in a dazzling display of virtuosity and superficiality, he roamed freely from pre-Socratic philosophical fragments to the *Critique of Pure Reason*. He reviewed generals from Alexander to Napoleon, not forgetting Gustavus Adolphus, and if any thor-

---

[53] Liang, "San-shih tzu-shu," 27b; Liang, "Hsin-ta-lu yu-chi chieh-lu," 38.2 and 38.74.

[54] Feng, *Ko-ming i-shih, I, 54.*

[55] Tsung Hyui-puh, "Chinese Translations of Western Literature," CSPSR, XII (1928), 369.

[56] Leon Wieger, *La Chine moderne,* I ("Prodromes") (Hsien-hsien, 1931), 8.

ough young student fell to musing about the ancient Germanic Wetenagemot or the courage of William of Egmont, the *Hsin-min ts'ung-pao* stood ready with corroborative detail. It had a wide circulation both in China and outside, and files of the periodical went through many printings.[57] But in 1903, publication was suspended. Liang was moving away again.

Liang in America

February 20, 1903, Liang sailed once more from Yokohama and on March 4 disembarked at Vancouver.[58] Pausing only briefly in western Canada, he sped across the continent to Ottawa, where he received an invitation from the leader of the Conservative Party to visit Parliament. Liang describes the formal organization of a parliamentary sitting and the beauty of the building. In these details, writes Liang, ever ready to make a pedagogic point, one can see the importance which the British attach to the legislative arm of government.[59]

The French-speaking population of Montreal interested him hugely, and he reported that, without having visited France, he had now seen a section of French society. What he thought about what he saw will interest us in the next chapter. It has a certain bearing on China that Liang asks where Canada would be if the Teutons were not its core, that he sees it brought low, like Brazil

[57] Britton, 119; Lin, 98; YPSWC, *passim*. The name of the newspaper was derived from a passage in the *Ta-hsüeh* [The Great Learning]. See Legge, I, 361: "On the bathing tub of T'ang the following words were engraved—'If you can one day renovate yourself, do so from day to day. Yea, let there be daily renovation.' In the announcement to K'ang, it is said, 'To stir up the new people.' "

Liang's discussion of Malthusian theory is an example of the occasional inaccuracy of the information he dispensed in the *Hsin-min ts'ung-pao*. He illustrates arithmetic progression by the series 2-4-8-16, which is actually geometric, and geometric progression by the series 2-4-16-32, which is nothing at all but a garble, a series which begins with squaring, then reverts to multiplication by the initial factor. See Liang, "Lun min-tsu ching-cheng chih ta-shih," YPSWC 182.2b [On the circumstances of the struggle of peoples].

[58] Liang, "Hsin-ta-lu yu-chi chieh-lu," 38.2-2b.

[59] *Ibid.*, 38.11.

or Peru, if the Latin element, "frivolous, unstable, willful, inexperienced," should be in command.[60]

On May 12 he arrived in New York, his headquarters for the next month and a half, during which time he made side trips to Washington, Boston, and Philadelphia. A New York appointment with Mr. J. P. Morgan seems to have been a paralyzing experience for Liang. He speaks with awe of Morgan's reputed power and strict business regimen. Liang had asked in writing for five minutes of his time, but, when he found himself in the financier's office, Liang confessed that he had really nothing to say and beat a retreat with minutes to spare.[61]

Liang was somewhat more vocal with the Socialists. Members of the Socialist Party visited him four times in four different places. They expressed their party's desire to affiliate with Liang's party and to make socialist organs of the Chinese newspapers published by the Chinese Reform Society. Liang accepted socialist tracts but dismissed these visitors with little homilies about the gradualness of progress.[62]

At the end of May, he came to Harvard and met the small body of Chinese students there. He had meant also to visit Yale, he writes, but he was extremely pressed for time, and had forced himself to pass Yale by while he hurried on to Cambridge.[63] Liang remained nine days in the Boston area. Part of the time he spent visiting historic sites, and he ruefully compares the consequences of the Boston Tea Party with those of the opium-burning by Commissioner Lin in Canton in 1839.[64]

Liang's visit was given considerable coverage by the Boston press, in a reportorial style of such elegance and distinction that one would be presumptuous to paraphrase. Following are several excerpts.

[60] Ibid., 38.11-11b.
[61] Ibid., 38.31b-32.
[62] Ibid., 38.30b-31b.
[63] Ibid., 38.32b-35.
[64] Ibid., 38.37b.

*Oriental Marc Antony Tells Chinamen How
They Have Only Been Slaves*

Surrounded in the reception room by a press of eager Chinamen, who lost all of their usual stolidity in the presence of the magnetic political agitator, Leong Kai Cheu made his response of welcome by unfurling a huge new banner. . . .

As four assisting Chinamen spread out the great banner before him like a lifesaving net, the young man stepped upon the rostrum before it and with his fiery eloquence pictured the toppling system that has burdened the empire for ages, and how with the flag enough would be saved from the conflagration to build an ideal government. The flag was white, with red stripes near the borders, and with three red stars in the field.

"The first star," said he, speaking in Chinese, "is self-edification. Few of our people have had the spirit to assert themselves and they have been bowed down into systems of caste until they are like sheep driven by their rulers. We want self-edification enough to say, 'I am myself,'" exclaimed the orator, smiting his breast, and then smiling as blandly as Emerson.

"And the next star," said he, bending down to the banner spread before him, and running his long gaunt fingers over it, like Mark Antony indicating the rents in Caesar's toga, "the next star is unity." Forsaking the mild-eyed papyrus of the mandarins, he promulgated the ideas that lead to American liberty. "We cannot gain liberty by acting alone. We must act together with the strength of us all. In union there is strength."

To hear the Chinamen cheering together at these sentiments, one would think the din came from Americans, if he did not see the crowd of high-cheeked-boned faces aleer with slanting eyes nearly closed in smiles.

"And the other star is equality. Wake up and get your liberty and be equal with your rulers. We have abolished the kow-tow so that one does not kiss the earth and rub one's forehead in the dust when an officer of the dowager goes by. There will be no ruler higher than the subject. Every one will be equal in rank."

This speech broke up in wild cheering, and the Chinamen, that are seen moving about Boston's streets stolid and undemonstrative as sheep, pressed forward and shook the hands of the orator.[65]

Not only was last evening's meeting attended by three or four hundred Chinese, but a larger number is expected tonight, and this afternoon all the business places in Chinatown were filled with China- men awaiting placidly the great reformer. In many stores there was a distinct resemblance to the crossroads general store of rural New Eng- land, as groups of men sat around waiting for something to turn up. Only for the whittling jackknife and the mastication of tobacco was substituted the stolid inaction of the Oriental and the puffing of the short-lived, tiny-bowled, bamboo-stemmed pipe. . . .

Leong Kai Cheu, although said to be a graduate of one of the great English universities, leaves his secretary to do the talking, alleging his own indifferent command of the English tongue.[66]

ANOTHER CHINESE INVASION THREATENED

Sam S. Shubert, the New York theatrical manager of the firm of Shuberts, Nixon, and Zimmerman, proprietors of "A Chinese Honey- moon," now playing at the Colonial Theatre, came over from New York yesterday to have an interview with Leong Kai Cheu, the leader of the Chinese Empire Reform Association, who is in Boston now in the interests of the local branch of the Bow Wong Woey Society. Mr. Shubert . . . desired to consult with the Chinese editor about the feasibility of taking "A Chinese Honeymoon" on an actual tour through China. . .[67]

This had certainly been a week of stimulating ideas among the "almond-eyed aliens of Boston."[68]

In Washington Liang talked for two hours with Secretary of State John Hay, who told him of his conviction, often ridiculed

[65] *The Boston Herald*, May 26, 1903.
[66] *The Boston Evening Transcript*, May 26, 1903.
[67] *Ibid.*, June 2, 1903.
[68] *The Boston Herald*, May 26, 1903.

by his colleagues, that China was destined to be a great power. President Theodore Roosevelt also received Liang. He expressed the not very graceful hope that the Chinese Reform Society would transform the customs of the Chinese immigrants in America.[69]

The Philadelphia Navy Yard and Independence Hall interested Liang.[70] He spoke to the Chinese population of Baltimore and then embarked on an extensive tour west into the heart of the United States:[71] July 1, Pittsburgh (trouble keeping clothes unsoiled); Pittsburgh to Cincinnati; New Orleans, St. Louis, Chicago (University and stock yards), Kansas City (speech to the Chinese population, about 200). He rode the Great Northern Railroad into Montana (excursus on the development of the Great Northern). He spoke in Billings, traveled to other Montana towns with Chinese populations and finally to Helena, the state capital. He mused about Indians in Idaho, and went on and on to Walla Walla, and on to Seattle.[72]

In Portland he read the newspaper accounts of Panama's declaration of independence from Colombia, of United States recognition and machinations about the Canal. There will be an annual payment of $250,000 to the new government, notes Liang (who for some reason quotes the figure in pounds sterling), in exchange for a grip on the country. He likens it to the British Suez maneuvers and the compromising of Egyptian independence. Back in Japan, he observes, the Chinese revolutionary party is publishing in its newspapers paeans of praise to Panama and asking why the Chinese cannot emulate the action of the Panamanian people. Here is Liang's opportunity for a magnificent innuendo. Alas, he writes, what difficulties stand in the way of our compatriots if they wish to imitate the Panamanians! The new Chinese government's annual needs would be so many times £50,000.[73]

[69] Liang, "Hsin-ta-lu yu-chi chieh-lu," 38.42b.
[70] *Ibid.*, 38.53-54b.
[71] *Ibid.*, 38.58.
[72] *Ibid.*, 38.58-73b.
[73] *Ibid.*, 38.76-76b.

After thus editorializing in Portland, Liang turned south for a month in California. In Los Angeles he was given a great welcome by the city. Many notables attended a reception for Liang at City Hall, and the mayor made a handsome speech, which nevertheless betrayed some misconception of Liang's political affiliations. Two years ago, said the mayor, Los Angeles had welcomed President McKinley. Subsequently it welcomed President Roosevelt. Now it is Mr. Liang Ch'i-ch'ao, he continued, carrying his sequence through in a generous crescendo. The touring representative of the "Protect the Emperor Society" made a short speech of thanks.[74]

Liang's excursion was drawing to its close. On October 31, aboard a Chinese vessel, he sailed from Vancouver. Exactly ninety-six telegrams and more than one hundred friends at the dock bade him good-by. On November 11, he disembarked at the old rallying-ground, Yokohama.[75]

[74] *Ibid.*, 39.19.

[75] *Ibid.*, 39.19. There is an episode with something of a comic-opera flavor which occurred during Liang's stay in America and which he fails absolutely to mention. The case is variously described in different accounts. Feng reports that, when Liang was in San Francisco, a retired army officer named Falkenberg offered his services to the *Pao-huang hui*. Liang, using the title of "Prime Minister of China," gave Falkenberg the title of "Grand Marshal of the Chinese Army of the Reform." Later, however, when Homer Lea, a critic of military affairs, sought him out, Liang gave the same grandiloquent title to Lea. Falkenberg heard of this, made bitter representations to Liang, and engaged in public controversy with the other Grand Marshal. The seals which Liang had given to both of them were published, and it was Lea's commission which bore the seal with Liang's personal signature on it. Lea thus got the position, but in 1911, disgusted with the *Pao-huang hui*, he had an interview with Sun Yat-sen in the United States and offered to collaborate with the revolutionary party. After the revolution occurred, Lea was Sun's adviser for a time in Nanking (Feng, *Chung-hua min-kuo*, II, 107).

Glick and Hong, in *Swords of Silence* (p. 131), tell another story, which is wildly melodramatic but at least advances reasons for all this maneuvering. According to this account, Lea met Sun in Japan in 1899 and plotted with him to return to the United States, pretend to join the supporters of K'ang Yu-wei there, and act as a secret agent for Sun. In 1900, Lea met K'ang in Japan, joined the *Pao-huang hui*, and was made commander-in-chief of the Chinese Imperial Reform Army.

In 1903, Liang, cognizant of rumors impugning Lea's loyalty, met Falkenberg. Liang gave Falkenberg his commission, stamped with what was supposed to be

Liang's account of his American journey has more in it than a bare outline of his itinerary. America called forth his comments on an immense variety of subjects, among them the question of revolution, monarchy, and republic, discussion of which we must defer to another chapter. He has random remarks on the benefits and evils of trusts, government policy toward them, and public concern. He discourses on the global scope of American capital accumulation, New York as the commercial center of the world, immigration and increase in population, and the character of immigrant groups, with particular attention to the problem of Jewish survival. There are cheerful facts about New York traffic, hotels, Central Park, the Statue of Liberty, the White House, the Capitol, and the Library of Congress. Liang writes a sketch of the career of Theodore Roosevelt. He describes the Monroe Doctrine and its development, as he sees it, with Roosevelt's big-navy

---

the Great Seal of China, lost by the Empress Dowager during the Boxer Rebellion. Falkenberg was told to say nothing about the commission. He would be called to command the bands of Chinese youths whom Lea was training if the rumors concerning Lea should prove to be true (*ibid.*, 166).

In 1904, Sun, traveling in the United States, appeared to be winning over the *Pao-huang hui*. K'ang therefore set Falkenberg in motion. The latter demanded Lea's resignation, but the Great Seal was proved a forgery and Lea remained in command of his cadets. Falkenberg filed suit against Liang in the United States courts, but the case was never tried. Sun took over the "Chinese Imperial Reform Army" (*ibid.*, 183-184).

The book by Glick and Hong purports to be based on Chinese documents (unnamed) and conversations with persons who took part in the events recorded. Unfortunately, Glick gives a different account of this episode in another book, *Double Ten* (New York, 1945; pages 137-175)—a book so fantastically garbled that, in the absence of corroborative evidence, little credence can be given to any of its author's statements. In this account, Falkenberg makes his bid in 1905, K'ang disowns him, and Lea, who has accepted his charge from the *Pao-huang hui* in good faith, agrees to work secretly for Sun only in 1905.

Frederic L. Chapin and Charles O. Kates, in a manuscript provisionally entitled "Homer Lea and the Chinese Revolution," based on personal interviews and intensive research in American archives and libraries, give the best account of this affair. Elaborately documented are the collaboration of Lea with the *Pao-huang hui*, beginning in 1900, the chequered career of Falkenberg down to 1905, and the attempts of Falkenberg, in that year, first to take over and then, failing this, to destroy the Chinese cadres which Lea was training.

talk, into a platform of world domination. The decline of traditional American anti-militarism worries him, and Yellowstone National Park, with its great geyser, Old Faithful, impresses him. Liang discusses the background of English colonial settlement and analyzes the social pattern of the South. He is aware of the states' rights question, gives statistics on Pacific shipping, and takes an interest in the projected St. Louis Exposition. Liang notes the general mediocrity of United States government personnel. Checks and balances and Cabinet salaries, American journalism and the Chinese mode of life in predominantly white communities, the Pacific underseas cable and the peculiar status of the District of Columbia—all these subjects and many more are grist for his busy mill.[76] Liang made the most of his months in America, and a broader and a wiser man he came back to Japan. The distance he had traveled from the old circumscribed Chinese world of his first speculations began to appear incalculable.

The Last Years of Exile

In 1904, in a letter to a friend, Sun Yat-sen wrote,

I have been engaged in a hard struggle against the reform party in the United States and have overcome them in five or six places. I intend to travel wherever there are Chinese and I believe that in three or four months I shall succeed in overcoming them all. I do not think it will be difficult for me to do this, because their influence was at its height when Liang Ch'i-ch'ao was there, but now the movement has gradually lapsed into decadence.[77]

In 1903, en route to America, Sun had visited Honolulu and there faced the bitter hostility of the *Hsin Chung-kuo pao* (New China), the organ of Liang's friends.[78] At San Francisco, he was obstructed in his attempt to disembark by the customs interpreter,

---

[76] Liang, "Hsin-ta-lu yu-chi chieh-lu," *passim*.

[77] Stephen Chen, and Robert Payne, *Sun Yat-sen, A Portrait* (New York 1946), 64-65.

[78] Feng, *Ko-ming i-shih*, II, 102.

who was a member of the *Pao-huang hui*.[79] Liang Ch'i-ch'ao's travels and his pen had everywhere exacerbated the conflict between revolutionary and reformer, and when Liang returned to Japan he came back to a factional struggle which grew more intense as the years passed by.

With the establishment of *Min-pao* (The People) in November 1905, Sun's forces, newly coördinated in the *T'ung-meng hui* (The Alliance), had their most potent weapon for the journalistic duel with Liang. Together with such material as an article on the life of Gambetta and a translation from Henry George, the first number carried in extenso a speech delivered by a Cantonese student on October 6, at a memorial meeting for the Chinese martyrs of 1898 and 1900. This speech was an impassioned denunciation of K'ang Yu-wei and Liang Ch'i-ch'ao. They were held responsible for the deaths and were charged with being false reformers, seeking their own and not their country's good.[80] Succeeding issues continued the personal attack, and in the realm of ideas, *Min-pao* engaged in a running battle of statment, refutation, and counter-refutation with the *Hsin-min ts'ung-pao*.[81]

In July 1907, Liang and several of his confreres organized the *Cheng-wen she* (Political Culture Association) and began to publish the *Cheng-wen she hsüan-yen* [Declarations of the Political Culture Association]. Essays in this publication elaborated on the

---

[79] Feng, *Chung-hua min-kuo,* I, 43.

[80] NCH, LXXVIII, January 19, 1906, 126-127. The speech was delivered by Hu Yen-hung of the *Wu-hsü chia-tzu chi-nien hui* (Society for the commemoration of 1898 and 1900). See Feng, *Chung-hua min-kuo,* II, 4.

[81] Tsou Lu, *Chung-kuo kuo-min tang shih kao* [Draft history of the *Kuo-min tang*] (Shanghai, 1929), 438-439, gives a list of *Min-pao* articles written specifically to refute articles by Liang. Among them are the following rather similar titles: Refutation of the *Hsin-min ts'ung-pao's* most recent anti-revolutionary article; Philosophical refutation of the *Hsin-min ts'ung-pao's* article on revolution; Second refutation of the *Hsin-min ts'ung-pao's* article on political revolution; Miscellaneous answers to *Hsin-min ts'ung-pao;* Discussion of the various opinions of the *Hsin-min ts'ung-pao;* Finances and state ownership of land—second refutation of the *Hsin-min ts'ung-pao's* criticism of the plan for state ownership of land; Banishing the errors of the *Hsin-min ts'ung-pao* on the subject of state ownership of land; Refutation of miscellaneous points in the *Hsin-min ts'ung-pao* no. 12.

four main principles of the *Cheng-wen she:* (1) organization of a parliament to establish responsible government, (2) collation of laws and strengthening of judicial independence, (3) establishment of local self-government and adjustment of the limits of the central power, (4) equal rights for China in foreign relations.[82]

When the *Cheng-wen she* held its first big meeting, in a Tokyo hall called the Kinkikan, some ten Japanese notables attended, Inukai among them.[83] These were not the only Japanese present; Liang, knowing that the revolutionists planned to break up the meeting, had come to the Kinkikan with a Japanese strong-arm squad for protection. After a few others had spoken, without interruption from the floor, Liang rose to speak. When he announced that the Chinese government had set a date for the presentation of a constitution and when he declared further that this was great grounds for rejoicing, Chang Chi, an associate editor of *Min-pao* (and later a prominent official and *Kuo-min tang* functionary), called out harshly "Baka! Baka!" (Japanese: "fool"), and hundreds of men rushed forward to the attack. Liang extricated himself from the melee and discreetly drifted off into the night. The revolutionists took over the meeting.[84]

Chang Chi mounted the rostrum, restored order, and made a speech of his own. Liang, he said, had been rescued by the revolutionists after the Peking *coup d'état* in 1898, but he had forgotten this great favor by now and was attacking the revolutionists. Although outwardly he advocated constitutional government, inwardly, it was alleged, he was working for absolutism. The audience loudly applauded.[85]

In spite of opposition of this nature in Japan, the influence of the *Cheng-wen she* spread widely. An affiliated society in Shanghai began to publish a monthly magazine called *Cheng-lun* [Political discussion], which was suppressed after seven issues.[86] Elsewhere

[82] Li, 131-132.
[83] Feng, *Chung-hua min-kuo*, II, 10.
[84] Li, 134.
[85] NCH, LXXXV, November 1, 1907, 293.
[86] Britton, 117; Lin, 98.

in China, pro-constitution student societies patterned after the *Cheng-wen she* mushroomed everywhere, even in Peking. Official opposition was expressed in a series of repressive orders, beginning in December 1907 and culminating in August 1908, with a stern decree enjoining governors of each province to interdict the *Cheng-wen she,* seize members, and treat them with rigor. The *Cheng-wen she* melted away, but certain other groups with similar aims, notably the *Yü-pei li-hsien kung-hui* (Public Society for the Preparation for the Establishment of a Constitution), whose leaders, to all outward appearance, had no connection with K'ang and Liang, continued unmolested by the authorities.[87]

The indefatigable Liang had new enterprises to organize. Returning to Japan in 1909 after another long period of overseas travel, he founded the magazine *Hsin hsiao-shuo pao* [New fiction]. The material which he published here had sometimes a rather revolutionary tone. In one story, *Hsin Chung-kuo wei-lai chi* [The future of New China], China becomes a republic called *Ta Chung-hua min-tsu kuo.* This appellation is not very far from the *Chung-hua min-kuo* which China eventually adopted, and in many other details the story seems to foreshadow events of the next few years.[88]

The year 1910 brought the last of his periodicals to appear before the Chinese revolution. This was the *Kuo-feng pao* [National customs], which came out every ten days in Shanghai.[89] Liang published here influential essays on cabinet government, representative institutions, bureaucracy, and other problems in constitutional and parliamentary theory.[90]

Early in the great year 1911, Liang made a trip from Japan to Taiwan. He went seeking instruction. It was important, he felt, to study Japanese techniques of colonization; they were of interest to China, in view of its plans for Manchuria and Sinkiang. And

[87] Li, 134-135.
[88] Britton, 120. In Britton's text there is a misprint for the character *shuo*.
[89] Lin, 98.
[90] For a list of such essays in the *Kuo-feng pao,* see Li, 154-155.

Japanese experience with reform of the Formosan currency might possibly have an application to Chinese currency problems.[91] In Taihoku, the capital, he investigated government bureaus and received a great welcome from the Chinese population.[92] On the voyage back to Japan, Liang's ship passed close to the Chinese coast, and nostalgia swept over him as he looked once more at his country.[93]

Events were brewing in China then which would put an end to his exile. As far back as 1904, a general amnesty had been declared for all persons implicated in the Hundred Days Reform, but naturally this could not apply to rebellious wolves, and K'ang and Liang were expressly excluded.[94] For his own official recall to grace, Liang had to wait for a petition of the National Assembly, October 1911, after the revolutionary successes at Wuchang had stripped the dynasty of all but a vestige of power and had left it with only the strength to pardon, no longer the strength to condemn. Liang made ready at last to go home.

Min-li pao [People's independence], a revolutionary paper of Shanghai, on November 16 reported an interview with Liang on the occasion of his leaving Japan for Peking. "The Manchu Government has lost the hearts of the people," said Liang, according to this account. "The whole nation has turned from them and it seems as though the Emperor would have to flee."[95]

Liang did not go to Peking. He went instead to Mukden, conferred there with friends, and returned to residence in Japan. There had been an ominous innuendo in the printed interview, an indication that Liang might not live if he went to Peking, an editor's note that said, "You are going to be a martyr for your King."[96] When Liang did at last return, in October 1912, he had

[91] Liang, "Yu T'ai-wan shu-tu," YPSWC 44.1-2 [Letters on the Taiwan voyage].

[92] *Ibid.*, 3.

[93] *Ibid.*, 5b.

[94] CSK, *Pen-chi*, 24.21b (July 3, 1904). THL has no entry for this date.

[95] J. Darroch, "Current Events as Seen Through the Medium of the Chinese Newspaper," CR, XLIII (January, 1912), 31.

[96] *Ibid.*

no longer a king or emperor, but he still had Sun Yat-sen to fight, journals to publish, and a standing to maintain, a name he had earned in almost two decades of intellectual agitation, a reputation as the first mind of the new China.

Liang's Influence in His Japanese Years

In the early years of the twentieth century, the Chinese student population of Japan swelled to impressive proportions. The *Japan Chronicle* reports that by 1905 their numbers had reached nearly 3,000, 9,000 in 1906, and 13,000 two or three years later, before the tide began to subside.[97] Although Sun Yat-sen competed, on the whole successfully, for their political allegiance, Liang's intellectual judgments permeated these student circles. As early as 1902, Ts'ai Chün, the Chinese minister in Tokyo, citing the danger of Liang's influence, recommended to the Throne that no more students be sent to Japan.[98] In that year, too, an association of returned students was founded in Shanghai, and in the publications of Liang they found their intellectual nourishment.

The Empress Dowager summoned Prince Tsai-chen, inspector of Chinese students in Japan, to give testimony on their allegedly reformist-subversive state of mind. Tsai-chen had himself come under the influence of Liang and protested the perfect loyalty of the students. He added, however, that curiosity about occidental things, permitted to an elite, should not be allowed to penetrate to the masses.[99]

In the introduction of Western thought, Liang was indeed prodigiously active. In his writing prior to his Japanese years, he had been much less concerned with exposition of an organized body

[97] *The Japan Chronicle*, November 23, 1905, 685; *ibid.*, August 24, 1911, 320.

[98] *The Japan Weekly Chronicle*, April 2, 1902, 295.

[99] Albert Maybon, *La Politique chinoise* (Paris, 1908), 152. In September 1902, Tsai-chen made an address to students in Japan which sounds much like the early Liang. In his conclusion, he said that the spirit of Western learning might be summed up in the motto, "Know thyself, know others, be diligent, conquer." There was nothing here, he said, which was inconsistent with the teachings of the sages. Islam, Buddhism, Christianity, and Confucianism all had the same basis— "Know thyself" (NCH, LXIX, September 17, 1902, 573).

of thought than with justification of the adoption of foreign modes, which were largely undefined except in most general terms. Now, with Japanese translations available and with a changing set of pedagogic ends, he was able to present, in some fashion, any number of European intellectual lights to his eager student public. Chinese thinkers—Mo-tzu, Wang An-shih, and others—he reinterpreted with new and unconventional standards of criticism, and he introduced a new method for the study of Chinese history; the fate of the people and the culture, not that of the ruling houses, becomes the true subject for the historian.

K'ang Yu-wei's role was small in this period, while Liang, from the Reform Movement of 1898 to the May Fourth Movement of 1919, was, according to one student, clearly the intellectual leader in a manner unknown to China since the Opium War; and the period 1902-1911, from the inception of the *Hsin-min ts'ung-pao* to the Revolution, was his golden age.[100] Hu Shih's autobiography corroborates this statement. Hu, writing of his Shanghai school-days in this decade, tells of his excitement at being given a book containing many writings of the Liang school.[101] The years 1902-1903 were Liang's most effective, according to Hu. Yen Fu (translator of Mill, Huxley, and other Western thinkers) was widely read but was not as influential among youth as Liang, because his literary style was too elegant in the antique manner. Liang's writings, however, appealed to the reader, for they were clear, lucid, infused with passion. Hu goes on to say:

[100] Ch'en Tuan-chih, *Wu-ssu yun-tung shih ti p'ing-chia* [An appraisal of the history of the May Fourth Movement] (Shanghai, 1935), 170. Much the same statement is made in Chu Ch'i-hua, *Chung-kuo chin-tai she-hui-shih ch'ieh-p'ou* [Anatomy of modern Chinese social history] (Shanghai, 1933), 242. Both these writers are Marxists, and the latter treats Liang to a full Marxist analysis. Chu says (p. 274) that in Liang's really significant period, 1902-1904, he was the spokesman of the new, rising middle class against the old order. His fresh, youthful spirit had to be dissipated because the expansion of the middle class in China was impossible; Liang became imbued with a class-spirit of the same restrictive character as that of the old regime which he had attacked. See also pp. 303-304, in which Liang's intellectual life, with what Chu calls its short period of new, youthful vigor, is made the prototype of the life of the Chinese middle class.

[101] Hu Shih, *Ssu-shih tzu-shu* [Autobiography at the age of forty] (Shanghai, 1935), 93.

He attracted our abundantly curious minds, pointed out an unknown world, and summoned us to make our own explorations. . . .

All sections of the *Hsin-min shuo* [Discourse on the new people]
opened up a new world for me; it made me believe at bottom that
outside of China there yet were peoples of a very high order and cultures of a very high order. The *Chung-kuo hsüeh-shu ssu-hsiang pien-
ch'ien chih ta-shih* [Changing trends in Chinese scholarship and
thought] also opened up a new world for me; it made me know that
outside the "Four Books" and the "Five Classics" China yet had
learning and thought.[102]

We learn that Liang's work was the seed of Hu's own subsequent researches in the field of Chinese philosophy.[103] Yet our
first concern is not to find out whom Liang inspired but to understand what he represented. If his essays convince, they also reveal,
and his contemporaries who found them meaningful could hardly
know then the meaning of the meaning.

---

[102] *Ibid.*, 100-105. For similar testimony to Liang's influence, see another autobiography, Chiang Monlin, *Tides From the West* (New Haven, 1947), 51: "His
style was clear, persuasive, and easy to follow and therefore very profitable reading
for students. I was one among thousands who came under his influence. I think
this great scholar did more than anyone else in his time to popularize modern
knowledge among the rising generation. His was the fountain of wisdom from
which every young man drew to quench his thirst for the new learning."

[103] Hu, *Ssu-shih tzu-shu*, 107-108.

G

CHAPTER IV

THE SUBSTITUTE FOR TRADITION

The Bankruptcy of the Chinese Tradition

IN THE FIRST PERIOD of his intellectual life, Liang Ch'i-ch'ao had clearly affirmed the value of the Chinese tradition. Nevertheless, one ineluctable conviction had begun to emerge: the world of the Chinese traditionalist was a world of dreams. None of the old rules worked. Liang had tried bravely to cover the breach between value and history, to lose westernization in a stream of Confucian continuity; but China's case was new, and if Liang's experiment with Confucianism is compared to that of the Jesuits, one can sense that Confucianism, after so many centuries, had at last been drained of any relevance to Chinese reality.

Some two centuries earlier, the Jesuits had made a first effort to syncretize Confucianism with a European tradition. Brushing aside centuries of commentary, they appealed to the pure and pristine classics, and they insisted that Christianity was fully compatible with the authentic classical Chinese spirit. Both Jesuits and Reformers, in much the same way, tried to make a Western idea seem properly Chinese. Where lay the difference between their respective rationalizations?

The intervening centuries of decline and fall had made the difference. In the Jesuit episode, a syncretism was necessary to Western thought to effect its entrance into the Chinese mind; when Liang wrote, a syncretism was necessary to the Chinese mind to soften the blow of the irresistible entrance of Western thought. In the first case, the Chinese tradition was standing firm, and the Western intruders sought admission by cloaking themselves in the trappings of that tradition; in the second case, the Chinese tradition was disintegrating, and its heirs, to save the fragments,

84

had to interpret them in the spirit of the Western intrusion. There was no longer a conflict between two sets of ideas equally vital, philosophically contemporaneous, but between one set of vital ideas and another of anachronistic fantasies. China in the nineties still had its many live thinkers of traditional ideas, but the ideas were none the less dead. We must know the thinker from the thought. An idea is alive, not simply when somebody thinks it, but when it has real reference to an objective situation, and the history of China in the nineteenth century had been the story of the retreat of its ideology from objective significance to a purely subjective one.

The way in which the reformers were challenged by some of the traditionalists betrays the lost world which the latter lived in. The modern Chinese word for "reform" is *pien-fa,* which means, literally, "change-law." But the very idea of changing the laws had a premise foreign to Confucian political theory, in which not laws but men, that is, human virtue, rule. If there is evil abroad, said the anti-reformers, change men's hearts, not the system; and this argument of obscurantists was put exactly in the terms of the ancient Confucianist-Legalist controversy, *te-chih* versus *fa-chih,* government by virtue versus government by law, a conflict enshrined in the *Yen-t'ieh lun* [Discourses on salt and iron], in the first century B.C.[1]

Thus, to the obscurantist, China was still a world, not a unit

[1] Ch'en Ch'iu, 80-81. See also ICTP 4.16, where Yeh Te-hui rails at the futility of "changing laws" (i.e., reform) rather than changing men. Tseng Lien, who in 1898 memorialized for Liang's execution, was one of the most forceful of those who put the question of reform in a Confucian-Legalist setting. Calling the Confucian paragon, the Duke of Chou, to witness, Tseng wrote, "In China it is in no wise the system which is defective; it is only that men's hearts are corrupt" (Ch'en Ch'iu, 81-82). This analysis seems of a piece with the moralism we have identified in Liang's early thought. How, then, does it appear as a sentiment combating Liang's ideas? The difference is subtle but crucial. Liang, though he values tradition, feels the pressure of new forces; he believes that the tradition must be justified, and moralism is his own subjective device to justify a tradition with which he is frankly tampering. Tseng, on the other hand, sees the tradition as itself the source of all justification, and his moralistic strain comes straight from the unchallenged tradition itself.

in the world. He saw the West and all its works solely in a Chinese context. We know that in the field of practical politics the West had once been seen that way—foreign relations, in traditional China, were tributary relations, and Western nations, it was thought, were simply a part of the Chinese political system, for they came to the Empire as suppliants, even as Korea and Annam. A series of wars and peace settlements had wiped out this political conception, but in China there was an intellectual lag behind political change, and with the coming of the twentieth century there still were Chinese so convinced of Chinese universalism that they could dismiss the whole body of westernizing, "reform" ideas under the pretext that the battle against them, or against their premises, had been fought and won by the molders of Chinese tradition two thousand years before.

It was Liang's purpose to convince these people that their ideas were as moribund philosophically as they were politically. Solipsism was hopeless. He knew that Western ideas could no more be waved away as Confucian cast-offs than Western ambassadors could be made into Confucian tribute-bearers. The day was past when China could hear the Legalist "Grand Secretary" and the Confucian "Literati" (antagonists in the *Yen-t'ieh lun*) and with a nice, fastidious taste decide the winner of the debate. Chinese tradition, for its own sake, had better be interpreted as receptive to reform, for drastic change could not be blocked; if the Chinese would not *pien* their own *fa*, somebody else would *pien* it for them. In 1902, Liang still found it necessary to insist that Western imperialists were something new, not Huns, Jüchen,

---

There is yet another consideration. Both Liang and Tseng are traditionalists in that both maintain that China's system should be *de jure* Confucian. Only Tseng considers that it is so *de facto*. Thus, he refers to corruption as being characteristic only of the participants in the system, while Liang looks for corruption among the architects of the system. Tseng, in effect, wants to repair the morals of the men of today—the system is sound; Liang wants to repair the damage, that is, the faulty system, caused by the immorality of the men of yesterday.

Mongols.[2] China's course in the actual world could never be set according to bygone preconceptions.

The Last Stage of Liang's Confucian Traditionalism

Before 1898, when the character *meng* appeared in Liang's writings, it almost invariably stood for "Mencius"; during Liang's exile in Japan, it usually meant "Montesquieu." As his knowledge of the West grew more complete and precise, it became impossible to cram it into the synthetic, always precarious Confucian-Western structure he had fabricated in the nineties. Eventually, he found a way to put the Chinese and European cultural relationship on a different footing, and with that he left his Confucian syncretic fancies behind him. But it took time for the solvent atmosphere of westernized Japan to do its work, and for a little while, especially in 1899, vestiges of the old theories persisted in his thought.

Pointing to Japanese example, he pleaded for Chinese study of the West, but he strongly enjoined that Confucius' teachings be the base.[3] Confucius, he said, had anticipated Western scholars who divide the peoples of the world into the categories of barbarian, half-civilized, and civilized; this schematization had been contained in the *Ch'un-ch'iu*, with its *chü-luan shih, sheng-p'ing shih,* and *t'ai-p'ing shih.*[4] And Liang, after outlining his version of true Confucian doctrine, explicitly called for a renaissance of the ancient Chou teachings to bring about the progress of human wisdom.[5]

Chinese thought in its pre-Ch'in efflorescence, he wrote, yielded

[2] Liang, "Hsin-min shuo," YPSWC 14.13 [Discourses on the making new of the people]. Portions of "Hsin-min shuo" and of other essays by Liang, to be cited below, have been translated freely by Leon Wieger in *La Chine moderne,* vol. I. In the present work, direct quotation of Liang's writings is always from the original Chinese.

[3] Liang, "Jih-pen heng-pin Chung-kuo ta-t'ung hsüeh-hsiao yüan-ch'i," YPSWC 44.45-46 [The origin of the Chinese *Ta-t'ung* school in Yokohama, Japan].

[4] Liang, "Tzu-yu-shu," YPSWC 45.6b [The book of freedom].

[5] Liang, "Lun Chih-na tsung-chiao kai-ko," YPSWC 28.52 [On religious reform in China].

nothing to Greece in caliber, but, since the Ch'in era, decline unchecked has led to China's present-day desperate intellectual deterioration. This comes from mistaking the spirit of the Six Classics and losing sight of the real aim of Confucius. Mean scholars perverted scholarship to their own unworthy ends, and rulers gave scholarship the task of dulling the minds of the people. Finally, after two thousands years of this, the true face of Confucius was hidden. This is the real reason why China is in its present straits.

If today we wish to rouse the East, we cannot but put forth the true teachings of Confucius. And K'ang Yu-wei is his prophet. Liang continues in the familiar vein, deriving from textual criticism. There are the time-tried references to the baleful influence of Hsün-tzu, to Confucius as a progressive and a democrat, and to the magic formula of the "three ages."[6]

In 1902, he pays a florid tribute to the concept of guidance by conscience, and here, too, he forces an analogy. The idea of conscience, the "inner light," writes Liang (making an error in theology), is a fundamental principle of the Roman Catholic Church, but it is also Confucian, and he cites the *Shih-ching* and Wang Yang-ming to prove it. There is no difference on this point between Eastern and Western doctrine.[7]

As a specimen of Western idea captured for Chinese tradition, everything seems to be in order here. But behind the appearance of standard Confucian-Western syncretism, beneath the polished surface, the worm has got into the apple. As we shall see below, Liang, by 1902, had come to hold no brief generally for the Catholic Church, and he pays Confucianism no tribute when he links the two together. The day was closing when a Confucian pedigree was necessary to make a foreign idea respectable. Classical references continue at intervals to crop up in Liang's writings, but they seem parenthetical, not central. For example, elsewhere in the work last cited, the *Hsin-min shuo*, he says that the *Ta-hsüeh* [the Great Learning] has discussed the absorbing and

---

[6] *Ibid.*, 47b-48.
[7] Liang, "Hsin-min shuo," 14.35-36; Wieger, 40-42.

significant problem of the relation to popular well-being of the proportion of producers to non-productive consumers. Wealth or poverty is regulated by this proportion. Liang quotes a phrase from the *Ta-hsüeh,* then deserts it for statements of the European classical economists on the relations of land, labor, and capital.[8] Why is the *Ta-hsüeh* mentioned? Liang does not maintain that it anticipated Mill or Ricardo; nor is a prior treatment in the classics necessary to make the workings of society a legitimate topic for discussion. Actually, in this section of his treatise, Liang is concerned with economic practicality, not with cultural justification, and the passage about the *Ta-hsüeh* is no more than rhetorical baggage.[9]

In another essay, a well-known account of Chinese intellectual history, written also in 1902, we again find the classics mentioned but shorn of their legitimizing function. Liang makes yet another elucidation of the famous *san-shih,* the three ages, and this time, indeed, there is an elaboration, for within each of the three ages are three ages, bearing the same names, respectively, as the major divisions. But this formula, of all classical themes the one most bound up with Liang's early syncretism, the one never cited previously without attendant exhortations to reform and pious references to the real Confucius and his prescription for modern China —this formula is now given simply as part of an outline of the Confucian system, pure history, with no imperatives attached.[10]

The plain fact is that an appeal to the *san-shih* doctrine had be-

---

[8] Liang, "Hsin-min shuo," 13.46; Wieger, 87-88. For the reference to the *Ta-hsüeh,* see Legge, I, 379: "There is a great course also for the production of wealth. Let the producers be many and the consumers few. Let there be activity in the production and economy in the expenditure. Then the wealth will always be sufficient."

[9] This is clearly indicated in an article written in the same year (1902). Liang prefaces a long description and history of economic theory with the statement that the Chinese know nothing of this study and must learn about it because of its vital relation to the question of the survival of the state. He insists that economic theory had originated and flourished only in the West. See Liang, "Sheng-chi-hsüeh hsüeh-shuo yen-ko hsiao-shih," YPSWC 11.1b-4b [A short history of the doctrines and successive changes in economic theory].

[10] Liang, "Lun Chung-kuo hsüeh-shu ssu-hsiang pien-ch'ien chih ta-shih," YPSWC 5.35b [On changing trends in Chinese scholarship and thought].

come a terribly stale argument for reform. It seemed to have de-
generated into a sort of convention, a ritual response whose words
Liang had learned by rote and repeated from force of habit. And
as far back as 1899 we find evidence that even habit was not
enough; Liang's memory of how the formula was supposed to
work appeared to be slipping.

In a discussion of "the right of the strongest," Liang flirts with
a *san-shih* explanation but at first does not use it. He says that in
a barbarous environment the strongest is measured wholly in
terms of physical strength; in a half-civilized environment,
strength is a compound of physical and intellectual power, and in
a civilized environment intellectual power is all.[11] Here we see
the old Chinese and early Liang delight in a well-ordered series.
And sure enough, just a few pages on in the discussion, the three
ages appear, not in a definition of the elements of power but in
the identification of who it is that holds it. The first age is that
of sovereign over people. In the second age, aristocracy dominates
people, male dominates female. The third age sees the conquest of
government by the governed; those who had once been weak
acquire power.[12]

Liang is clearly tired of this formula, so tired that somehow he
has reversed what used to be the order of the first two ages (first,
"many sovereigns"; second, "single sovereign"). The lapse is
significant. It indicates directly the gentle crumbling of Liang's
Confucianism, but it points, too, indirectly, to the gradual per-
meation of his mind not only by Western ideas but by their con-
texts. The order of the ages which he sets forth here applies neatly
to England, where the barons, extorting Magna Carta from the
king for their own purposes, laid the groundwork for popular
government. Of all Western countries, England was the one which
he most admired and studied hardest. More and more, in his
Japanese period, Liang turned from explaining away China's failure to explaining English success, and here we have an early
specimen of this change of emphasis. If the *san-shih* sequence of

[11] Liang, "Tzu-yu shu," 45.23.
[12] *Ibid.*, 45.25.

historical epochs really is as here expounded, English history may be its illustration, but it has no relevance whatever to Chinese. As long as the *chü-luan shih* and the *sheng-p'ing shih* were equated with the periods of feudalism and of imperial despotism (an indisputably historical Chinese sequence), reform, which Liang had advertised as the harbinger of the *t'ai-p'ing shih,* could look like the natural and traditional culmination of Chinese history. But if the order of the first two ages is not true for China, then it does no good to advocate the third, and Liang's reformist position must be justified on other grounds than tradition.

And so, finally, the old rationalizations go into the discard. When in 1902 Liang writes of the decline of Chinese feudalism and the beginning of centralization, he does not speak of the transition from *chü-luan* to *sheng-p'ing*[13]—a chance he never would have missed a few years earlier. When he calls modern Europe the reflection of ancient Greece[14] and Athenian civilization the prototype and spiritual father of modern British civilization,[15] he again implicitly rejects the *san-shih* formula; for, it will be remembered, his belief in the three-age theory of history had once forced him to undervalue Greece while he admired Britain, to insist that th ancient West was no nearer to the *t'ai-p'ing* age than ancient China had been.[16] And at last he comes out with it frankly: history is the story of struggle, race against race—there is no *ta-t'ung* or *t'ai-p'ing,* he says, no Great Harmony, no Great Peace.[17]

[13] Liang, "Chung-kuo chuan-chih cheng-chih hsin-hua shih lun," YPSWC 35.4 *et seq.* [On the history of the transition to autocratic rule in China].

[14] Liang, "Hsin shih-hsüeh," YPSWC 34.37 [The new history].

[15] Liang, "Ya-tien hsiao-shih," YPSWC 36.15b [A short history of Athens].

[16] In this connection, see also Liang, "Lun li-fa ch'üan" [On the legislative power] (YPSWC 20.47b-48), an essay which breaks completely with the early syncretic efforts either to deny that Greece had had a parliamentary spirit or to affirm that China had possessed it: "Western government is superior to Chinese on more counts than one, but if we seek the root of this superiority, it is in the early development of the legislative arm. This really is most important. In the West, from antiquity Greece had a so-called council of elders, the Gerontes. . ."— and Liang continues with a history of European representative institutions.

[17] Liang, "Hsin shih-hsüeh," 34.33b.

The real break with his past had already been made. In 1901, he wrote:

The abdications of Yao and Shun are the premier instances of generous action in Chinese history. It is not only the standard old scholarship which unites to praise them. Thus, the modern "people's rights," "great harmony" group, too, does not fail to cite Yao and Shun to prove that China had a democratic system in antiquity. Their intent cannot but be called laudable. [Yet] I consider democracy to be a world universal principle. Where universal principles are concerned, one must not consider as a matter of any importance whether or not the ancients previously applied it. Thus, the abdications of Yao and Shun actually have no bearing on the modern doctrine. That is, even if Yao and Shun really did abdicate, that still is entirely different from modern democracy.[18]

Liang gives no *mea culpa*. Nevertheless, this passage is a devastating commentary on his own past thinking and a milestone on the way to a new Chinese appreciation of Chinese history in the modern world of European encroachment and pervasive European influence. Textual criticism has served its turn. If the Confucian tradition of the reactionaries has been drained of meaning, so, too, has the "authentic" Confucian tradition of the reformers, and a Chinese adjustment to the modern world which will leave China its dignity and autonomy must take place under some other ideological aegis.

In his thirtieth year, wrote Liang, many years after that year had passed, he ceased discussion of the "false classics."[19]

The Break with Tradition

At last he comes to a new position. China's disasters do not stem from betrayal of the genius of Chinese culture, from willful resistance to the authority of the classics; they come rather from

[18] Liang, "Yao Shun wei Chung-kuo chung-yang chün-ch'üan lan-shang k'ao," YPSWC 35.25 [A consideration of Yao and Shun as the fountainheads of the central monarchical power in China].

[19] Liang, "Ch'ing-tai hsüeh-shu kai-lun," 63.

insistence on that authority. Liberation is needed—from "false" classics, from "true" classics, from domination by any dead hand of the past. Evolution is the law of life, he writes, even for China, the world's most laggard and unprogressive country, where today's thoughts, customs, script, tools are still those of thousands of years ago. China's evolution has been peculiar but unmistakable; it consists of the development of authoritarianism in government.[20] "Wash out the poison of thousands of years."[21]

"China today is in a period of transition," he repeats and repeats. It has been static for so many centuries (he piles up phrase upon phrase, one after the other, all meaning "immobility"). Now China is a "ship leaving shore." The people have only exasperation with and contempt for the old political, intellectual, and cultural forms. Not all the people, that is; for Liang divides the nation into two groups: first, the "old and worthless," the bitter foes of transition, and second, "youth," the spearhead of the new movement.[22]

Here indeed is the new Liang. No idea of categorical conflict of generations could have been part of his early thought. He had never spoken of a cleavage between young and old. Rather, the old were expected to embrace reform, since it would come in the guise of the truly traditional. China could be revivified, he thought then, by devotion to the real implications of the classical thinkers. But, in these latter days, China had another and far different requirement. The first essential for the attainment of social progress, he declared at last, was freedom of thought.[23] "Freedom of thought," that western shibboleth—to understand how Liang came by it, we must discuss once more his intellectual relationship with K'ang Yu-wei.

[20] Liang, "Chung-kuo chuan-chih cheng-chih chin-hua shih lun," YPSWC 35.1 [On the history of the development of autocratic government in China].

[21] Liang, "Shih chung te-hsing hsiang-fan hsiang-ch'eng i," YPSWC 15.52b [Contradictory and complementary principles of ten types of morality].

[22] Liang, "Kuo-tu shih-tai lun," YPSWC 16.14b-16b [On periods of transition].

[23] Liang, "Wang Ching-kung," YPSCH-CC 7: 27:114 [Biography of Wang An-shih].

K'ang Yu-wei's last political act was an attempt to restore the Manchu Emperor in 1917. He may be judged by his work prior to 1898; he strained tradition that far and no farther. Liang's ideas became gradually more and more independent, and in 1921 he identified the root of their divergence from K'ang's.

The perennial weakness of Chinese thought lies certainly in its penchant for dependence (*hao i-p'ang*) and in its confusion of name with reality (*ming shih hun-hsiao*). If we inject Buddhism into Confucianism, if we are prone to forge books, the impulses all originate in a spirit of this sort. For Ch'ing scholarship, Yen Yüan, though close to Mo-tzu, must nevertheless be described as stemming from Confucius; Tai Chen belongs entirely to western thought, but he must be described as stemming from Confucius; K'ang Yu-wei's "great harmony," an unprecedented discovery, must yet be described as stemming from Confucius. . . . If these flawed bases of our thinking are not rooted out, there will be in the end no hope of independence and freedom of thought.[24]

Liang first came frankly to this point of view in the intellectual climate of Japan and the great world, but even before his flight from China, when he seemed to be still K'ang's second self, there were signs that Liang might slip his Confucian moorings and eventually leave K'ang behind him. In 1898, Liang wrote an article, "Tu Meng-tzu chieh-shuo" (see above, p. 38), to corroborate K'ang's idea of the "three ages." Liang considers the work of various philosophers and identifies the teachings of each with one of the ages. In the interests of establishing the formula, Liang insists that these writers be distinguished from one another.

It is then apparent that in the intellectual activity of the ancients, each school had its writers not mutually without order and sequence. How unclear on this issue were scholars of later generations! They strained to pull all threads together in a uniform pattern. If, in order to read all kinds of books, one does not look critically upon the ancients, one falsifies the ancients.[25]

[24] Liang, "Ch'ing-tai hsüeh-shu kai-lun," 65.
[25] Liang, "Tu Meng-tzu chieh-shuo," 15.

Dangerous thoughts for a man who is working for K'ang Yu-wei! Liang was a convincing publicist, and it was only a matter of time before he convinced himself.

K'ang was a naturally endowed philosopher, Liang wrote in 1901. This seems a compliment, but it is spoiled by condescension, for the natural endowment, Liang suggests, is in his being a philosopher of his particular bent without having penetrated Western culture, understood Western speech, or read Western books.[26] The tone of this essay is consistently one of eulogy; Liang buries as he praises, and it seems very much like an *ave atque vale* when Liang proclaims: "In Chinese political history and in the history of world philosophy, he must occupy an extremely important position."[27]

But the kiss of death for K'ang Yu-wei is in a later essay, one of 1902. Liang remarks on K'ang's emphasis on the *san-shih* doctrine, with its evolutionary overtones, and he praises K'ang in these terms: "The proclamation of this by Nan-hai [K'ang], *before Darwinism came to China* [italics mine], cannot but be called a great discovery."[28] Here is the final relegation of K'ang's doctrines to the museum after their brief appearance on the battlefield. Now they are history, not current truth. Western thought has supplanted them. Darwin does more than Confucius can to justify social change to man. Yet, Darwin is not the only European prototype of K'ang Yu-wei; in his biography of the latter, Liang has said, "My teacher is the Martin Luther of Confucianism."[29]

Now at last we may understand how Liang could escape Confucianism, whether orthodox or reinterpreted. Darwin and Luther, as Liang exploits them, are the symbols of his liberation. Darwin stands for knowledge, the new world of Western thought which Liang really studied for the first time in Japan. It was natural that Darwinism, a system more complete, more coherent, more incon-

[26] Liang, "Nan-hai K'ang hsien-sheng chuan," 68b.
[27] *Ibid.*, 81.
[28] Liang, "Lun Chung-kuo hsüeh-shu ssu-hsiang pien-ch'ien chih ta-shih," 6.34.
[29] Liang, "Nan-hai K'ang hsien-sheng chuan," 64b.

trovertible than K'ang's application of Confucianism, should commend itself to an open mind. As Liang and China became exposed to more and more of the non-Chinese knowledge, Chinese tradition had to crack under the strain of assimilating so much new content, so much hopelessly foreign content, for sentimentality could cover just so long the infinite discrepancies.

Nevertheless, the mere accessibility of Western knowledge was not enough, the inadequacy of Chinese explanations was not enough to account for Liang's drift from tradition. The process of acculturation, of the erosion of a traditional way of life and traditional beliefs, is never the product of some hypothetical free competition of ideas. Liang had no simple choice—truth over falsehood, reason over absurdity, Darwin over K'ang Yu-wei. How was he to get the open mind? People believe not what they must but what they can, and Liang no more than any man could proceed from devotion to tradition to denial of tradition except by way of concern for that tradition. A conviction of the equivalence of China and the West had been a necessity before 1898, and it was still a necessity now. In the first instance, to assert this equivalence he had clung to a simple belief; if the Western tradition seemed to have all the answers, the Chinese tradition must have all the answers, somewhere. No abstract apprehension of flaws in this conclusion could shake it as long as the premise remained unshaken. We have seen already that in his earlier phase Liang had at least an intimation of a vulgarized Darwinism and that his whole syncretism was a tissue of logical incompatibilities, but for all that, he was a traditionalist then. Increasing knowledge of the West per se could never make him forsake his Chinese affiliations.

What knowledge of the West could do was to convince him that the Western things he valued issued not from fulfillment of something known as the Western tradition but from the rejection of it. Europe had had its medieval orthodoxy and, as Liang believed, its concomitant stagnation. European development had been inhibited by an intellectual despotism with pretensions at least as ecumenical as the Confucianists'. If European progress hinged on the shattering of this tradition, progress in China would seem to require something of the same. The European Reformation was the key point to study. Although the Reformers maintained that they were the real traditionalists, yet, by their challenge to institutionalized orthodoxy, they indirectly introduced the possibility of freedom of thought and of those secular advances which Liang admired. How does Liang stigmatize K'ang Yu-wei? He is a captive of tradition, an obstructor of freedom of thought. And how does he praise him? As a Martin Luther.

This is clearly not the whole story of the search for a new principle of equivalence, but it was Liang's beginning. Although the solution was incomplete and theoretical difficulties still abounded, he was at last emotionally able to quit an intellectually insecure position. If he could bring the European tradition down to China's level of futility, it would be just as comforting as to raise Chinese tradition to Europe's level of success. Instead of comparing European vitality to Chinese stagnation and being forced to explain the latter away, he could compare European vitality to European stagnation. Then, China, away with the need to redeem the past! If the achievement of Western values required frank admission that the Western dogma was an incubus, surely a Chinese could sacrifice his own canons without feeling any more futile than the next man.

It is no surprise, then, to find Liang celebrating freedom of thought, in double-edged commentaries expressing contempt for the European Middle Ages and condemnation of Chinese worship of the past. He writes an account of Western history in terms of the triumphs of heroes of thought, and he ignores the Middle Ages. Modern history, the history which Liang admires, begins with the Renaissance. Renaissance expansion of thought, fed by the revival of Greek knowledge, leads to a complete change in the European spirit; and this is caused by Luther and the Reformation. Bacon and Descartes join Luther in the pantheon.

They put an end to the age-old slave mentality of the scholarly world. Not a vestige was left. Freedom of thought in all Europe entered swiftly thereby on its development; its glory daily grew brighter, until finally we see its present-day flourishing.[30]

Elsewhere Liang calls Bacon and Descartes the two heroes of modern times, who delivered thinking men from slavery to the ancients.[31] A traditional teaching deceives.

The theories of men of the past are often the source of error. Generally those who trumpet the words of a "master" are like puppets on the stage.[32]

The old books, he thunders, the old education will not produce minerals, make cannon, build railroads. Tear down the old Chineses structure, and let progress be possible. Luther, Bacon, Descartes, Smith, Copernicus—men like these had set Europe on such a course.[33]

But it is in the following passage, more clearly than in any other, that we may see the point of his emphasis on European anti-traditionalism:

Whence comes the movement to preserve the Confucian doctrine? It comes from fear of the incursions of Christianity and a belief that this is the way to resist it. To my way of thinking, this anxiety is out of date. . . . As the strength of science daily waxes, the strength of superstition daily declines. As the frontiers of freedom daily expand, the frontiers of religious domination daily contract. Today the strength of Christianity in Europe is only one or two tenths of what it was in centuries past.[34]

Here is how Liang frees himself from the Chinese past. All he needs is the conviction that China and the West remain equiva-

---

[30] Liang, "Lun hsüeh-shu chih shih-li tso-yu shih-chieh," YPSWC 6.38-39b [On the power of learning to control the world]; Wieger, 140-142.

[31] Liang, "Chin-shih wen-ming ch'u-tsu erh ta-chia chih hsüeh-shuo," YPSWC 9.20 [Theories of the two great founders of modern civilization]; Wieger, 117.

[32] Liang, "Chin-shih wen-ming ch'u-tsu erh ta-chia chih hsüeh-shuo," 13b; Wieger, 113.

[33] Liang, "Hsin-min shuo," 13.30-33; Wieger, 74-76.

[34] Liang, "Pao-chiao fei so-i tsun K'ung lun," YPSWC 28.58b [To preserve the Confucian doctrine is not the way to honor Confucius].

lent, that whatever China pays for progress, it costs the West as much.

Thus Liang prepares for his forward march, slowly, deliberately, shoring up the defenses behind him. The forces of logic may batter as they please; he yields no ground until he has an emotional lodgment newly prepared. The watchword for China still is westernization without capitulation, and his old syncretistic position is not so much abandoned, which would have meant calling an end to Chinese history, as it is transmuted, changed but retained, and preserving the continuity of the civilization of China. That civilization dies and Chinese history stops when innovation ceases to be explainable as somehow proper to China. Once let it be felt only useful to China, necessary only for its value, with no history but an occidental one, and China becomes an appendage of Europe. Its civilization will be the European civilization lived by the Chinese people, those new recruits, with no more feeling for their own real past than Egyptians had after the Ptolemies. And so, when Liang calls for rejection of Confucian tradition, the manner in which he does it, still holding Europe the same arm's-length away, shows that he does not mean China really to break with its past but only to add to it. He has not broken with his own past; he simply moves gingerly beyond it, and he carries much of the old equipment with him. "Analogy of patterns of culture-growth" and "analogy of cultural values" are still in service.

Liang draws an analogy of the first type when he declares that the revival of basic ʿConfucianism by the *chin-wen, kung-yang* school—that body of "false-classics" textual critics of whose number he had been the latest—was related to the new Chinese thought in just such fashion as the revival of Greek learning in the Renaissance was related to modern European thought.[35] Here we

---

[35] Liang, "Lun Chung-kuo hsüeh-shu ssu hsiang pien-ch'ien chih ta-shih," 6.32b. See also Liang, "Tzu Mo-tzu hsüeh-shuo," YPSWC 7.41b [The theories of the sage Mo-tzu], where Liang declares, "The civilization of the modern West stems from the period of the renaissance of antiquity. We are following this example."

see, in utter clarity, the dialectical quality of the continuity of Liang's ideas. It was the *chin-wen* school which had produced the *san-shih* theory, the universal law of the succession of the three ages, whereby Liang had been able to contend that modern improvements were as much in the stream of Chinese history as of any other. This theory, which asserted that all societies go through the same historical stages, had been the whole basis for Chinese sanction of Western-type reforms by analogy of patterns of culture growth. The *chin-wen* school had provided a formula to explain historical facts; now, with the next turn of the screw, it was no more than a fact which the formula explained. The school had taught Liang that Chinese history ran parallel to the history of the West, would never simply taper off into it, and the fact that it had taught him so was a fact which proved it true.

An analogy of cultural values permits Liang, in another pivotal maneuver, to transcend traditionalism and yet, by using old materials in a new way, continue without a break his assertion of Chinese independence. In the argument by this type of analogy, it will be remembered, one locates in the Chinese past counterparts of things which Europe boasts of. Now Liang matches the West's Jesus against China's Confucius, and he finds for the latter, because he, unlike Jesus, did not preach, says Liang, a doctrinal despotism. The ideas of Jesus as applied by the Church produced the Middle Ages, darkest period in world history. The authoritarian doctrine which has come down as Confucian is false, not the teaching of Confucius, for he detested authoritarianism, and this is why he should be revered.[36]

This is a paragraph full of plums. Here are the two champions, subjects for analogy, just as they might have been in the nineties. Then and still now, the rationale of such a comparison could only be the following: (*a*) Liang recognizes that some principle, spirit, or achievement has value; (*b*) most people, ill-informed Chinese among them, consider this thing to be associated in history exclu-

[36] Liang, "Lun Chung-kuo hsüeh-shu ssu-hsiang pien-ch'ien chih-ta-shih," 5.43-43b; Wieger, 155-156.

sively with the West; (c) actually, an equivalent or superior example of it can be found in the Chinese tradition, which therefore makes it perfectly proper for modern Chinese to revive it. But what does the Chinese tradition authorize here? It authorizes the rejection of the Chinese tradition. Do not listen to the voice of the past, says Liang. It is perfectly proper not to listen; the voice of the past has told us so.

More Blows against the Historical Culture as the Basis of Comparison

Liang's attack on Chinese tradition as a corrupting orthodoxy has been able to proceed only as fast as his attack on a corresponding Western orthodoxy. As long as the ideals which he cherished were supposed to belong to a monolithic unit known as the West, China, too, had been considered as a great unit, and everything in its past had somehow to be accounted for, either praised or blamed and explained away. Relief from the impossible pressures of such a task comes when the concept of the monolithic West breaks down. The assault on the Christian tradition splinters the West in time. Liang, in this same period, was finding in his studies material with which to splinter the West, also, as it were, in space.

Where once he had seen nothing but a vast homogeneous culture-area, he now introduces distinctions, some crude, others fine and subtle, which qualify out of existence the idea of a simple "West." Now, instead of one civilization there are several races, or many nations, or a myriad of individuals. The vision of a unified West is lost amidst these fragments. One day Liang would again face up to the fact that China and the West were the irreducible units of comparison, but, in this period of Chinese history, when Liang and many others were ready to change the face of Chinese culture, they could feel themselves released from an obligation to cultural loyalty only when "European civilization" had become a meaningless abstraction.

Liang's essays are studded with comments on racial differences;

the broadest distinction, that of color, he had mentioned before
(see above, Chapter II, note 20). Now, in 1902, he asserts roundly
that white peoples are active, others are phlegmatic; whites are
belligerent, others peaceful; whites advance and invade, others are
conservative; whites are able to propagate their civilization, others
can only create one.[37]

Liang goes on to make a further breakdown in the racial pattern, and another essay includes a diagram of subdivisions among
races. He admires most the Aryan branch of the white race, represented in antiquity by the Greeks, and he remarks that, after the
Greco-Roman period, first place in world history was taken indisputably by the Aryans, particularly by their Teutonic segment.
The Teutons today are preëminent among Aryans, who are
preëminent among whites, who dominate nine-tenths of the
earth.[38]

In capacity for self-government, he declares, Teutonic peoples
far surpass the Latin,[39] and in a point-by-point comparison of
racial characteristics, this item on colonization practice sets the
general tone: Latins first set up wine-shops, Teutons first repair
the roads.[40] (We have already heard Liang in this vein in his discussion of the races of Canada; see above, pp. 69-70). But he analyzes the Teutonic race itself, and the group he praises above all
others is the Anglo-Saxon.[41] The Anglo-Saxon race assuredly
possesses the characteristics of freedom, Liang maintains,[42] and
only the Anglo-Saxons, well adapted to self-government, can stage
a revolution without succumbing to mob rule.[43]

[37] Liang, "Hsin-min shuo," 12.43; Wieger, 29.

[38] Liang, "Hsin shih-hsüeh," 34.34b-39.

[39] Liang, "Chin-shih ti-i nü-chieh Lo-lan fu-jen chuan," YPSWC 42.57b [Biog-
raphy of Mme Roland, the outstanding heroine of modern times].

[40] Liang, "Ou-chou ti-li ta-shih lun," YPSWC 37.55-55b [On European geographical conditions].

[41] Liang, "Hsin-min shuo," 12.41b-43; Wieger, 29-30.

[42] Liang, "Ta mou-pao ti-ssu-hao tui-yü pen-pao chih po-lun," YPSWC 30.6b
[In answer to the criticism of this newspaper in issue no. 4 of a certain news-
paper].

[43] Liang, "Chung-kuo wan-pu-neng shih-hsing kung-ho lun," [China can

This racist strain in Liang helps him to focus on less than a whole civilization. Yet, Liang's new unit of equivalence, smaller than civilization, was not the race but the nation. Let the West decompose into nations, little watertight units best described in the abstractions of political philosophy; then Europe is only a geographical expression, emptied of cultural content.

Liang had always, of course, been aware that the West was not a political unit. He had even written little histories of several individual European nations. Nevertheless, he had seen these nations as parts of a unified culture-area, and it was this area's cultural challenge which Liang had felt forced to meet. His method then, stripped of all camouflage, had been simply to acknowledge in his inmost heart that what China really had was not sufficient to match the West, that he must invent triumphs for China and thus inflate his country to Western dimensions. Now, as he became more steeped in Western learning, he realized that he could no longer make his misleading or false reconstructions of China's past; instead of building China up, he would, by dint of the same Western learning, cut the West down to size. For the first time Liang makes a systematic classification of nations, and political constitution becomes the index of differentiation between them. All nations, China among them, are visualized as historical instances of universal, culturally neutral types. One no longer, for example, compares China, the society, which lacks the scientific spirit, to Europe, which is imbued with it. Rather, compare China, the nation, which one terms a monarchical autocracy, to, let us say, Thebes, an aristocratic autocracy. This comparison is not so invidious, and Thebes seems somehow less formidable a rival. Between China and the West the broad and embarrassing distinctions, such as between the nonscientific and the scientific, tend to be passed over when the unit of equivalence is not society but state, when the criterion of the quality of the state is its political

---

never adopt the republic], quoted in Tseng, 128. This essay, which was published in Shanghai in 1906, cannot be found in subsequent collections of Liang's works, YPSTC ("ts'ung-chu"—1916), YPSWC (1925), or YPSHC (1936).

constitution, and when the distinction between China and some European state is no different in kind from the distinction between two European states themselves.

In 1899 Liang made a tentative attempt to parcel up the world in this fashion and file the pieces in a set of pigeonholes. He stated that the modern world was made up of nations of two types, republics and monarchies, and that the latter were divided between the categories of authoritarian and constitutional.[44] This scheme of classification was purely elementary for Liang. By 1905 we see in him a nicer taste for qualification. He remarked then that authority could be institutionalized only on a national basis, and he went on to make such an elaborate set of distinctions that the allegedly homogeneous West seemed fragmentized indeed.

Liang held that, broadly speaking, there were two types of nations, autocratic and nonautocratic. Nonautocratic nations were subdivided further into nations comprising (a) monarchy, aristocracy, and people (b) monarchy and people, or (c) people. Autocratic nations might be (a) monarchical despotisms (China, Russia, Turkey), (b) aristocratic despotisms (Sparta and other oligarchies appearing in Greek and Roman history), or (c) popular despotisms (Cromwell's England; Marat's, Danton's, and Robespierre's France; the second French Republic during the presidency of Louis Bonaparte).

Even these refinements were not enough for Liang. He persisted in his discriminations, relentlessly worrying the categories he had set up, defining their sections one from the other. For example, nonautocratic popular rule he disintegrated into regimes which provided for direct popular participation or for indirect popular participation, and the latter type was further dissected along the lines of universal or restricted suffrage, and so on.[45]

This tragico-comico-pastoral partition of the world could go far

[44] Liang, "Ko-kuo hsien-fa i-t'ung lun," YPSWC 23.1 [On the differences between the constitutions of the various nations].

[45] Liang, "K'ai-ming chuan-chih lun," YPSWC 29.37-38 [On "explanatory despotism"]. See note 223 below for a discussion of this term.

to lift the burden of guilt from a China committed to foreign ways. Western cultural successes could not be compartmentalized in such a fashion; hence no Western political unit could claim these successes as its own. The Chinese political unit could certainly not so claim them, but where was the embarrassment in that, when so many others were joined in her company? Liang considered that, of all individual nations, England came closest to being an independent creator of values—for example, he writes that England was the initiator of constitutional government,[46] England the country where democratic rights had made their earliest progress.[47] China had lagged behind England, Liang was ready to admit, but so, after all, had even France and Germany, and they did not seem to be stumbling with shame because of it. China could borrow, without sense of pressure to find a native pedigree for innovations, and likewise with no feeling that everyone had dignity except its poor old broken-down self. Thus was the cultural challenge that had once obsessed Liang (and really did so still) obscured by the division of the world into nations and by the peculiar implications which, as we shall see, this national orientation possessed.

Nevertheless, even more than his concepts of race and nation, Liang's interpretation of the role of the individual in history served to strip from the West its cultural prestige. In 1899, he made a theoretical statement on this subject and offered a confused, ill-defined, and analytically worthless doctrine of mutual interaction of genius and trend. His conclusion was that great men shape the times and that, on the other hand, the times determine what men can do. Liang stated both the Carlylean position, that the hero makes history, and the Hegelian position, that the hero is never more than the creature of a predetermined and inexorable process of historical development, and confronted with this contradiction, he fell back on easy synthesis, the traditional device of tired minds. Pretending to philosophy without doing the

[46] Liang, "Ko-kuo hsien-fa i-t'ung lun," 1b.
[47] Liang, "Ai-kuo lun," YPSWC 15.21 [On patriotism].

philosopher's labor, he theorized as though the simple existence of two extremes guaranteed the truth and clarity of any amorphous platitude he might put in the center.[48]

Despite the indecisiveness of his abstract reasoning, however, Liang showed himself a Carlylean when he faced practical problems of historical interpretation. In the very same essay in which he took such an inexplicit theoretical stand, he explicitly declared that, without Montesquieu and Rousseau, France could not have achieved its revolution, and that, if the school of Adam Smith had not existed, England could never have come to a free-trade regime.[49]

If the mainsprings of historical events lie in individuals, the implications are considerable. When we say that a thing would not have happened had a particular human agent not caused it, we are saying that the agent's act was itself spontaneous, uncaused; for if suprapersonal historical causes lay behind the individual's effort, the same effect would ultimately ensue whether he lived or died. Therefore, the great-man theory of history requires its adherents to assume that genius is not a function of socio-cultural events, not the product of cultural efflorescence but the cause of it. If a hero were not autonomous, one would have to examine the history of his culture to find the cause of his appearance, and comparative values for cultures would be set according as each provided the causes of the emergence of genius. But when genius causes the cultural triumphs and not vice versa, the question of culture really vanishes. When great events are caused by great men, these heroes represent not their cultures but themselves. If the Western values he admires are the fruits of their efforts, Liang knows Chinese culture has not failed, for it is not Western culture which has succeeded. Only men have succeeded, men who existed by chance, and there are men in the East and brains in the East. One need claim no longer that Chinese culture had really made provision for all Western feats. Let Chinese people only do them, and the West will have met its match well enough.

[48] Liang, "Tzu-yu shu," 45.7b.
[49] Ibid., 45-47.

Thus, it is of the utmost importance to recognize the unqualifiedly Carlylean strain in Liang's approach to history. We have already noted that tremendous causal implication he attributed to Luther, Bacon, and Descartes. He spoke of many others in the same manner; for example, of Montesquieu:

Until the 18th century, the political and legal base was very narrow. In the hands of the sovereign and his ministers lay sole responsibility for ruin or prosperity. Then came Montesquieu, the first to distinguish between the three types of power . . . legislative, executive and judicial. Thereafter, every civilized country followed this procedure [i.e., separation of powers].[50]

In another essay, Liang described the United States' system of government as constituted after the American Revolution, the abolition of slavery in British colonies and the United States, the abolition of serfdom in Russia, and penal reform. He concluded each section with the refrain, "Who brought about this happy circumstance? Montesquieu!"[51]

Of Rousseau: He introduced the idea of the rights of man. . . . When this doctrine was once abroad in European intellectual circles, it was like a clap of thunder over level ground, like a ray of light in the darkness, the wind speeding the clouds away. Just some ten years later, the French Revolution came, launching the whole 19th century world on its course of history. What implications Rousseau had for the world![52]

Of Bluntschli: With Bluntschli, the definition of the nation was fixed—its character, its spirit, its action. Thereupon nationalism had its great flowering in the world. . . . He made patriotism the primary duty, and at that point arose the great powers.[53]

Of Voltaire, Tolstoy, and Fukuzawa Yukichi: If these men had not lived, it is doubtful whether their countries could have advanced.[54]

[50] Liang, "Lun hsüeh-shu chih shih-li tso-yu shih-chieh," 39b. See also Liang, "Lun li-fa ch'üan," 49b.

[51] Liang, "Fa-li-hsüeh ta-chia Meng-te-ssu-chiu," YPSWC 9.25b-26 [The great legal philosopher Montesquieu].

[52] Liang, "Lun hsüeh-shu chih shih-li tso-yu shih-chieh," 39b-40.

[53] *Ibid.,* 41.

[54] *Ibid.,* 42b.

Of Cromwell: If Cromwell had not lived, then England would not have the constitutional government it has today; if Cromwell had not lived, England would not have the spirit of empire it has today.[55]

In the early writings, Liang had mentioned only rarely specific personalities involved in the history of the West. (He had, after all, been able to learn the names of only a few until he gained access to Japanese books.) In the nineties, aspects of culture were his subject—literacy, democracy, efficiency—and the appeal to Chinese tradition, while it mentioned names, Confucius and Mencius and the like, really invoked them as symbols of the total Chinese culture. As years went by, he realized that this type of defense for China was hopeless. Yet, just when it appeared that his traditionalist-culturalist rationalizations could no longer even be imagined valid—that European culture was supreme and must be unconditionally acknowledged so—the opponent disappeared from the field. The native culture, which in China is rejected, in Europe is extracted, and only all-powerful individuals remain. That China has lacked the individuals is not to be culturally explained, for the successful individuals of Europe have not derived from its culture; they have created it.

How, then, does China come to face the world? We have already suggested the answer—nation to nation, with a new way of life and no Chinese sugar-coating, for means of survival are the ultimate national values. Liang has fought his way through from culturalism to nationalism, but his apparent rejection of Chinese culture as the focus of loyalty is paradoxical testimony that Chinese culture was his tenderest concern. The tradition into which a man is born is the most inalienable thing he has. When the tradition is in decay, he can either dream that it still is vital, as Liang did once, or pretend that it doesn't matter. Either he holds it dear and will not see it die, or he must see it die and so wrenches his heart away from it. One method or the other spares him the pain of mingling frankness with affection. If a way of life is in-

[55] Liang, "Hsin Ying-kuo chü-jen K'o-lin-wei-erh chuan," YPSWC 42.59 [Biography of Cromwell, a great man of modern England].

supportable, blame the nation for it and lash the nation into changing it. No great distress need come from this. The nation is only one's relatives, but one's culture is oneself.

Culturalism and Nationalism

We have seen, in Liang's thinking, how he disposed of Chinese culture as the basis of Chinese equivalence with the West. We have still to consider how well the nation played the culture's erstwhile role. But first it is necessary to distinguish between Chinese culturalism and nationalism and to show how the one shaded off into the other.

Chinese nationalism is sometimes simply described as "anti-foreignism," as though that were its whole content, and since anti-foreignism is nothing new in China, the distinction between a traditional culturalism and a modern nationalism may seem illusory or, at best, incomprehensible. Also, since Europeans generally faced different intellectual and emotional problems in their age of incipient nationalism, this Chinese distinction did not figure prominently in European history, except in that of certain peripheral areas, and consequently the problem has been, as yet, extremely ill defined. Certain basic differences between culture and nation and between their respective claims on the individuals who belong to them must be catalogued.

A nation is a corporate thing, which can exist only as a sum of its parts and only if the parts will it. A culture can be complete, down to its last detail, in the individual. A man can consider himself a participant in the Chinese culture and yet have no concern for anything but his own fortunes; but if he thinks that his membership in the Chinese nation is the most important single status he has, he must feel himself involved in a larger world than his own life defines. A man is born into his culture, enrolled into his nation, and while a nation is something which must be served by human action, a culture is the content of it. Liang is always quite convinced that a Chinese culture exists; it is the nation's existence which he says he fails to see when he finds no group consciousness in China, no capacity to recognize a common public interest transcending differences on issues of less than total national significance.[56]

A culturalism bars foreign ideas, but it may actually invite or not actively oppose foreign material force. Nationalism reverses these relations; it may admit foreign ideas, but it will blaze against foreign material incursions. In the T'aip'ing Rebellion (1850-1864), we see these two sentiments ranged against each other. The rebels flouted Chinese tradition but protested that they battled in the Chinese national interest against foreign Manchu rulers. Yet, the Chinese defenders of tradition and the Ch'ing dynasty knew that, culturally speaking, the Manchus were more Chinese than the T'aip'ings would ever be. Though there was a significant difference between the circumstances which led first the T'aip'ings and then Liang to break with tradition (a subject to which we shall return), they came, in the end, to make the same distinction between culture and nation. Let a Chinese action be culturally unorthodox if only it be nationally useful.[57]

When a man holds such a conviction, it means that he feels that his people has rivals. A sense of rivalry is the essence of nationalism; no man trumpets "my country" unless he realizes that other countries exist, with loyal populations of their own and a dangerous capacity to threaten. But a genuine, old-fashioned Chinese culturalist had no conception of rivalry. Chinese civilization was all the civilization there was: I think; therefore I am Chinese. When so much could be assumed, what need was there to insist? If all other peoples in the world were so thoroughly unimportant, how could the fate of the Chinese people loom as a

[56] Liang, "Hsin-min shuo," 13.43-44; Wieger, 84 and 32-33.

[57] Liang represents the very adoption of nationalism as one such action. He calls on Kossuth of Hungary, Mazzini, Garibaldi, and Cavour of Italy to give China lessons in patriotism. See Liang, "Hsiung-chia-li ai-kuo-che K'o-su-shih chuan," YPSWC 41.49b-69b [Biography of Kossuth, the Hungarian patriot], and "I-ta-li chien-kuo san-chieh chuan," YPSWC 42.1-47b [Biographies of the three heroes of the building of Italy].

subject of much importance? This confidence, of course, did not issue from any feeling of military impregnability. Barbarians could conquer China, that the Chinese knew, but they knew also that barbarism could not. Conquerors generally were so effectively denationalized by the compelling attractiveness of Chinese culture that the Chinese failed to think in national terms, and so, with national China nonexistent and cultural China impervious to challenge, immediate personal interest was the only cause which could rouse a Chinese to much of a fighting pitch. The Kwang-tung coast, which lay under threat of British cannon, had a lively interest in the Opium War, but few men in Yunnan rushed to the colors to defend their nation's integrity. To Liang, it seemed as though the Chinese could look with equanimity on foreign invasion.[58] Patriotism could hardly flourish when the world was only China and appendages, Chinese and barbarians who would become Chinese if they could ever get the chance and had the intelligence.

But when China was not alone, then the Chinese traditional culture was not enough. Liang Ch'i-ch'ao knew that China had rivals, and, though his first position was syncretism, the stated assumption that there was no contest, the intrusion of the very idea of contest put an end to Chinese pretensions of universalism. As Chinese knowledge of the world expanded, China contracted, and it is clear and explicit in the writings of Liang Ch'i-ch'ao that this process was synonymous with the rise of the Chinese nation from the embers of the Chinese culture.

In 1900, he wrote that Europe and Japan stigmatized China as a nation without patriotism. The sickly state of Chinese patriotism, maintained Liang, was the root cause of the nation's accumulated weaknesses. Nationalism was lacking because the court, not the nation, was the traditional focal point of allegiance and because the Chinese had been unaware that signficant peoples other than themselves existed in the world.[59]

[58] Liang, "Hsin-min shuo," 13.6b-13; Wieger, 50-54.
[59] Liang, "Chung-kuo chi jo su-yüan lun," YPSWC 15.23b-25 [On searching for the origins of China's accumulated weaknesses].

This latter theme received extensive treatment in Liang's influential *Hsin-min shuo* essays of 1902. He made there the key statement that the concept of nation can emerge only if the mind sees the world as fragmentized, if there is knowledge of and, he implies, respect for other peoples.[60] He went on to point out the reason for nondevelopment of patriotic nationalism. In centuries of foreign occupation of all or part of Chinese territory, the idea of "China" was obliterated. Under the influence of the literati, the Chinese began to think of China as a world (*t'ien-hsia*) rather than as a nation (*kuo-chia*); nationalism and, by extension, patriotism were destroyed.[61]

Although there were numberless barbarian peoples, in neither area, population, nor culture did they approach China. Beyond the Onion Range [in Turkestan] there existed Persia, India, Greece, Rome—all civilized countries—but there was no contact between them and China and no mutual knowledge. Hence, China looked on its country as the world.[62]

In 1911, just before the revolution, he was still insisting that there could be no consciousness of national identity or of patriotism when all the world was considered potentially a single country.[63] This was the conclusion he drew from a comparison between China and ancient Rome.

Among our countrymen, patriotism has long ceased to grow; universalism has been the obstruction. Gibbon is a great English historian. His history of the fall of Rome is read everywhere [literally, "where there is well-water to drink"] in Europe. In it he says, "From the time of Rome's conquest of Italy, its people never again knew patriotism. It is not that there was no love for Rome; but the object of love was the Roman culture and not the Roman people or the Roman nation. Its people always considered the preservation and expansion of this culture, its extension to the world, as their mission. It was immaterial

---

[60] Liang, "Hsin-min shuo," 12.51b.
[61] *Ibid.*, 12.51-51b; Wieger, 44-45.
[62] Liang, "Hsin-min shuo," 12.51b.
[63] Liang, "Chung-kuo ch'ien-t'u chih hsi-wang yü kuo-min tsc-jen," YPSWC 18.49b [China's hopes for the future and national responsibilities].

what the national origin was of the man who had the responsibility of consummating this purpose. The Romans, then, granted power with no reservations. For this reason, half the emperors in Roman history were of foreign origin."

And all this, said Liang, could be applied to China.[64]

Actually, in 1899, the very beginning of this period of Liang's life, he had seen the problem of Chinese nationalism in full perspective. He wrote then of China's abasement before the foreign powers. Because they believe that the Chinese have no concept of patriotism, foreigners feel they can be perfectly open in proclaiming their predatory intentions. Here, too, Liang explains his countrymen's lack of national feeling by Chinese historical experience, in which, prior to the western invasions, her contacts were with peoples who could not compare in cultural standing; this led to the inference that China was the world. Patriotism is the source of European independence and prosperity, he continues. There must be mass patriotism and education if a country is to be strengthened, and Chinese patriotism is identical with willingness to adopt Western-style reforms. There follows a reverent recapitulation of the great reform decrees of the Emperor Kuang-hsü.[65]

In this one article Liang fully comprehends the implications of nationalism for China. Nationalism commands recognition of the reality and formidableness of foreign peoples and, at the same time, supplies the means to fight them off. It is interpreted in the beginning as organized resentment, a device to make Chinese close ranks and resist enslavement; in the end, it is the spirit which moves a people to take nontraditional measures to implement resentment. That is, nationalism first induces realization that there is a nation whose interests should be at the heart of every citizen, and, secondly, it induces willingness to recognize and adopt the measures (like rejection, in the interests of national efficiency, of the old Chinese calendar)[66] which will enable the nation to pros-

[64] *Ibid.*, 49.
[65] Liang, "Ai-kuo lun," 12-21b.
[66] Liang, "Kai-yung t'ai-yang-li fa i," YPSWC 28.29-30b [Discussion of a law for the adoption of the solar calendar].

per. The first of these processes is not necessarily subversive of culturalism; but the second one is. In a nation's fight for life, its people's way of life is nothing sacred.

The nationalist proposition that the world is divided and that the world's divisions are nations has a corollary—that China must be undivided, that only in its wholeness can it be a nation. As Liang wrote in 1911, "Therefore, nationalism, in re internal considerations, is incompatible with localism; in re external considerations, it is incompatible with universalism."[67] Liang had to dramatize the idea of one China, the sum of its parts, if he was to make China distinguishable as one part of a sum.

Accordingly, more than once, he remarks sadly that the Chinese people seem to be rather parochial localists than nationalists,[68] and he approved of K'ang Yu-wei for his insistence that China is indivisible and for his opposition to the advocates of provincial autonomy.[69] He bitterly quotes Marquis Ito of Japan as saying, "China is one country in name, eighteen countries in fact."[70] He analyzes the poisonous effect of provincial coinage on the national power, and in a discussion of possible systems of indirect suffrage for China, rejects the old United States method of senatorial election by state assemblies, on the ground that its application to Chinese provinces would strengthen provincialism at the expense of nationalism.[71]

Thus, in Liang's mind, China was neither a world nor a geographic expression for a clump of contiguous but incohesive localities. In actual fact, it was not a world, but until the Chinese acknowledged as much, they could never take steps to rule out the

[67] "Chung-kuo ch'ien-t'u chih hsi-wang yü kuo-min tse-jen," 49.

[68] Liang, "Cheng-chih-hsüeh ta-chia Po-lun-chih-li chih hsüeh-shuo," YPSWC 10.33 [Theories of the great political philosopher Bluntschli], and Hsin-ta-lu yu-chi chieh-lu," 39.11b.

[69] "Nan-hai K'ang hsien-sheng chuan," 78b.

[70] "Chung-kuo chi jo su-yüan lun," 30-30b.

[71] Liang, "Ko-sheng lan-chu t'ung-yüan shao-shih," YPSWC 25.41b-49 [A short history of excessive coinage of copper by the individual provinces]; Liang, "Chung-kuo kuo-hui chih-tu ssu-i," YPSWC 22.31 [Private deliberations on a parliamentary system for China].

second description, which was, alas, too objectively true. China must realize that it is a nation; then it can try to become one.

Now one may see how the transition is made from Chinese culturalism to nationalism. It is in the decaying culturalist stage that an appreciation of foreign values appears. This is the period of syncretism, when a fusion of Chinese and foreign cultural values is attempted. As this attempt becomes more obviously impossible, China must be taken down from its lofty pedestal (its position as *t'ien-hsia,* world) so that it may be elevated again to another pedestal (its position as *kuo-chia,* nation). As a nation and not a world, China subscribes to a new world view: that history is not the story of the one great society but of the conflicts between autonomous societies. This is a new line of retreat for a partisan of China, but it is serviceable. If the old grand China of the obscurantists is dead, so is the mean China of the "self-effacement" defeatists; for, if China is not the great society, as the traditionalists had thought, neither is the West. It is still the syncretists' equivalence which is sought, but now it is the equivalence of nations, not cultures.

> It seems, as one becomes older,
> That the past has another pattern, and ceases to be a
>   mere sequence—
> Or even development: the latter a partial fallacy,
> Encouraged by superficial notions of evolution,
> Which becomes, in the popular mind, a means of disowning
>   the past.[72]

If nationalism is necessary to fit China for the struggle, the Social-Darwinist, survival-of-the-fittest, evolutionary explanation of struggle serves admirably to scuttle the debilitating traditionalist culturalism. When Liang agrees with Benjamin Kidd that the agent of progress is death, removing the useless and superannuated forms,[73] the Chinese past may indeed be in a fair way to be

---

[72] T. S. Eliot, "The Dry Salvages," from *Four Quartets.* Quoted with the permission of Harcourt, Brace, and Company, and Faber and Faber Ltd.

[73] Liang, "Chin-hua lun ko-ming che Hsieh-te chih hsüeh-shuo," YPSWC 10.5 [The theory of Kidd, a revolutionary in the discussion of evolution]; Wieger, 132.

I

disowned. And when Social-Darwinism ordains that the nation is the highest unit of struggle, not only does nationalism supplant culturalism as the spirit of action, but nation supplants culture as the end of action. Liang is most explicit in affirming that struggle for existence is the one great issue of life and that the world of nations is the scene of combat. In 1901, we find a simple spelling out of the doctrine of the survival of the fittest. First, there is a reiterative insistence that all is new; then, tiny steps for tiny feet—

All men in the world must struggle to survive. In the struggle for survival, there are superior and inferior. If there are superior and inferior, then there will be success and failure. He who, being inferior, fails, must see his rights and privileges completely absorbed by the one who is superior and who triumphs. This, then, is the principle behind the extinction of nations.[74]

In the *Hsin-min shuo,* Liang stated categorically that, in compliance with the general law of struggle for existence and of natural selection, men must come into conflict with men and nations with nations. Because struggle exists at all levels, the struggle of nations, the largest natural focal point for loyalty, dwarfs all more petty struggles, and patriotism is the great necessity. Private interest must be sacrificed for public. This battle is the mother of civilization, the prerequisite for progress.[75]

Elsewhere he wrote,

I have thought and thought again about the popularly accepted system in China today; there is almost not a single aspect of it which ought not to be destroyed and swept away, root and branch. . . According to the universal principle of evolution, when a race cannot meet the exigencies of the times, it cannot endure.

China, he went on, had for millennia been beset only by insignificant peoples, who could never really leave their mark on China.

[74] Liang, "Mieh-kuo hsin-fa lun," YPSWC 16.28b [On the new law of the extinction of nations]. See also Liang, "Tzu-yu shu," 45.30, where he remarks that there exist two principles, one the "world principle," which banishes the idea of combat and which belongs to theory, and the other the "national principle," which is based on the idea of military hostility and which belongs to fact.

[75] Liang, "Hsin-min shuo," 12.49-50; Wieger, 43-44.

Thus, China was unprepared for the onslaught of powerful foreign races. Some blame the government, some the mandarins; but
that is false analysis. Here is the real reason:

Our country's civilization is the oldest in the world. Three thousand
years ago, Europeans were living like beasts in the field, while our
civilization, its characteristics pronounced, was already equivalent to
theirs of the middle ages. Because of our self-satisfaction and our
inertia, the blindly cherished old ways have come down more than
three thousand years to our day. Organization of the race, of the
nation, of society, our customs, rites, arts and sciences, thought, morality, laws, religion, all are still, with no accretions, what they were
three thousand years ago.

Liang calls this a state of senile decrepitude. By the laws of struggle
for existence and of natural selection, China must perish if this
state persists.[76] For,

In the world there is only power—there is no other force. That the
strong always rule the weak is in truth the first great universal rule
of nature. Hence, if we wish to attain liberty, there is no other road:
we can only seek first to be strong.[77]

If China is involved in a struggle, then she must learn to fight
and learn to enjoy it. When Liang blasts the Chinese pacifist tradition, he shows us one of the links between the "conflict" element in nationalism and the nationalist's readiness, mentioned
above, to break with cultural orthodoxy. Praising Japan, Liang
notes that all Japanese poets speak of war's joys, and all Chinese
poets speak of its bitterness.[78] One root of weakness is cowardice;
this is part of the Chinese national character, which exalts letters,
while Europeans and Japanese, prizing the military virtues, are
free of the taint. What else can be expected of China as long as
it follows Mencius and maintains that filial piety enjoins avoidance
of risk?[79] Actually, though the Chinese have never seemed to

[76] Liang, "Hsin-min i," YPSWC 15.2-2b [The principle of the new people];
Wieger, 102-103.
[77] Liang, "Tzu-yu shu," 45.24b.
[78] Ibid., 45.29; Liang, "Chung-kuo chi jo su-yüan lun," 32.
[79] Ibid., 31b.

know it, a man owes less devotion to his parents than he does to his country, which guarantees his life and property.[80] Liang hates the old saw, "Good iron is not used for nails, and good men are not used for soldiers."[81] China has the reputation today of being unmilitary, she deserves it, and Liang is ashamed and indignant.[82]

He likes Bismarck and his "blood and iron." Without such a policy any nation, no matter how great its civilization, its wisdom, its population, or its area, is doomed to destruction in this world of combat. In this world of the jungle, where the strong feeds on the weak, in this world of the hawk and the tiger, the most ineffectual attitude is submissiveness. Germany was right—build the army and rise to power. And see Japan, so small compared to China, reaching such heights because of its *bushidō* and *Yamato-damashii*, the Japanese military code and spirit.[83]

Yet China once had had its own *bushidō*. In the days of the great pre-Ch'in struggle for power, the Spring and Autumn and the Warring States periods, the way of the warrior had flourished.[84] The concept of *ming-yü*, honor, a standard motif in modern Japan and widely recognized in the West, was current in China in those early times, when a warrior would rather lose his life than his honor.[85] Liang's search for precedents in these instances should not be confused with his earlier culturalistic attempts. When Liang says that the military spirit is not really foreign to China, he is trying not to make it seem acceptable for his contemporaries but to make it seem possible. This is the implica-

[80] Liang, "Hsin-min shuo," 12.46b; Wieger, 32. See also Liang, "Lun chiao-yü tang-ting tsung-chih," YPSWC 29.13b [On the educational aims which should be determined upon]: "For children are the public possessions of the nation, not the private charges of their parents."

[81] Liang, "Chung-kuo chi-jo su-yüan lun," 31b; Liang, "Hsin-min shuo," 14.15b.

[82] Liang, "Chung-kuo chih wu-shih-tao," YPSHC-CC 6:24.17 (China's *bushidō*).

[83] Liang, "Hsin-min shuo," 14.10b-14b.

[84] Liang, "Chung-kuo chih wu-shih-tao," 21; Liang, "Chung-kuo ch'ien-t'u chih hsi-wang yü kuo-min tse-jen," 47b.

[85] Liang, "Te-yü chien," YPSHC-CC 6:26.13 [The mirror of moral culture].

tion of his statement that the spirit has withered in China but that he believes it can be revived, for its roots are deep.[86] Even though he tries weakly to cull militaristic statements from the classics,[87] his first justification for urging the revival of martial virtue is that it will preserve the nation today. If the ancient sages can be lured to join the chorus, their help will be accepted, but Liang shows himself, in this matter, too frankly utilitarian to let us suppose that, in pursuit of his aims, he would not sweep away any cobwebs of tradition. As stated above, means of survival are the ultimate national values; if adherence to tradition is incompatible with the adoption of these means, tradition will go.

In his acceptance of these Social-Darwinist values and his invocation of them in the question of war and peace, Liang shows most revealingly the distinction between culturalism and nationalism, for the Chinese tradition, in the last analysis, was one of disdain of war. When Liang disdains this part of the tradition, it must seem, to many Western minds with feelings of guilt about Western wars, the almost unbelievable discard of China's highest card.

With Social-Darwinism as the solvent of one and the core of the other, nationalism issues from culturalism in a sequence that is logical as well as chronological. Liang's decaying culturalism (that is, cultural loyalty which he feels he must justify) and his nationalism are linked to each other and distinguished from each other by the fact that both presuppose an idea of progress and that each defines progress in its own separate way. In the space of less than a decade, China makes the European intellectual journey from Condorcet to Spencer. In its Social-Darwinist guise, Liang's

[86] Liang, "Chung-kuo ch'ien-t'u chih hsi-wang yü kuo-min tse-jen," 48.

[87] See Liang, "Chung-kuo chih wu-shih-tao," 24b.1-2, where he notes Confucian injunctions to courage, e.g., in the *Hsiao-ching,* in which Confucius is recorded as saying that a man who lacks courage when he stands in battle array is not filial; Liang also lists references in Chuang-tzu and Mencius ascribing similar ideas to Confucius. See also Liang, "Hsin-min shuo," 14.19-19b, where he emphasizes that Confucius by no means stood unqualifiedly for "weakness and softness." Liang says that the military virtues were not ruled out in Confucius' philosophy.

idea of progress is tied no longer to a set of values, ends which are considered intrinsically good, which China must have, which tradition enjoins, for there are no more freely chosen ends. His values now are only means, means to nourish the nation-state, which is itself no more than a means to engage in the blind process of evolutionary change. The latter is the only value we know or need to know. Progress, now, is nothing but passage of time, but that was not so in the early phase. Then, to progress was to choose an end and close the gulf of time to reach it.

With superficial notions of evolution, Liang has indeed disowned the past. When time and progress are a chain of conflicts, the entire past is nothing but a series of clashes contained in the present and pointing to some future resolution, and what this resolution will be is the only question that matters. If China proves to be the fittest of nations, no rationalization or denial of alleged failures in its past will be necessary. And if China should not survive, nobody will be interested to hear that Mencius knew all about city-planning. Liang the nationalist looks on the great figures of Chinese history with a new and different vision. They are still great, but they are no longer the eternal spokesmen of the Chinese culture. Now they are heroes of the Chinese nation, and there is a tremendous difference between hero and prophet. They differ in just such measure as nationalism differs from culturalism.

A hero is one whose thought or action is peculiarly effective at some given moment in time. In later ages, his admirers feel bound to direct their own efforts toward repeating not necessarily the content of his achievement, which belongs to history, but the spirit of it. Culturalism demands prophets, who deny the significance of time's passing, whose achievements tyrannize over those who come after them. But nationalism demands heroes, who inspire but do not dominate, who bequeath to succeeding generations a universal form of action, heroism, but leave the substance to those generations' own choosing. When Liang, in his early writings, kept his recommendations still subject to a Confucian imprimatur, he was acting as a culturalist, and Confucius was his prophet. But at last he insisted that China should think as Confucius would think today, not as Confucius had thought when he lived; he should be revered for his creativity, but if modern China would revive his spirit, she must abandon what he had created and create for herself. Confucius deserved to elicit all the patriotic pieties of the Chinese people, but the nation owed him no quasi-religious veneration. His doctrines were not eternal. Time had passed.

This change in the status of Confucius is very apparent in Liang's newer writings. We have already remarked how appeals to Confucian precedent gradually disappeared, although Liang occasionally cited the classics as containing an apt comment along the lines of his present thought. In the *Hsin-min shuo,* Confucius is praised, along with Moses, Jesus, Columbus, Tseng Kuo-fan, Darwin, Montesquieu, and others, as a man of courage and perseverance.[88] Confucius, then, has been transformed in Liang's mind from prophet to hero, just one of the species of good men in their day.

In the same work Liang insisted, as we know, on the absolute rule of progress, which, he repeats, ordains that, with the passing of time, thought reaches new heights, wisdom goes deeper. The greatest philosophers are imperfect, and succeeding epochs point up their imperfections.

Do not be slaves of the ancients. The old sages, the old heroes all had great merit and virtue, and it is fitting that we should love and respect them. But they were they and we are we. . .[89]

He once more attributed China's stagnation to its homogeneity, its lack of rivalries and clashes, a fatal lack in a world in which "battle is the mother of progress." Western triumphs he relates to constant strife among the Greeks and its carry-over into the succeeding centuries in Europe. The closest Chinese approximation to this situation occurred in the Warring States period, when

[88] Liang, "Hsin-min shuo," 14.2-5b; Wieger, 97-98.
[89] Liang, "Hsin-min shuo," 13.19b; Wieger, 61.

Chinese thought was at its apogee. China's decadence, continuing to the present, began with the unification of the Empire by Ch'in.[90] When Liang says this, there is a tribute implied to Confucius as a creative thinker, as a force, for the fact that his philosophy and that of his school proved so influential is one of the evidences that the pre-Ch'in period was indeed the most active in Chinese intellectual history and most nearly analogous to the great age in Greece. However, this compliment to Confucius as a great thinker contains within it a condemnation of what his thought furthered, the centralized bureaucratic organization of the Empire. His success becomes testimony to the greatness of the age he represented, and yet, insofar as he sought to end that age, he is an imperfect figure, a hero when he lived but by no means a prophet for all eternity.

"To Preserve the Confucian Doctrine Is Not the Way to Honor Confucius"—This is the meaningful title of an essay of 1902, Liang's most explicit distinction between nationalism and culturalism, between hero and prophet. Therein he says:

> I venture to regard the task of preserving the country, and that only, as the one on which we ought to expend effort from now on. . . The doctrine and the nation are not the same. . . A country must rely on the strength of its citizens for protection. It is not the same with a doctrine. A doctrine is something to protect men, not something requiring men's protection.[91]

The purport of this essay is unmistakable. Nationalism thrives on hero-worship, and in his devotion to the Chinese nation, he holds Confucius in honor. He is a great man, nothing less. But for Confucianism, Liang has only a slight regard. Confucius is a great man, and nothing more.

[90] Liang, "Hsin-min shuo," 13.25b-29; Wieger, 70-73.

[91] Liang, "Pao-chiao fei so-i tsun K'ung lun," 28.57-57b. Cf. this famous passage by Lu Hsün: "A friend of mine has once said: 'Before we can be expected to preserve our national essence, our national essence must have qualities that will preserve us'" (Wang, Chi-chen, tr., *Ah Q and Others*, New York, 1941, p. xviii).

The Chinese Nation Confronts the West

When nationalism supplants culturalism, however, converted prophets are not the only men on the roster of heroes. Anyone can qualify, those whom the tradition has ignored and those whom tradition condemns, as long as they are members of the Chinese people and meet the standard of greatness which the nationalist applies. Liang, therefore, celebrates non-Confucian Chinese individuals and institutions (like the feudal *bushidō*), and he compares them favorably with Western counterparts. Although these analogies may sometimes seem like the old assertions of cultural equivalence, they really have a quite different character. They are the nationalist's expression of pride in Chinese achievements and his exhortation to their emulation, rather than the fading culturalist's apologetic camouflage for his introduction into China of the achievements of the West. This distinction was stated categorically by Liang Ch'i-ch'ao in 1904:

It would be strongly hypocritical to consider all doctrines which Westerners possess today as doctrines which we Chinese possessed in antiquity. This is an attitude which seriously falsifies the ancients and furthers self-deception on the part of our countrymen. Let us suppose, however, that there really is something to which the vision of our forefathers extended. We proceed to bring it out, polish it—this places a responsibility on the people who come later, and, moreover, it is one method of increasing patriotism. . .[92]

These two themes, pride and exhortation, are present in an article by Liang in which he recognized the exploits of Western heroes of exploration and pointed out that China too had had a few. He told the stories of the Han Dynasty's wide-roaming Chang Ch'ien and Pan Ch'ao and asked for the revivification of their spirit; for, said Liang, if China stays torpid, she will simply be bait for Teutonic imperialists.[93] Likewise, he devoted other

[92] Liang, "Tzu Mo-tzu hsüeh-shuo," 41b.
[93] Liang, "Chang Po-wang Pan Ting-yüan ho-chuan," YPSWC 41.1-14 [Joint biography of Chang Po-wang and Pan Ting-yüan].

articles, half tribute and half warning, to praise of Yüan Ch'ung-huan (1584-1630), a Ming general in the wars against the Manchus —Liang calls him China's greatest soldier[94]—Cheng Ho, the famous fifteenth-century navigator, and Chinese emigrant-colon-izers who had crossed the Pacific to settle new lands. Liang lamented the fact that after Columbus and Vasco da Gama came many other great Western sailors, but there had never been a second Cheng Ho,[95] and he pointed up the disgrace of Western domination over countries largely settled by yellow races. Chinese had broken the ground for colonization, and now they were only as "oxen and horses."[96] The English and the Dutch rule now where Chinese had led the way.[97]

Patriotic pride rather than culturalistic self-justification animates Liang's tribute to the pre-Ch'in Legalist philosopher Kuan-tzu, who was of course beyond the pale of Confucian acceptability. The great political realities today, said Liang, nationalism, the spirit of law, systems of local government, economic competition, imperialism—all of them associated in men's minds with their Western efflorescence in the last two or three centuries—were thought out first in China. Read Kuan-tzu. Consider national sovereignty, the principle behind the existence of the great powers. Did the West think of this some thousands of years ago? No, only our Kuan-tzu did.[98]

Elsewhere, Liang equated Hsün-tzu and Hobbes, whose pre-mises about the nature of man and conclusions about the nature

[94] Liang, "Ming-chi ti-i chung-yao jen-wu Yüan Ch'ung-huan chuan," YPSWC 41.20-37b [Biography of Yüan Ch'ung-huan, most important personage in the declining years of the Ming dynasty].

[95] Liang, "Tsu-kuo ta hang-hai-chia Cheng Ho chuan," YPSWC 41.49 [Biography of Cheng Ho, our mother-country's great navigator].

[96] Liang, "Chung-kuo chih-min pa ta-wei-jen chuan," YPSWC 41.41b [Biographies of eight heroes of Chinese colonization]. Chinese emigrants are called "oxen and horses" again, while English emigrants are said to bring self-govern-ment with them, in Liang, "Lun Chung-kuo kuo-min chih p'in-ko," YPSWC 16.7b [On the character of the Chinese people].

[97] Liang, "Lun Chung-kuo jen-chung chih chiang-lai," YPSWC 16.11b [On the future of Chinese migration].

[98] Liang, "Kuan-tzu chuan," YPSHC-CC 8:28D. 1-2 [Biography of Kuan-tzu].

of government, he said, were similar. He pointed out, too, the agreement of Mo-tzu and Hobbes on the contractual basis of sovereignty, but he added that Mo-tzu's doctrine of the supremacy of Heaven limited what in Hobbes's theory was the absolute power of the monarch. These comparisons permit Liang to boast that the ideas of Hobbes, a great name in Western intellectual history, a product of the seventeenth century, were in the same category as some Chinese ideas (and in a sense inferior to these) enunciated as far back as the Warring States period. "Then we may say, 'How early did our Chinese thought develop!' "[99]

This essay of Liang's, we may say, is a demonstration of how he used Chinese history to express equivalence in a nationalistic way. He is not trying to sell Hobbes to China, to maintain that Hobbes could be accepted easily by Chinese because the truths he spoke had been spoken as well in the Chinese past. Liang actually had no great interest in the content of Hobbes' philosophy, but he was perfectly willing to borrow for China some of Hobbes's prestige as a philosopher. Making our old distinction between appreciation of hero and appreciation of prophet, Liang exalts the spirit not the deed; the process of powerful thinking—Hobbes' and Hsüntzu's and Mo-tzu's—not the substance of their thought.[100]

Here, then, is the indication of what it means to face the West as a nation and not as a culture. Instead of straining to find an

[99] Liang, "Huo-pu-shih hsüeh-an," YPSWC 8.46b-47b [The theories of Hobbes].

[100] In this connection, see also Liang, "Tzu Mo-tzu hsüeh-shuo," 29-30, where Liang rejoices in "our Mo-tzu's" speculative achievement in anticipating by almost two thousand years Hobbes, Locke, and Rousseau; and *ibid.*, 5b, 24, and 30, where Liang maintains that the conception of God in both Mohism and Christianity is one of an omnipresent, omniscient, and omnipotent being; where Liang, in a carefully balanced way, speaks of "Mo-tzu in the East, Jesus in the West," both standing for the principle of universal and impartial love; and where Liang says, finally, of Christianity and Mohism: "The essence and form of the two are entirely the same."

It should be remarked that not only the spirit of this analogy but also the use of Mo-tzu as its Chinese principal testifies to its nationalistic character, for Mo-tzu, indisputably a member of the Chinese people, had been ignored by the Chinese tradition.

equivalence in specific values (argument: democracy, which is good, is Western; it is also Chinese, if you look hard in the right books and disown the heretical rascals), Liang asserts an equivalence in abstract potentialities. Anything you can do, we can do (better), sometimes sooner. (Item: the great tools of modern European civilization, says Liang—compass, firearms, printing—came to Europe via the Arabs, who learned their secrets from the Chinese.) [101] Tradition, the experience of the past, retains no shred of dominance over China's choice of what she shall do, but experience of the past may convince her that she has the power to do it. An equal chance in the evolutionary struggle is all the equivalence China needs, and reference to Chinese precedent can give her that feeling of equal power which may help her to capitalize on this chance. If there really is no Chinese precedent for a Western course of action which China should take, Chinese equivalence, we have seen from Liang's writings, is not to be prejudiced by that fact alone. If Liang refuses to worry about whether or not some contemplated innovation of his has been preordained by Chinese culture, he will not consider it pre-ordained by Western culture, no matter how well established it may be in the West. No event "belongs" to any history until it occurs there, and by the same token, once it occurs anywhere, it belongs there as much as anywhere else.

Thus, in 1907, a Liang discussion of parliamentary government proceeds along nonculturalistic lines and establishes the Chinese nation on the firm ground of self-respect. Instead of considering parliamentary government the inevitable outgrowth of Western history, a value peculiarly associated with a civilization foreign to China, something which must, by rationalization, be located in the Chinese tradition, he looks on it as the product of just the last century in the West (except for its prior gradual development in England). Liang gives a list of individual nations which have

[101] Liang, "Ti-li yü wen-ming chih kuan-hsi," YPSWC 37.29-29b [The relation of geography to civilization]; Liang, "Lun Chung-kuo kuo-min chih p'in-ko," 5b.

acquired representative institutions in the past century. The oldest development of this type dates back a hundred years; others go back thirty or forty, while the most recent, like Russia's, are only a few years old. "Before they had parliamentary bodies, their governments were bad, and they were no different, all of them, from our country today."[102]

Therefore, if China adopts these institutions, she is only one nation in a series to do so. The difference between culturalism and nationalism now seems analogous to the theological distinction between realism and nominalism. The culturalistic approach makes parliamentarianism a Western institution, of which individual Western parliaments are instances; but the nationalist criterion recognizes only individual parliaments, whose large incidence in the West might conjure up the idea of a Western parliamentary spirit. The nationalistic Liang must be a nominalist and reject this idea as false. There is no Western parliamentarianism, there are only parliaments in the West, and so, to be equivalent, China need only institute one herself. She need not feel called upon to vindicate her culture by finding a parliamentary spirit in the Chinese past.

We seem to be standing at a point we reached before. This frame of mind, now susceptible of explanation as the positive fruit

[102] Liang, "Cheng-chih yü jen-min," YPSWC 19.11b-12 [Government and people]. In this connection, see also: Liang, "Shao-nien Chung-kuo shuo," YPSWC 16.3-3b [Discourse on Young China], where he pays homage to Mazzini, the architect of the "risorgimento" of a nation whose situation had been analogous to China's ancient glory and modern low estate; "Kuo-tu shih-tai lun," 15b-16, where he analyzes, country by country, the eighteenth- and nineteenth-century process of transition to freedom and independence in the West, and remarks that two countries, Russia and China, are in transition today; "Tzu-yu shu," 46.4b, where he discusses, in an obvious comparison of independent equals, the United States, changing from republicanism to imperialism, and China and Russia, changing from authoritarianism to libertarianism. These three nations are to be the great powers of the twentieth century. His comparison of China and Russia carries an interesting implication to readers today. He indicates many points of similarity between them—both peoples determined to succeed though suffering for it, both weighed down by broad and long-continued monarchical power—and concludes: "Therefore, if today there is to be a plan for China, we can well decide upon it by scrutinizing Russia."

of nationalism, is exactly that to which Liang came in his fight for emancipation from the tyranny of tradition. Here is the final proof that, in this Chinese instance, rejection of traditionalism, of culturalism, did not simply lead to nationalism—it was identical with it. Denial of the one was equivalent to affirmation of the other. Because of its inner strains and contradictions, Liang's culturalistic syncretism of the nineties had to give way; nationalism, however, was not only the attitude which did follow but the attitude which had to follow. In Liang's writings in Japan, the simple expressions of nationalism show that follow it did. When these expressions are subjected to analysis, however, when we seek out the presuppositions, stated or unstated, which had to be the basis of the nationalism expressed, we know that follow it must. Nevertheless, though it had to emerge, this form of nationalism, like the syncretism which had gone before it, had eventually to disappear. It, too, was torn apart by logical incompatibilities, vitiated by hopeless discrepancies—all of them, like the early ones, natural in the circumstances—and, again as in the former case, Liang waited only for the possibility to come of a new estimation of the rival West before he abandoned the position he had won with such long travail.

The Logical Contradictions in Liang's Second Position

There are two types of inconsistency which we may expect to find in Liang Ch'i-ch'ao's ideas. By far the more interesting is the inevitable type, which derives from the historical situation; he is forced to abandon culturalism, he must justify what he is doing, and the only arguments available for rationalization of his new position turn out to be, on examination, basically irreconcilable (as discussed in the next section). The other type of inconsistency is much more simple and innocuous. Human frailty accounts for it. Anachronistic lingering of outworn ideas, perpetuation of a few stray enthusiasms which have no place in the brave new nationalistic world—these can have little bearing on one's judgment of his work. As a truly catholic mind, in possession of one intellectual empire and in bold quest of another, he may be permitted some woodnotes wild without our questioning the coherence of his collected thoughts.

Liang's eulogy of Immanuel Kant, written in 1903, is an example of this minor form of inconsistency. *The Critique of Pure Reason,* says Liang, inaugurated a new era in European intellectual history. Kant's life is like Socrates', his dialectic like Plato's, the breadth of his knowledge like Aristotle's. Bacon, Descartes, Hume, Leibniz, Hegel, Herbarts, Rousseau, Goethe—all are comprehended in Kant. His theoretical ideas are like the Buddha's, his practical injunctions like Confucius', and in his union of theoretical and practical philosophy he resembles Wang Yang-ming. He belongs not to Germany but to the world; he is not of the eighteenth century but of all time.[103] Liang cites with highest approbation Kant's five-point plan for permanent peace, and he agrees with the great philosopher that war is the relic of a barbarous age and has no place in civilization.[104]

In both spirit and substance, this tribute clashes with the Social-Darwinist nationalism which Liang had fairly well articulated by 1903. There is an air of the 1890's in Liang Ch'i-ch'ao's universalism, in the whole-hearted acceptance of this finest representative of Western culture and his naturalization for China by the reference to his Chinese equivalents. And, more to the point, this disparagement of war and this intimation that its disappearance is the criterion of progress come strangely from one who disavows elsewhere his old devotion to the doctrine of the "Great Peace" and calls war not the precluder but the mother of civilization.

There is something old, something new in his high praise of Buddhism at this time. First, he makes every effort to represent Chinese Buddhism as a domestic Chinese product. When he

---

[103] Liang, "Chin-shih ti-i ta che K'ang-te chih hsüeh-shuo," YPSWC 10.16b-17b [The doctrines of Kant, the greatest philosopher of modern times].

[104] *Ibid.,* 30b-31. For a summary of Liang's views on Kant, his comparison of Kant's philosophy with Buddhism and with the Sung Confucianism of Chu Hsi, see Forke, "Ein chinesischer Kantverehrer," MSOS, XII (1909), 210-219.

speaks of Buddhism, he means the Mahayana, which he says is Chinese, not Indian,[105] and he calls himself proud of China's role as the home country of the great Buddhist sects which have persisted, especially in Tendai, Hossō, and Kegon branches of Japanese Buddhism.[106]

Then Liang compares this Chinese creation to certain European ideas. He identifies the high-mindedness of Benthamite utilitarianism with that of the Hua-yen (Japanese: Kegon) Sutra, which, he says, warns man, as Bentham does, not to seek transient pleasures, leading only to grief, but to suffer small troubles to attain long happiness.[107] Bentham stands up against Buddhism more successfully than some other Western worthies do. The doctrine of karma, an immanent causal principle banishing the idea of external agency, is a formulation, says Liang, which Darwin and Spencer only approach.[108] In Liang's strongly Buddhist statement of his views on life, death, and immortality (1904), he claims for Buddhism improvements on modern scientific conceptions of evolution and heredity and a vast superiority over Christianity, with the idea of karma excluding the Christian idea of the soul.[109] Chinese Buddhism couples philosophy with religion, but Christianity, very thin philosophically, is almost all superstition.[110]

As for its political implications, Buddhism, which calls for no submission to a superior and insists on the equality of all in their

[105] Liang, "Lun Chung-kuo hsüeh-shu ssu-hsiang pien-ch'ien chih ta-shih," 5.3; Wieger, 150. Liang makes here the strange comment that China, in developing the "scientific" Mahayana, was wise enough to reject the superstitious Hinayana, which, he says, prevails in Tibet and Mongolia, as well as in Burma and Siam. Actually, the Buddhism of Tibet and Mongolia is Tantric, which is more like a super-Mahayana than anything else.

[106] Liang, "Lun Chung-kuo hsüeh-shu ssu-hsiang pien-ch'ien chih ta-shih," 6.21b-15b.

[107] Liang, "Lo-li chu-i t'ai-tou Pien-shen ch'i hsüeh-shuo," YPSWC 9.39b [The doctrines of Bentham, the leading light of utilitarianism]; Wieger, 126.

[108] Liang, "Lun Fu-chiao yü ch'ün-chih chih kuan," YPSWC 28.68-68b [The relation of Buddhism to popular government]; Wieger, 191.

[109] Liang, "Yü chih ssu-sheng kuan," YPSWC 45.28-37 [My views on life and death].

[110] Liang, "Lun Chung-kuo hsüeh-shu ssu-hsiang pien-ch'ien chih ta-shih," 6.15b.

capacity as potential Buddhas, is the equivalent of modern Western libertarianism; or, rather, it is really more advanced, for citizens of a Western-style free society are yet individuals, and as
such, still in their *chü-luan* age, barred from the vision of unity
which the Buddhist sees when he teaches that all men are one in
the Buddhahood.[111]

Liang seems here to be treating Buddhism as he had previously
treated Confucianism. He heavily overinterprets a Chinese tradition to make it accord with western values which he cannot
gainsay. Is not this the same old form of syncretism, based on the
same last-ditch culturalism which admits innovation but which
must endow it with a Chinese pedigree? And with his new tool
of nationalism ready now to enable China to stand her ground,
has not Liang just explicitly forsworn, as a vicious instigator to
self-deception, such assertion of cultural equivalence? Perhaps,
however, one may say that these encomiums to Buddhism are
really nationalistic, delivered by Liang only as "one method of
increasing patriotism," as a proud recognition that "there really
is something to which the vision of our forefathers extended."[112]
Nevertheless, that is hard to concede, Liang's analytical efforts here
are so unimpressive, his comparisons of Buddhism with utilitarianism and Darwinism so strained—as though evanescence and evolution were the same, just because neither can be reconciled with fixity
—that we must tend to see in these remarks not a sincere and proud
belief that China has anticipated Western successes but precisely
an effort at self-deception, a culturalistic compulsion to make the
Chinese past at least co-author of that modern civilization which
China must embrace.

Yet, though the evidence of inconsistency seems so strong,
Liang's remarks on Buddhism can be vindicated. The key to the
puzzle lies in one of the articles on Buddhism which we have

---

[111] Liang, "Lun Fu-chiao yü ch'ün-chih chih-kuan," 67-67b; Wieger, 189-190.
For a more detailed outline of Liang's Buddhist metaphysics, see Forke, 606-611;
d'Elia, *passim;* and D. T. Huntington, "The Religious Writings of Liang Chi-tsao,"
CR XXXVIII, 9 (September 1907), 470-474.

[112] See above, p. 123.

K

already cited. Liang tells us, in a revealing admission, why he makes these enthusiastic murmurs: he recognizes that a perfectly civilized people needs no religion, but, being as yet, like all others, short of this ideal, China should have a religion, and this should be Buddhism, which is superior to all its rivals.[113]

Now the problem has a new aspect. However much he may have argued about interpretations of Confucianism, Liang had never had to push China to revere Confucius. On the contrary, in his early syncretic manner, he would recommend that China listen to Darwin, for example, because he spoke like the honored Confucius. But in the nineteenth and twentieth centuries, at least, Buddhism was almost as alien to the traditionalist Chinese mind as anything Western could be. What Liang is actually doing in these Buddhist essays is reversing his old procedure; he is recommending that China listen to the Buddhists because they speak like the honored Darwin. It is no longer Liang's saying in effect, "Men of Chinese culture, this doctrine is true (which is not of unique importance), and it is acceptable because it is Chinese." Now it is "Chinese nationalists," which he seems to say, "this doctrine is acceptable because it is true, and (special added patriotic attraction), it is Chinese." If Liang the Kantian is guilty of only a casual inconsistency, the inconsistency of Liang the Buddhist is at bottom no more than illusory. But let the crepe-hangers not despair. Liang Ch'i-ch'ao's system will crack because it has to, in small ways and large, before their very eyes.

The Role of the Individual in History

We have seen that, in order to avoid making a cultural analogy which would damage China's claim to equivalence with the West, Liang often reasoned back from a general situation to an individual hypothetically responsible for it. He made cultural excellence seem to depend not on a historically determined wave but on the operation of uncaused genius. This was another form of

[113] Liang, "Lun Fu-chiao yü ch'ün-chih chih kuan," 63b-64; Wieger, 182-183.

the voluntaristic theory by which he had, in the early days, protected China from the imputation of failure. Then he had criticized China morally rather than institutionally and had blamed China's backwardness on free-will sins and lapses; now he wrote off Western supremacy as the product of free individual action. Whether he was exculpating China or crying down the West, his end was the same, his method the same—and so were the inconsistencies in which he trapped himself. The requirements of his first position had made him at once a determinist and a voluntarist. When he moved to new ground, he carried this conflict with him.

As a necessary consequence of his adopting a nonculturalistic (hence, nationalistic) explanation of Chinese equivalence, Liang was moved to assume simultaneously that great events issue from the doings of great men and that a man can be called great who has had no discernible historical influence whatever. The first assumption is voluntaristic, and it may best be characterized as an arbitrary statement of *post hoc propter hoc*: political freedom became widespread after Montesquieu urged it, so it became widespread because Montesquieu urged it. But what of Mo-tzu, whom Liang considers great enough to win the palm for China when he is matched, in the quality of his doctrine, against such a key figure in Western history as Jesus? [114] Liang seems to need a new *hoc* for his formula; no longer can it be the hero, for Liang realizes very well that, in Chinese history, what came after Mo-tzu certainly never came because of him. When he calls Mo-tzu great and at the same time acknowledges by "rediscovering" him the fact that Mo-tzu has been sunk without a trace for twenty centuries, Liang proceeds according to the deterministic assumption that the course of history refuses to be deflected by freely exercised genius. These opinions on Mo-tzu and Montesquieu issue naturally from the new nationalism, but in the world of abstract logic, from which time, place, and personality must forever be excluded, the opinions are irreconcilable. Individual greatness can-

[114] See note 100 above.

not be posited as the certain cause of historical consequence if in certain circumstances the one does not follow the other. Liang explains away as immaterial, because a man's greatness must have caused it, a case of inequivalence in effects—Western progress, Chinese lag in the development of political freedom, for example. But he is webbed in inconsistency when, at the same time, he points with pride to a case of equivalence in greatness—Mo-tzu and Jesus, let us say—a case which could never be cited if the idea of greatness were not entirely divorced from any consideration of effect at all.

The Aims of the Historian

If China was to have the nationalism which Liang conceived of, the Chinese people would have to be convinced of three things: first, that they formed a nation; second, that the Chinese past was so splendid that the Chinese people should wish to identify themselves with the nation and act in its interest; third, that the Chinese past was so dubious that the Chinese people, in their nationalistic desire to act in the nation's interest, should change their way of living and use any methods, however alien, to implement that desire. These uncongenial propositions (which we shall soon examine at length) were the basic elements in Liang's explosive formula, and the Chinese historian was called upon to authenticate each one of them. Liang urged the application of three conflicting versions of historical method.

First, he criticizes the old Chinese historiography as one which focused on the Court and the lives of individuals, while it obscured the fact of the existence of the nation and ignored the Chinese people in their collectivity. Because the collective strength, wisdom, and virtue of the people were not set forth in the histories, the Chinese never cultivated a consciousness of themselves as a collective body.[115]

Next, filling out a passage in which he calls China the oldest

[115] Liang, "Hsin shih-hsüeh," 26b-27. As a statement of the ideal from which Chinese historians have in practice deviated, Liang has already in the course of this

and largest country in the world, with magnificent human resources and a general eminence which no other country can hope
to attain, Liang remarks that one or two great men are enough to
shed luster on a nation's annals. It is vital, he says, to lead the
people to honor their forbears. To know how to study these ancestors is the historian's duty.[116]

Finally, he reverts to his insistence that the historian's duty is
to tell the broad story of the people and the culture, but in this
passage (in the very same essay as the one first cited), he condemns the old histories not for failing to celebrate the Chinese
people but for failing to chasten them. The histories blame certain
ministers for weakening the nation or injuring the people. This
leads to the false inference that if these one or two men had been
eliminated, the Chinese government would have been equal to
those of the most highly civilized modern Western nations. This
is the delusion, says Liang, that is sown by the false ideas of the
old historians. They lead the Chinese people to complacency instead of to a zeal for renovating action, for measures to implement nationalism and make a strong nation.[117]

Thus, just as pride in the past and rejection of the past were
logically incompatible but historically necessary ingredients of
Liang's early nationalism, so emphasis on individuals and emphasis on the anonymous mass were simultaneous requirements of
his historical method. And it is easy now to see why the role of
the individual in Chinese history and his role in European history
could be pictured at times so differently. If the Chinese people,
lacking now the protective shield of culturalism, were to be emotionally able to accept innovations from the West, they had to
believe that the Western successes had occurred fortuitously—

---

article said: "The subject investigated by the historian is the broadest and most
important subject. It is the clear mirror of the folk, the well-spring of patriotism"
(ibid., 25-25b).

[116] Liang, "Kuan-tzu chuan," 28 A.1.

[117] Liang, "Hsin shih-hsüeh," 45.

hence the long roster of European heroes which Liang has given us. But if the Chinese people were ever to see the practical need to accept innovations, they had to be disabused of the belief that the Chinese disasters had occurred fortuitously. "Wicked ministers" was not the answer. All Chinese were in it together, and their patriotic duty was to shake off the old life, take their lead from Liang's great masthead, and become, collectively, a "new people."

"Patriotic Schizophrenia"

The mutual incompatibility of the aims which Liang set for historians was but a single symptom of the one great over-all inconsistency. Just as he had failed to banish that old impossible methodological dualism, rationalization by determinism and by freedom, so he remained caught in his first dilemma, the conflict between the abstract, logical necessity to choose between two alternatives, history and value, and the practical, historical necessity to cling to them both. In his first position, syncretism, he had attempted to smother the conflict by denying its existence, by maintaining that the good was really traditional and the really traditional, good. When, with the passing of time, the logical weakness of this solution became established and the practical possibility of doing without it emerged, Liang moved on to nationalism. But the conflict was still with him, for only the method of repression had been transcended, not the conflict itself, and now the latter tore Liang's thought apart. Liang's nationalism, concocted for a situation which differed decisively from the classical European nationalistic situations—a difference we shall subsequently explore —had to be concurrently pragmatic and romantic. He called on the Chinese to be a new people; but, as we have suggested already, the impulse to implement nationalism by adopting new methods and attitudes (however much they may clash with those of the Chinese past) can move only a people which is emotionally nationalistic to begin with. The emotional substance of Liang's nationalism, like any other, was a sense of community with his fellow-countrymen, a community based on belief in the existence of a peculiarly Chinese, wonderful national essence. And this national essence, which should inspire the Chinese to a "new-people" appreciation of value, can only be a bequest from the old people and must be enshrined in their history. A romantic attachment to the Chinese past, in this anomalous nationalism of Liang Ch'i-ch'ao's, is the ground of a pragmatic contempt for it.

At this time in his life, then, Liang made uncompromising statements of two positions which were polar opposites. On a few occasions, however, without having recourse to the old syncretistic bromide that the Chinese founding fathers had made provision for everything, Liang contrived, by tenuous and over-subtle analyses, to harmonize these two positions. The reasoning which he used to achieve this coup, apparently for the first time in 1899 and again in 1902 and 1903, may be described as a technique either of praising the Chinese past and rejecting it for its very virtues, or —one is not sure which—rejecting the Chinese past and praising it for its very flaws.

Before the founding of the Ch'in Dynasty in the third century B.C., wrote Liang in the first of these compositions, political processes in China and Europe were in large part the same. Thereafter, from the time that Ch'in dissolved the Chinese feudal system, there were many differences between China and Europe. One of the two most important of these was the distinction between European division and Chinese unity; even in periods in which China was politically disunified, warfare was usually on a small scale, and reunion was always eventually accomplished. The second important distinction was that Europe had class divisions, post-feudal China had none.

After making this breath-taking generalization,[118] Liang goes on to say that happiness generally pertains to a homogeneous, classless society. However, progress comes from conflict, which

[118] Which he repeats in "Tsa-ta mou-pao," YPSWC 31.20b [Miscellaneous answers to a certain newspaper], saying that China, unlike the West, does not have classes representing extremes of wealth and poverty.

was endemic in the European system of disunity and class-differ-
entiation. The spirit and wisdom of the European people, then,
was developed to a high pitch through conflict, until finally they
were able to dispel the accumulation of corruption "and to reach
in one leap the sphere of the *t'ai-p'ing* [the Great Peace] and the
jen-shou [long life attendant on perfect virtue: cf. *Han-shu,* 'Yao
and Shun performed acts of virtue, and then the people attained
jen-shou']". The Chinese, on the other hand, not receiving direct
harsh treatment, were brought into indirect subjection. Since natural rights had never been lost, so were they never fully imple-
mented.

Now, says Liang, as between a divided culture-area and a unified one, the unified is to be preferred. As between a class society
and a classless one, the classless is to be preferred. Yet we have the
spectacle of European progress and Chinese stagnation. The secret
lies in the European tradition, extending back into classical times,
of popular representation, an institution unheard of in China, and
this because the Chinese masses, not feeling themselves impelled
to engage in conflict, never battled to extend their rights nor
sought redress for usurped prerogatives. Thus, they did not know
when they had lost their rights, for in not seeking extension of
their power, they did not recognize what power the others had.[119]

China comes out of this analysis very well indeed. Blemishes are
not inordinately embarrassing when the imperfection issues from
perfection. Much the same impression is left by Liang's other
essays in this vein. In one of them, after discussing the early
withering of Chinese aristocracy, he points out the contrast with
Europe and Japan. These areas had only recently begun to rid
themselves of this institution, a fact which redounded to China's
credit, for, Liang reminds us, "Government by an aristocracy is
the most inequitable government, the least free. Our China at an
early date had already rooted it out." Yet, contrary to what one
might think, freedom and equality were absolutely crushed in

[119] Liang, "Lun Chung-kuo yü Ou-chou kuo-t'i i t'ung" YPSWC 17.28-31b [On
the differences and similarities of the national structures of China and Europe].

China, while good government, prospering the people, flourished early in the West. The reason is that the European aristocracy, although it battened on the common people, yet was the bitter enemy of monarchical despotism, so that in Europe there was almost no parliament which was not founded by an aristocracy's action.[120]

Liang has conveyed the idea here that no discredit is reflected on the age in which, we know from hindsight, China went wrong, for no mistake discernible to that age had been committed. This, too, is what he implies when, judging from its organization in San Francisco, he analyzes the defects of Chinese society. The major defect is that, operating under a regime of clan law dating from the Chou period, China had preserved the family as its basic unit. The Chinese had made themselves incapable of organizing a self-governing nation, while the Aryan race had shown itself preeminently able to do so. The reason for this sad fact is that the Aryans emphasized self-government of the community organization, but the Chinese emphasized self-government on a family basis.[121]

This analysis clearly mitigates the failure of China to attain the Western set of values which Liang admires. The Chinese development was the inevitable consequence of an original choice of a line of action which in itself was morally equal to the Western choice; they meet on the common ground of an emphasis on self-government. As a means of rationalizing innovation, this argument is an advance on those of his earliest period. He no longer intimates, "We both have the idea of self-government," as he had in the early "Mencius" essays, but, "We had an idea of self-government of a certain kind." It is no longer a call to the people to go back to the well-springs of their tradition, which will be found miraculously sweetened with all the typical nineteenth-century virtues; it is a call to dilute the springs with Western waters. Instead of blurring the distinction between history and

120 Liang, "Chung-kuo chuan-chih cheng-chih hsin-hua chih-lun," 17.
121 Liang, "Hsin-ta-lu yu-chi chieh-lu," 39.11-11b.

value, he recognizes their independence of each other and tries to soften their mutual antagonism. Nevertheless, these efforts were too sporadic and the reasoning employed in them too clever by half to mask the tension in Liang's thought. Sincerely anxious to build a new people, he could ultimately be neither so tender with the old nor so cavalier with it. This is the conflict which wracked his nationalism. An idea of one man, at one time, driven to two extremes, will not be distinguished for its coherence.

We have seen occasionally, in the course of this exposition, some of Liang's acid commentary on the heritage of old China. There is a great abundance of this material in his writings. For example, he cites Montesquieu's dictum that in all half-despotic countries the sole purpose of education is to make the people obey; and he quotes approvingly, as an illustration, Fukuzawa's statement that the old teaching in China emphasized rites and music—rites to make men yielding and submissive, music to soothe men's anxious or ruffled spirits.[122]

Liang is no admirer of the Chinese character forged in the crucible of history. In his frequent, ringing praise of Britain, he means to shame China by comparison; witness his comment that Chinese have none of the English virtues, neither self-respect, common sense, nor the ideal of the "gentleman," who treats others, of whatever status, with politeness and respect.[123] And from antiquity to the present day, the Chinese have lacked a spirit of enterprise and initiative. Retelling the old homilies, Liang mocks their counsels of peace, caution, you-can't-be-too-careful, take care of that precious vessel of filial piety, your ancestors' only hope, yourself.[124] When someone tells him in Los Angeles that the United States had trained Filipinos to fight Filipinos, Liang is revolted by this example of what he calls the slave mentality of Eastern peoples. Chinese are by no means exempted from this scathing condemnation.[125]

[122] Liang, "Tzu-yu shu," 45.27b-28.
[123] Liang, "Hsin-min shuo," 13.40b-41; Wieger, 82.
[124] Liang, "Hsin-min shuo," 13.5b-6; Wieger, 50.
[125] Liang, "Hsin-ta-lu yu-chi chieh-lu," 39.19.

What shall we think of the society which this model race has created? It is thoroughly decadent, and Liang assigns to novels a major responsibility for this condition. The Chinese people have learned from novels to celebrate the career of the scholar-official with no equipment for office but useless rhetorical baggage. Novels have encouraged political adventurers and bandits and have confirmed the people in superstition. It is the mentality fostered by the novels which makes men prepare for examinations all their lives and which encourages brigands to think themselves heroes straight from the pages of the "Three Kingdoms." [126]

In 1907, after the Japanese had all but completed their destruction of the independence of Korea, Liang published a merciless dissection of Korean social and political organization. The commentary was pointed up at intervals by the parenthetical remark: "How like our country!" Liang made no expression of hostility toward Japan, no moralistic condemnation of her as an aggressor. The fall of Korea was a thoroughly domestic responsibility, and so, from the point of view of that pragmatic nationalist who was more concerned to make his country great than to muse about its greatness, would be the fall of China. Foreign invasion and Chinese disaster might be the occasion for some Chinese nationalists to play the injured innocent and prate about beauty and honor brought to the dust, but Liang, one of our Liangs, as the blast at Korea clearly implies, would point out coldly the nation's faults. The irresponsibility of the monarchy in Korea, the lucrativeness of official position, the lack of legal protection for citizens—"how like our country!" [127]

In his country, says Liang, those who are incapacitated are only burdens. But in civilized countries (he wields the lash), there are special schools and institutions to attempt to salvage them for society. In China, too, prisoners are brutalized instead of being fairly treated, as in the West, and constrained to work. [128] And

[126] Liang, "Lun hsiao-shuo yü ch'ün-chih chih kuan-hsi," YPSWC 17.18-19 [On the connection between novels and rule of the masses]; Wieger, 101-102.

[127] Liang, "Chao-hsien mieh-wang chih yüan-yin," YPSWC 37.1-6 [The causes of the destruction of Korea].

[128] Liang, "Hsin-min shuo," 13.51b-52; Wieger, 91-92.

who are they who set the styles in this brilliant social system and stand at its pinnacle? "The literati," says Liang. He has a great deal to say about the literati:

Do they say that they lead the people to knowledge? I see the nation becoming daily more stupid as the literati increase. Do they say that they instruct the people in virtue and the right path? As the literati increase, I see manners daily more corrupted. . . Venal, shameless gluttons, the literati are, in fact, a species of parasitic insect, worms on the people, grubs on the nation.[129]

So Liang despised the Chinese way of life. If he feels it at all, his contempt must be uncompromising now, for, with his non-culturalistic, Social-Darwinist nationalism, he has burned his bridges behind him, and no longer can he reject the Chinese present while he happily explains it away as a mistake. The present is what it was bound to be, and he despises it. Yet, any foreigner could do the same and there let the matter drop. Liang could not let it drop. He was a Chinese nationalist, and if he felt his country to be unworthy of respect, he must devote his life to making it respectable. The Chinese nationalist's obligation to go beyond mere condemnation, however, meant more than this. A man who merely loved the Chinese way could not be a nationalist; but a man who merely despised it could not be Chinese.

Together, then, with his anathemas, Liang issues praise. He pays magnificent tribute to China, most populous of nations, largest, most central, with the longest continuous history. Other vaunted "mothers of civilization" were long ago destroyed. Thanks be to heaven, he exclaims, for having chosen Liang to be born in this most beautiful of countries. Chinese were the first to think and write. Liang will never believe that a country with this past will not one day again come to the fore in the arts and sciences. Oh, the thrill of being Chinese, and the duty we have of augmenting and enriching the precious inheritance of the ancients! Do not abandon it for subservience to foreigners. Every

[129] Liang, "Hsin-min shuo," 13.53-53b.

civilized country is conscious of and proud of its national essence. Patriotism imposes this duty on the Chinese.[130]

Here is a contrast, shame and pride. What is the consequence of shame? It is the practical, utilitarian, nonsentimental adoption of any measure which may effect a good change: in order to suggest what such measures might be, Liang pays tribute to foreign heroes. What is the premise of pride? It is the belief in the existence of a "national essence," for the Chinese heroes whom Liang invokes to stimulate pride would serve that purpose, would justify the modern Chinese in feeling pride, only if the latter felt a bond with them. The bond could have no connection with the value of the old achievements—foreigners could be admired for as much— but had to be forged from emotional conviction that the men who achieved were the direct precursors of the men who felt pride, the voices of their past and of no other, the architects of their history, theirs alone.

The concept of national essence leads easily to a thorough-going conservatism. How can the nature of this mystic essence be identified except empirically, by the appeal to history to see what the people have actually done? If some projected action has no precedent in the nation's annals, men who wish to maintain the status quo can fight the new idea, as conservatives have done in the course of all national histories, by calling it demonstrably alien to the spirit of the people. Liang, the great iconoclast and renovator, who felt that the new ideas were demonstrably vital to the survival of the people, spirit and all, could never tolerate that interpretation, and, insofar as he could find Chinese precedents for innovation in spirit if not in fact, insofar as he could maintain that pride in past achievement implied no desire to perpetuate the achievement anachronistically in modern times, he was able to stay out of the impasse into which the extreme view would have forced him. Nevertheless, although he resisted its invitation to complete conservatism, the doctrine of national essence, thrust on

[130] Liang, "Lun Chung-kuo hsüeh-shu ssu-hsiang pien-ch'ien chih ta-shih," 5.1-2b; Wieger, 148-149.

Liang by his need to believe in the greatness and uniqueness of his country, was at hopeless odds with the denationalized utilitarianism which, he felt, the interests of his country demanded.

If there was to be any pedagogic purpose in telling China what the West had done to become great, the logical premise must be the conviction that, if a procedure works among men in one place, it will therefore work among men somewhere else. Naturally, however, if the two groups of men are not united by their common humanity but separated by their distinctive national spirits, a course of action may be congenial to one of them and impossible for the other. When the nation tries to plan its future, only the national history counts. Foreign precedent is thrown out of court. And just as no foreign-inspired innovation can be justified because it is allegedly "good"—as though a value could be abstracted from the particular circumstances of its creation and labeled universal—so no sacrifice of a native institution can be justified because it is allegedly "bad." Utilitarians may say that men are men and that the good here is the good there, and they may say that no institution, however much a product of the nation's history, deserves to be perpetuated once it becomes merely vestigial or actively injurious; but those who prize a national essence will be very wary of universalist abstractions, and they will never let continuity with the past be snapped by one mortal generation's base criterion of unfeeling, unromantic practicality. Jeremy Bentham and Liang Ch'i-ch'ao may think society a mechanism—one may tinker with its parts and make it work; but Edmund Burke and Liang Ch'i-ch'ao will find it an organism, with a life of its own on which no other may impinge.

Liang knew he was in a dilemma, but there was nothing he could do except to wish himself out of it. He wished hard and talked fast. A 1907 article shows him deep in trouble, faced flatly with the problem of the incongruity of his standards. If, as Western experience seems to indicate, the phonetic method of reducing a language to writing is most workable, should China abandon its traditional script? Liang boldly raises the specter, then backs timidly away.

There seems, at first, to be an unequivocal answer to the question, a Burkian answer. A people, he says, stands independently in the world only when it possesses special characteristics, and these really derive from the people's history. The Chinese written language, thousands of years old, is the repository of the spirit of the national history and of countless heroes and thinkers. Would the hypothetical benefits of changing it overnight be a recompense for the loss? [131]

This is a straight answer—but for the "hypothetical." Liang cannot really face a choice between practical benefit and national spirit, and his tactic here is evasion. From this point on, having already remarked that the written language was a unifying element in a nation in which dialects differed, he reiterates, with various justifications of his opinion, that the alleged benefits of reform would not really materialize.[132] The possibility of a collision between the irresistible force and the immovable object in Liang's nationalism, a prospect that had seemed tantalizingly near at hand, has vanished.

There was one other way for Liang to shy away from his difficulties, and if we remember his soothing statement in the case of the great man versus the spirit of the times, we may guess very well what it was. He proclaims himself to be on "middle ground" —a comfortable, safe, easy, and trivial maneuver. Faced with the problem of resolving extreme opinions, he says, in effect, that the solution to the problem is a simple announcement that the opinions must be resolved.

An educational system, says Liang, should be fitted to a nation's peculiar characteristics. Chinese educators should combine an examination into the nation's characteristics with an assay of educational trends in the world, and these two strains should be "melted together."[133] A legal system should be constructed in the same

[131] Liang, "Kuo wen yü yüan chieh," YPSWC 12.1-3 [The original cleavage between the nation's writing and speech].

[132] *Ibid.*, 3 *et seq.* Cf. Liang, "Hsin-min shuo," 13.27b-28 (written five years earlier), where he charges that the Chinese written language is inadaptable for the expression of new ideas.

[133] Liang, "Lun chiao-yü tang ting tsung-chih," 2.

manner. Liang believes that China's most urgent task is to reform its law code; he writes, "Although law is a product of development, not of creation, assuredly we cannot but adopt the long points of others to compensate for any short-comings in ourselves; and we cannot but examine profoundly the mental cast of our fellow-countrymen and seek only that which suits it." [134]

There seems to be much practical wisdom in this sort of compromise, until we realize that Liang's reasoning is purely tautological. If he were asked what it is that "suits" the nation, he could only answer, "That which the nation will not reject." Although he makes his impartial nod in the direction of "development," he cannot take a line of absolute historicism and decide that what suits the nation is what the nation has not rejected; for when he speaks of shortcomings, the implication is that certain things which the nation has rejected must now be supplied, and it is required that they be none the less suitable for that. Very well, then —Liang must be settling on the reasonable process of selection by trial and error. He seems to believe that no ready-made yardstick exists, neither foreign nor domestic, whereby one may measure suitability. But why, then, if this were the case, should Liang be attempting to construct just such a yardstick, an *a priori* formula which should govern his legal or educational philosophers in their researches? He means to tell them what to look for, not to have them look for anything and then see how it works. Stepping gingerly around the conflict of history and value, he has talked himself, with eloquence, around a logical circle. Try only suitable measures, he says; and a suitable measure is that which appears so after it has been tried.

Liang's best defense of his synthetic position occurs in the "Hsin-min shuo," and here, ironically enough, his plea for at least a modified doctrine of national essence is bolstered by a universalistic invocation of Anglo-Saxon example. In urging the creation of a new people, says Liang, he does not intend that China

[134] Liang, "Chung-kuo fa-li-hsüeh fa-ta shih-lun," YPSWC 8.2b [Historical discussion of the development of Chinese legal philosophy].

should reject its own past. Rather, it should conserve what it has while it takes from others what it lacks. The peculiar treasures of a nation are its morality and law, its customs, literature, and art. This heritage is the basis and source of nationalism. It must be preserved, but China is not to remain stationary. Let there be new fruits on old boughs. China's only chance of survival is to learn what has made other peoples so strong. Borrow—but assimilate, make the borrowings one's own, make them Chinese, for, to be living and to be workable, institutions must be an inner part of a nation.[135]

Some say "conservatism," some say "progressivism." Liang calls for a mean position.

> Thus were formed the great Anglo-Saxon nations, which, in a manner of speaking, make their way with one foot on the ground and one foot going forward, or which hold fast to things with one hand and pick up things with another. Therefore, our so-called new people must not be like that class of men infatuated with western ways, who, in their zeal to equal westerners, throw away the morality, the learning, and the customs of some thousands of years. Nor should we be like that class of empty conservatives who say that they cherish only the morality, learning, and customs of these thousands of years and that consequently it is sufficient to have their feet planted on the ground.[136]

Liang has chosen a good example for his purpose. England (the "Anglo-Saxon nation" par excellence) had indeed managed to preserve its sense of continuity with the past even while it led the world into the future. Nevertheless, the very fact that Liang had to cite England as a model for China is an indication that the English situation was no true prototype of the Chinese. In England, and in Europe in general, it was possible for the antagonism between tradition and change to be blunted; paradoxically, where no man had to believe in both, a middle ground could be really discovered. But in China, where Liang had to breach

[135] Liang, "Hsin-min shuo," 12.40-40b; Wieger, 26-28.
[136] Liang, "Hsin-min shuo," 12.41.

L

tradition in the name of utility and to qualify utility in the name of tradition, his espousal of the idea of a middle ground was but an evasion of the impossible task of finding it.

What Liang says in the passage last quoted, he says elsewhere in more pithy fashion, in two precepts which he delivers to the Chinese:

(1) Do not be slaves of the old thought of China.

(2) Do not be slaves of the new thought of the West.[137]

Liang would have himself believe that the procedure which he prescribes for China is analogous to that which the English had used. But let us transpose these instructions into an English key. We shall find the melody very strange:

(1) Do not be slaves of the old thought of England.

(2) Do not be slaves of the new thought of the East.

Now it is apparent just where the distinction lies. No one in nineteenth-century England, except persons deemed eccentric, needed to be warned away from any civilization foreign to his own. If a Westerner favored innovation, this innovation would be, after all, a product of his own civilization. He might expect, certainly, opposition on the part of those who felt that tradition was being deserted; nevertheless, the new departures were European, and it was still a European Europe if not a pre-modern one. China, on the other hand, once it ceased to be pre-modern, could not remain a Chinese China. A British, a French, a German nationalist could feel, as Liang did, that, in the interests of the nation, old institutions must go, but only the Europeans could really feel that the thread of the past was being extended, not snapped. Therefore, since the claims of a national past did not seriously inhibit their efforts for the national future, they could indulge themselves, without much strain, in the normal nationalistic love of that past. In China, however, the claims of the past nurtured not only the common European garden-variety of romantic hostility to change but the powerful obstructive impulse buried in the

[137] Liang, "Chin-shih wen-ming ch'u-tsu erh ta-chia chih hsüeh-shuo," 20b; Wieger, 118.

natural desire of a people to own the ground it stands on; so that Liang was driven to hate the past, for it thwarted his plans for the nation's greatness, plans which stemmed from his devotion to the nation, a devotion which led him, paradoxically, to a nationalist's love of the past.

In his drive to bring changes to China, Liang made extensive efforts, as we have seen, to banish the idea of cultural concern. He could not deliberately set out to make a modern China unless he could call it a Chinese China, continuity with the past still preserved. Before he could be a nationalist at all, before he could expose himself to inconsistency, he had to believe that the innovations which he sponsored, though introduced first, perhaps, in Europe, were yet absolutely in the public domain; the right to use them was not to be purchased with Chinese self-respect. If he succeeded in making this case for China, if he could throw off Chinese traditional restraints without feeling, any more than a Western modernist did, that he was giving the game away to a foreign civilization, why was he forced into the "patriotic schizophrenia" which Western nationalists escaped?

He was forced into it not necessarily because his rationalizations were unconvincing, but because they had to be made at all. To raise China to a point of equivalence with the West, Liang made a tremendous intellectual effort, but the effort itself symbolized his basic awareness that no such equivalence existed. A Chinese nationalist had to run very fast just to get to the western starting line. A man whose doubt makes him ask a question will never feel as secure, no matter how brilliant the answer he receives or gives himself, as the man to whom the question has never occurred. A doubt may be canceled but never expunged, and when Liang, driven from culturalism to nationalism, tried to make acculturation psychologically possible by telling himself that the integrity of a way of life was a matter of no importance, he was not really expelling his need for cultural loyalty but sweeping it under the bed.

Some time still in the future, when this period had passed in which it seemed impossible to demonstrate such equivalence, Liang would openly declare again that recognition of cultural as well as national equivalence was a basic claim of China on the West. When, in the last great phase of his intellectual career, after the First World War, Liang set out to vindicate the worth of Chinese culture against the pretensions of European civilization to supersede it, he revealed at last that conviction of cultural equivalence had always been a heart-felt need. In the dry years which stretched between the time for syncretism and the time for disparaging the success of the West, Liang could only smother the need and kindle a conflict. Something of this same malaise afflicted nationalists among certain peoples in Europe who were themselves not entirely a part of the standard expanding modern European civilization. Irish patriotism's occasional brush with the Church, the "generation of '98" and its despair over Spanish sterility, the hostility of Russian westernizers to the Slavophils, Zionist indifference to Jewish orthodoxy give us cracked-glass reflections of the situation in China. But no conflict in the Chinese manner rent the central nationalisms of Western society. The central nations never felt the Chinese need.

It should now be clear that Chinese nationalism was nothing which the Chinese people, in their zeal to copy Western ways, imported from Europe like the double-breasted suit. Chinese nationalism was a way of thought molded by Chinese history, pressed into exotic shape by the Chinese need to cope with importations. Just because he used concepts of Western thinkers, often outdated in the world of their origin, Liang was not merely rethinking European thought and China was not fighting old European battles. Liang's nationalism has a background of Chinese culturalism, not European feudalism, and when, to support that nationalism, he weaves together strands of European thought —Smith and Spencer, Rousseau and Darwin, Bentham and Burke—which in Europe belong to different ages, different minds, it is Chinese intellectual history which he makes. The fact that European thinkers are involved is a Chinese fact.

Philosophy deals with thought, but history deals with thinkers. We may expect pragmatic and romantic ideas both to emerge in a single society, as they did in nineteenth-century England and in twentieth-century China, but with all this similarity, the intellectual situations of that England and that China were very far apart, for the ideas were thought of in different combinations. Sometimes history demands what philosophy will not permit, the attempted compromise of two mutually exclusive premises. That was China's dilemma and the reason for the abortiveness of Liang's conclusions. But when history permits (and therefore demands) that these premises be held each independent of the other, and that they be developed each to its own conclusion, a compromise can be arranged between these conclusions. That is what happened in England, with its separate schools of Bentham and Burke, following untrammeled premises through to conclusions consistent within themselves; England was able to see that each conclusion was true insofar as it exposed the falsehood of the opposite extreme. Liang's theory had to follow English practice, but the latter was the product of the mingling of two streams of thought, and these two streams had not been merged in their theoretical beginnings.

How do the two conclusions bear critically upon each other? Bentham saw correctly that sheer traditionalism, as represented, for example, in certain romantic apologia for the pre-Reform British electoral system, was the cloak and abettor of human injustice. Burke, too, showed a genuine insight when he realized that the dehumanized abstractions so dear to the French revolutionaries could be the ultimate pretext for dehumanized action, for the exercise of tyranny over poor, particular, time-ridden, historically conditioned individuals who had the misfortune not to fit easily into a preconceived, theoretical mold. If the views of Burke and Bentham are indispensable correctives of each other, then one may be driven to follow both of them. This would be disconcerting, for they are incompatible. Liang was caught in this inconsistency. Why were not Bentham and Burke caught themselves?

Bentham could remain apart from Burke, because, after all, innovations which the former proposed, while later in time of origin, were just as English as the institutions which Burke defended. Continuity with the past was not so deliberately broken as Chinese continuity must be. Utilitarianism in the West permits enough scope to romanticism so that the enemy's teeth are drawn, and the utilitarian may go a straight way, without any dealings with rivals. Liang's utilitarianism was so arid, however, that he had to slake his thirst for romanticism with a pure Burkian draught.

Burke could remain apart from Bentham, because his traditionalism was not only sentimental but practical and useful. Traditionalism had a definite function, the rationalization of conservatism, and conservatives in Europe could succeed in their aims as long as they maintained the status quo. But traditionalism served no practical interest in China, Liang felt, not even that of the Confucian conservatives, for Confucianism was an anachronism and the preservation of the status quo impossible. Only one question was relevant: would the status quo be changed by Chinese or foreigners? Traditionalism in China was so completely a species of sentimentality that for practical justification Liang needed Bentham.

Both Bentham and Burke, then, expressed a truth about human history. The premises of both, in Europe, were self-sufficient, and the adoption of either one alone was psychologically feasible; there was no compulsion, therefore, for any individual to embrace both at the same time. By the same token, however, since both theories were so amenable to admixture, there was no bar to the fusion of their consequences, the mitigation of each by the truth expressed in the other. Liang's ideas, in the period of incipient Chinese nationalism, came to no such consummation. For no one mind can be truly compartmented, and these two premises canceled each other out before the truths could emerge from their separate conclusions.

Off-Stage Trumpets: First Heralds of a New Synthesis

The basic inconsistencies in Liang's work were put there, not by his carelessness, but by his historical condition, and these constitute the element in it most significant for the historian. Inevitable inconsistencies make pressure on the future. One might think of intellectual history as a product of tension between abstract logical universality and historically compromised (particular) efforts to attain it: a thinker's idea, depending in part on what he can see in the objective world around him, is an unstable version, as it were, of a hypothetically possible "final" idea. If only the objective context be modified, pressures will work, tensions ease, ideas change. There is a perpetual disequilibrium which makes it impossible for a man to rest quietly with the only idea he can possibly think. The inconsistency in Liang's ideas could not, on the one hand, prevent their being thought, and could not, on the other, permit them to stay unchanged.

Before Liang's thought could yield to the pressure of its inconsistencies, something had to happen to let him dispense with an axiom which had been thrust on him. When Liang says in 1902 that the role of the historian is to explain human progress, document it, and seek to arrive at the general principles behind it,[138] he shows us what this assumption is, this mental block. According to the criteria of the day, a belief in progress had an inevitable corollary, a belief that Europe represented the flower of unfettered progressive growth.

The First World War, which so profoundly shook the West's belief in its own traditional values, came as a godsend to those Chinese who had been reluctantly reëxamining the Chinese values. The West had made material progress, but the fruits seemed evil. Why, then, need Europe be taken as a standard? Why should China make all the apologies and Chinese history

[138] Liang, "Hsin shih-hsüeh," 30-32.

fear comparison with a history that had looked so grand and had culminated in such catastrophe? If moral sickness was the end product of an obsession with material development, perhaps the innovations which China required were not testimony to the greatness of their creators but to their decadence. If that were true, Liang could resolve his conflict at last; for, although Western techniques would still be necessary for the implementation of Chinese nationalism, Liang would no longer be forced by helpless acknowledgment of Western prestige to be ashamed of the country in which he took pride. To this position Liang came when the bubble of European optimism finally burst. Now he gladly associated "material progress" with the West. China could seek the nontraditional things while the West bore the responsibility for them and the stigma of "materialism."

A sense of drift and despair, a mocking revulsion against material, hollow victories never worked their way deep into the consciousness of the modern West until the First World War loosed them, but the nineteenth century had its bitter and skeptical voices. Liang, too, even in this period of his early nationalism, when the conviction of Western virtues governed his thinking, gives us hints and guesses of Western defeat. They foreshadow his last great period, when West and East become Matter and Spirit.

In 1904, in one of his remarkable specimens of tortured analysis, Liang seems unconvinced of the soundness of the Western system. He says that earnestness in personal action is incompatible with a belief in determinism. The most important cause of modern Western social progress is "free competition," which is based on a deterministic assumption (that is, given free competition, society will of necessity move in a certain direction). This, then, will impair the zeal which is part of the competitive spirit, and cynicism, pessimism triumph, the mortal foes of effective personal action. In this somewhat mysterious passage, he indicates, then, that Western success gradually eats away the spirit which gives it life. Here is certainly an ingenious version of the doctrine of capitalism's inevitable demise through the development of its inner contradictions![139]

He struck a more significant note when he called for a new Chinese morality, an amalgamation of the best product of antiquity and modern times, China and the outside world. Something terrible would happen, he felt, if that were not achieved: "I fear that mental training will gradually become more important, while moral training decays, that the materialist civilization of the West will invade China, the 400,000,000 people be led away and become as the birds and beasts."[140] This is very much akin to his old protest against both obscurantism and self-effacement, but it goes beyond it. Now the possible collapse of their own civilization is not to be considered only as a great emotional deprivation of the Chinese but as the sacrifice of something precious in exchange for dross. For the first time, the pejorative "materialist" is used to describe the West, and the whole passage looks forward to the day when Liang would no longer emphasize to the Chinese that they must reconstruct their civilization, but would insist that the Chinese never malign the civilization they were inevitably transforming. That day came, and with it a mass of apologetics, like the *China's Destiny* of Chiang Kai-shek, giving to the West the task of revealing the secrets of sordid material power, while China gets the halo for its spiritual achievement in traditionally neglecting the search.

Liang and the Revolutionaries

A theory more suited to the discouragement of social revolution could hardly be devised. In this latest stage of the fight to claim an equivalence with the West, China gives away as much as she can when she accepts the introduction of science. If the

[139] Liang, "Tzu Mo-tzu hsüeh-shuo," 33. The next year, in "Tsa-ta mou-pao," 16b, he says that Europe and America, economically and socially, stand today on the brink of inevitable revolution, and he speaks (*ibid.*, 20b) of evil consequences as having attended the Industrial Revolution in Europe.

[140] Liang, "Hsin-min shuo," 12.47b.

balance is to be maintained, or the scales tipped a bit in chauvin-
ism's direction, morality and the social order, the human side of
life, must be kept in line for traditional China. And there, too,
lived the spirituality which enabled her to borrow with an air of
condescension rather than one of meek humility. Yet, Liang had
worked for a new China, and, in his strictures on the old and
his discovery of nationalism, he had much in common with revolutionaries like Sun, and the T'ai-p'ings before him, and the Communists after him. How did they justify their breaks with the
past if their ends were different from his? How could his judgments be so like theirs, yet avoid their revolutionary conclusions?

Liang was certainly hostile to revolution, not only in his matter-
spirit phase, but in the time of his syncretistic theories and his
fight for the Reform Movement, and in the years of his exile and
ambivalent nationalism. On just a few random occasions he
wrote as though the idea of revolution were congenial to him.
Once he declared that the progress of the West to enlightenment
was a product of the French Revolution,[141] and at another time
he stated that progress was in the direction of satisfying the
majority and that the current struggle between laborers and capitalists was the latest in a long series of battles which have pointed
to that end.[142] These assertions, however, were more than coun-
tered by the constant, passionate reiteration of his hostility to
political revolution and to sudden change in the existing system
of property relations.

His biography of Madame Roland begins with an elaborate
Chinese rendering of her famous apostrophe before the guillotine:
"Oh liberty, what crimes are committed in thy name!"[143] The
French Revolution stained the nation's history with blood, says

---

[141] Liang, "Pen-kuan ti-i-pai ts'e chu-tz'u ping lun pao-kuan chih tse-jen
chi pen-kuan chih ching-li," YPSWC 17.9 [Speech in honor of the one hundredth
issue of this newspaper and discussion of a newspaper's responsibilities and this
newspaper's history].

[142] Liang, "Cheng-chih-hsüeh hsüeh-li chih-yen," YPSWC 19.18b-19 [Various
notes on the doctrines of political philosophy].

[143] Liang, "Chin-shih t'i-i nü-chieh Lo-lan fu-jen chuan," 48.

Liang, and for more than a thousand years, people who hear of it will tremble and grieve.[144] As for revolution in China, Liang is convinced that it would only lead to foreign intervention.[145] He demonstrates that Chinese rebellions, which have generally lasted much longer than European and wrought more havoc, show an amazingly high correlation with foreign invasion and spoliation.[146] What China needs for its defense is the expansion of the production of wealth, and to this end capitalists should be encouraged, not harassed by revolutionaries seeking more equitable distribution.[147] Liang attacks as economically unsound a speech of Sun's advocating nationalization of the land,[148] and another blast against this proposal develops into a condemnation of public ownership in general.[149]

Since revolution and republicanism were always associated in Liang's mind in the years before the Empire fell, he lost no opportunity to discredit republics. Liang foresaw a disastrous train of events if an attempt should be made to set up a republic in China; there would be war between the military and the people, lower classes and upper classes, province and province, party and party, with a revolution likely, on the South American model, after each presidential term.[150] Saying that the French and Latin American revolutions had led only to mob rule or personal despotism, he cautioned against a belief that American liberties

[144] *Ibid.,* 57b.

[145] Liang, "Pao-tung yü wai-kuo kan-she," YPSWC 30.59b-60 [Insurrection and foreign intervention].

[146] Liang, "Chung-kuo li-shih shang ko-ming chih yen-chiu," YPSWC 35.34b-35 [An investigation of revolutions in Chinese history]. This is an interesting anticipation of the work of Karl Wittfogel, Owen Lattimore, Franz Michael, and others concerning the race for the throne between rebels and invaders at the end of the "dynastic cycle."

[147] Liang, "Tsa-ta mou-pao," 22-24.

[148] *Ibid.,* 26-35b.

[149] Liang, "Tsai po mou-pao chih t'u-ti kuo-yu lun," YPSWC 32.6b-55 [Second refutation of a certain newspaper's article on the nationalization of the land]. A professor from the University of Chicago helps Liang out with his argument. See *ibid.,* 49b.

[150] Liang, "Pao-tung yü wai-kuo kan-she," 62b-63.

stemmed from the American Revolution. Actually the American republic, with its spoils system and its politics for profit, was decidedly inferior to the British constitutional monarchy.[151] England was the nation with the most flourishing democracy in the world, and the English people loved their monarchs like father or mother.[152]

He flatly denies the revolutionary *Min-pao's* allegation of a necessary connection between nationalism and republicanism,[153] and he avers just as firmly that autocracy and monarchy are not synonymous. In modern Europe, except for France and Switzerland, all countries are monarchies; but, except for Russia and Turkey, none still have autocratic governments.[154] Of the ten great powers in the world, all are constitutional monarchies except Russia, France, and the United States.[155] For monarchy is clearly the best polity, says Liang, discussing Aristotle's classification of the types of government. The post-Greek devices of constitutionalism can bar it now from that lapse into tyranny which Aristotle felt to be its logical tendency.[156]

Liang's antipathy to the idea of revolution may be explained in two ways: first, as an extension of his theories concerning the Chinese culture and the Chinese nation, and second, as a product of the historical situation which originally gave rise to his theories. To explain it in the first of these ways, let us consider Liang's refusal, for the most part, to turn his nationalism against the Manchus.

[151] Liang, "Hsin-ta-lu yu-chi chieh-lu," 39.20b-21. See Liang, "Ta mou-pao ti-ssu hao tui-yü pen-pao chih po-lun," 7b-8, for another reference to Latin American experience as an object-lesson to China.

[152] Liang, "Li hsien-fa i," YPSWC 20.45 [Discussion of the establishment of a constitution].

[153] Liang, "Ta mou-pao ti-ssu hao tui-yü pen-pao chih po-lun," 15.

[154] Liang, "Lun chuan-chih cheng-t'i yu pai-hai yü chün-chu erh wu i li," YPSWC 20.41 [That an autocratic system of government brings a hundred injuries to monarchy and not one benefit].

[155] Liang, "Li hsien-fa i," 42b.

[156] Liang, "A-li-shih-to-te chih cheng-chih hsüeh-shuo," YPSWC 10.9-10b [Aristotle's "Politics"].

Just as, once in a while, he seemed to tolerate the general idea of revolution, so he permits himself, but only rarely, an anti-Manchu hint or statement. Praising Mazzini, Garibaldi, and Cavour for their parts in the making of modern Italy, Liang commends their example to the Chinese[157] and he tries to encourage the latter by pointing out historical parallels between China and Italy. Both had been once the supreme countries in their worlds, the oldest and most honored; both had fallen into decay, and become subject to division and rule by foreigners.[158] Liang does not press the comparison, but deliverance from the Manchus would be the obvious Chinese equivalent of that expulsion of Bourbons and Hapsburgs which his Italian heroes effected.

This muted call to arms, however, seems faint indeed compared to the one really inflammatory anti-Manchu diatribe in all Liang's writings before the dynasty fell. In 1902 he expatiates on the wretchedness of life in China, with its misery never so intense as in the past century. More people die in China from famines, caused by administrative negligence, and from the epidemics and brigandage which follow the famines, than any revolution can kill. So declares the surprising Liang, and finally: "Daily we perform the ceremony of the three bows and the nine kowtows to that people, and we receive scarcely enough to half-fill our bellies."[159]

This invective against the Manchus could hardly be improved upon by Sun Yat-sen. Nevertheless, as a specimen of Liang's opinion, it is decidedly atypical. When, in his anti-culturalist nationalism, he arraigned the Chinese people for the deficiencies of its character and its way of life, he meant what he said. Liang believed, and not without justice, that if the Chinese indulged themselves in the luxury of blaming the Manchus for Chinese ills, this was self-delusion and cant and a courting of disaster. Do not

[157] Liang, "I-ta-li chien-kuo san-chieh chuan," 1b.
[158] Ibid., 44-44b.
[159] Liang, "Hsin-min shuo," 13.33-35b.

blame "robbers," he says, or "wolf and tiger nations" for the destruction of Chinese freedom;[160] and he remonstrates that the expulsion of the Manchus would not mean necessarily the expulsion of bad government.[161]

Liang scouts the claim of Sun's newspaper in Japan that old China had had a nationalism which despotism and the principles of monarchy had stifled; he notes that no facts are attested to prove this. However, granting the revolutionaries' premise for the sake of argument, Liang insists that if the poisons of absolutism and monarchy have so blighted the nationalist spirit, then blighted it is. The simple fact is that the spirit of the people must change from what it is today.[162] It is natural that Liang should insist on this. Everything in his being that made him long for a "new people" made him turn from the nationalist's easy way out, from the deceitful temptation to think the old people good enough, if only the Manchu incubus could be taken off their necks.

To this end, then, Liang ridicules the idea that, at this late date, any significant distinction remains between the Chinese and Manchu peoples. Using six criteria for telling whether a certain group constitutes a homogeneous nation, he points out the substantial uniformity of Chinese and Manchus according to all six: (1) same blood (Liang hedges on this), (2) same language, (3) same living area, (4) same customs, (5) same religion, (6) same spirit.[163] China should look at her Manchu monarch as England looks at her Norman one.[164] And even when Liang cannot quite conjure the Manchus out of existence, he is at pains to indicate how inconsequential a body they really are. In discussing how much more fortunate in her natural endowments China is than

[160] Liang, "Tzu-yu shu," 45.19.

[161] Liang, "Cheng-chih-hsüeh ta-chia Po-lun-chih-li chih hsüeh-shuo," 46b-37.

[162] Liang, "Ta mou-pao ti-ssu hao tui-yü pen-pao chih po-lun," 14-14b.

[163] Liang, "Shen-lun chung-tsu ko-ming yü cheng-chih ko-ming chih te-shih," YPSWC 33.24-25b [Further discussion of the gains and losses attendant on racial revolutions and political revolutions].

[164] Liang, "Chung-kuo-pu-wang lun," 31.49b [China does not die].

certain other countries, he remarks that, unlike their counterparts in the Austrian Empire, with its war of Germans against Slavs, the people of China are one; there are, to be sure, two races in China, Chinese and Manchus, but the few millions of the latter make up but a tiny portion of the population.[165] This circumstance, we note in passing, which to Liang is a source of gratification, is humiliating in the eyes of Sun Yat-sen. According to his version of nationalism, the Chinese may not congratulate themselves that the minority is small and the nation strong in virtue of its freedom from racial struggle, but should feel ashamed that a minority so small could dominate so many.

To counter the Sun party's branding of the Manchus as ineradicably foreign intruders, Liang insists that the transfer of power in the seventeenth century is not properly described as a transfer from Chinese to Manchus; one ought to say only that Ch'ing eclipsed Ming, that the rule of the Chu family ended and the rule of the Aisin Gioro began. There was a Manchu government from 1616 to 1644. It was extinguished then. But there has been a Chinese government since the rise of Ch'in, and that is the government in China today.[166]

Liang's decision about the Manchus is more than a by-product of his basic decision about the condition of Chinese culture and more than a simple prop to his antirevolutionary bias. In no other aspect of Liang's thought is the distinction made so subtly between his nationalism and the culturalism from which it had emerged. He writes somewhere that a Chinese nationalism which expresses itself in an anti-Manchu form must logically be extended to anti-Mongol, anti-Miao, anti-Mohammedan, anti-Tibetan

---

[165] Liang, "Lun Chih-na tu-li chih shih-li yü Jih-pen tung-fang cheng-ts'e," YPSWC 18.21b [On Japan's Eastern policy and the actual strength of China's independence].

[166] Liang, "Tsa-ta mou-pao," 2-5b. It was in 1616 that Nurhaci, with the Manchu power still based on the region beyond the Great Wall, declared himself founder of the Chin (later, Ch'ing) dynasty. In 1644, the capture of Peking brought one of his grandsons to the Chinese throne. "Aisin Gioro" is the family name of Nurhaci's clan.

forms. Can this be the way to build a nation? China should have
not a nationalism of a narrowly defined Chinese community
oriented against other peoples within its borders, but a nationalism
of all groups within the country oriented against the nations outside. Common speech, script, and customs are the most important
of the social uniformities which make a population into a strong
nation, and both Chinese and foreign scholars have recognized
the marvelously solvent character of Chinese culture. The
Manchus, at least, have become completely Sinified: "Today,
among the Manchus south of the Wall, those who can read
Manchu script and cope with the Manchu speech are already as
the phoenix's feathers and the unicorn's horn."[167] If the Chinese
can learn to think of themselves as citizens, the Manchus can do
the same.

On the surface, this seems to be a vindication of antinationalist
culturalism, the basic tenet of which always was that acceptance or
rejection of the Chinese culture was the one criterion of in-group
or out-group status. Actually, however, Liang has taken a stand
here against culturalism as it was manifested in China. He does
not show himself attached to any specific cultural content, certainly not to the traditional Chinese content. Cultural uniformity
becomes just a device to power the nation, which has the real,
fundamental claim on the allegiance of the Chinese, whatever
their culture may be. Liang asks, as a minimum, that it be the
same among the parts of the nation. In other words, the culturalist
tinge which he exhibits is "simultaneous," not historical. In his
remarks on the Manchus, Liang never implies that the Chinese
culture need be identical with the Chinese culture of the past; it
need only be identical with the cultures lived by other peoples
within the Chinese borders. But true culturalism is historical.[168]

Pro-Manchu sentiment was not the only expression of an anti-

---

[167] Liang, "Cheng-chih-hsüeh ta-chia Po-lun-chih-li chih hsüeh-shuo," 38-39.

[168] This view of Liang's leads, of course, to cultural aggression, which makes
for just the internal struggle of people against people which, in his strictures on
the anti-Manchu, he deplores.

revolutionary spirit which was bound up with the nationalism of Liang Ch'i-ch'ao. Traditionalism and antitraditionalism, the inconsistent components of his nationalism, both could be used to nurture that spirit. The traditionalist argument is obvious. If a man believes, with Liang, that the state is a kind of organism, totally unlike an inorganic machine, that it develops from within with a steady growth, rooted in history,[169] he cannot proceed, as the revolutionary must, to hack at its roots and fabricate at will.

Liang's antitraditionalism was embodied in his appeal to the Chinese to become a new people, and this appeal, in its own quiet way, had antirevolutionary overtones. "New people" can be a clarion call not only against the Confucian conservatives, who are content with the old people, but against revolutionaries too, who fight for a new system. For one thing, Liang's repeated warnings that a people must learn before it can operate a new system constitute a sort of delaying action against revolution.[170] There is something, however, in the "new people" doctrine more significant than this. When we examine closely the most vitriolic criticism of the Chinese social order which Liang can make in this period, we find that, as in the old days, the criticism is moral, not institutional. If certain people do not play well their roles in Chinese society, Liang asks them to become new people; but the revolutionaries ask for a new society.

[169] Liang, "Cheng-chih-hsüeh ta-chia Po-lun-chih-li chih hsüeh-shou," 34-34b; Liang, "Hsin Chung-kuo chien-she wen-t'i," YPSWC 34.2b [The question of construction of a new China].

[170] For such warnings, see Liang, "Ta mou-pao ti-ssu hao tui-yü pen-pao chih po-lun," 1-4, 10, 33b; "K'ai-ming chuan-chih lun," 81b, 86b-90b; "Chung-kuo kuo-hui chih-tu ssu-i," 22.28b; "Hsin-min shuo," 13.25-25b, and Wieger, 70.

By k'ai-ming chuan-chih (explanatory despotism), Liang meant precisely what Sun meant by chih-hsün (political tutelage), an idea which Sun came to emphasize only after the revolution had taken just such a disastrous course as Liang had predicted for it. Both terms imply that "honest brokers" should hold the power of government in trust for the masses until the latter had been taught how to govern themselves. The term k'ai-ming chuan-chih occurs in Liang's writings as late as 1913. See Liang, "Ou-chou cheng-chih ko-chin chih yüan-yin," YPSWC 47.40b [The causes of European political advances], and Liang, "Shuo yu-chih," YPSWC 48.12 [Tell the young].

M

The king-pins of Chinese society were the literati. We have already seen a specimen of what Liang thought of these gentry. A few more examples of his eloquence on the subject will serve a purpose here. Literati are intellectually petrified, politically corrupt, economically parasitical. Every producer carries a hundred leeches on his back. Liang despises the great families in which the sons all wish to live together, gambling, drinking, whoring, doing nothing else, draining the strength of the one or two members of the household who work.[171]

It is a member of the household, we may observe, who is said to be exploited, not the vast peasant population outside which can never live in great-family groups. The proportion he quotes of "leeches" to producers shows that he means it to apply within the gentry class. All he says, then, is that the household contains parasites; he fails to indict the household itself as a parasite on society. Liang is convinced that there will always be a gentry. In the early years of the Republic, when he berates the literati most bitterly, he makes it even more clear than he does now, in 1902, that he wants them only to do their duty, not to disappear. The revolutionary, striking against an organization of society which makes its intelligentsia corrupt, obscurantist, and parasitical, tries to pull the rug out from under the feet of the landlord-literati. But for all his slashing attacks on the traditional leaders of society, Liang Ch'i-ch'ao only beats the rug, and the landlords stand where they always did.

We can now see what the social content was of radicalism, vintage '98. Liang sponsored revolutionary change in the Chinese way of life, but the change was to take place within the prevailing class system. In the classical revolutionary situation, standards of value pass away when the class which sets the styles, as the French aristocracy did, is ousted from power by a new class with its own ideals. Change might have come to China in this way, if the vast, inchoate nineteenth-century peasant rebellion could have matured and triumphed. It failed, and since Chinese isolation could

[171] Liang, "Hsin-min shuo," 14.24b-27b and 13.50b; Wieger, 37 and 89-90.

be only a dream, westernization, which had to come under somebody's auspices, was ushered in not by social revolution but by
the "national revolution," the property of the Kuomintang, which
fought Liang politically but which ultimately emerged as his
ideological beneficiary. The fall of Ch'ing marked the passing of
the antique conservatives, for whom Confucianism was the air
they breathed. After the warlord interregnum, the establishment
of the Nationalist government marked the rise to power of the
modern conservatives, for whom Confucianism, diluted, reinterpreted, and in strange company, was a tool they used. Yet,
the first set of conservatives, as a class, had never been displaced,
but lived on in the second, its social constitution somewhat modified, as its ideas had been, by the impact of the West. Like their
prototypes in all Chinese history since the death of feudalism and
the inception of the bureaucratic society, the new financial power
and industrial power allied themselves with the landed power,
and Western ideas came with them into the intellectual heritage
of the ruling class. The gentry-literati, revamped but by no means
discarded, had come a long way, like Liang Ch'i-ch-ao, intellectually. But, in their long march out of old China, the ruling orders
had carried with them their old enemies, the perennial Chinese
agrarian rebels, who were like the gentry now in having urban
auxiliaries. Like the gentry, they had been catalyzed into a new
sort of action by the intrusion of the West, and they were just as
ready, parallel to the conservatives, to make the transition from
antique to modern.

The nineteenth-century Western military and commercial invasions had given a new urgency to two problems: the relation of
Chinese classes to each other, and the relation of China to the
world. In our search for the roots of likeness and difference between Liang Ch'i-ch'ao and the social revolutionaries, these two
problems are supremely relevant. To take up the first problem:
for a variety of reasons,[172] the economic lot of the peasantry was

[172] For instance: (1) Inflation caused by export of silver to lubricate the opium
trade. (2) Destruction of peasant handicraft industries by the flood of foreign

worsened to the point of becoming unbearable. At the same time, the traditional culture's command over men was beginning to break down, an irreversible trend toward iconoclasm was beginning to set in, symbolized in the doubts of the textual critics and materially hastened by the intrusion of the West, which exposed to minds that were losing their certainties the reality of an alternative way of life. These two processes combined to end the stability which the Chinese imperial system had enjoyed since its beginnings in the third century B.C. For, despite the riots and alarums which had punctuated all Chinese history, stability was the word for traditional China. Not until the great T'ai-p'ing Rebellion (1850-1864) was a Chinese revolt converted from a *jacquerie* into a revolution.

No longer did men seek only to rise in the established hierarchy or to lessen the strains in an accepted system; they began, confusedly, to reject both. And, more important, the T'ai-p'ings rejected orthodox Confucianism and invented a pseudo-Christian synthetic ideology which was anything but old-Chinese. This is the beginning of a secession of one class from a hitherto unified complex of classes; it is the beginning of a feeling that the Confucian tradition is not Chinese tradition but gentry tradition, that the interests of the entity China and those of the body of the old tradition are not only not identical but are diametrically opposed.

As for the problem of China's relation to the world, the literati, the gentry, could no longer, in this last century, think of China as a world but were forced to think of China in the world. They were the guardians of the Chinese tradition; their interest, then, unlike that of the seceding revolutionaries, was not to scrap the

---

machine-made goods, subject to only a nominal tariff. (3) Increased burden of taxation, caused by the central government's war expenses and indemnity obligations. (4) Increased rapacity of officials, great numbers of whom attained their posts solely by purchase and for profit as the financial condition of the government became more and more hopeless under the pressure of wars and treaties. (5) Series of unusually severe natural disasters, invited by the government's inability to take preventive and ameliorative measures.

tradition but to justify it in the face of the foreign onslaught. Justification could be either by simple affirmation (the obscurantists' way) or by rationalization in the series of stages through which we have seen Liang Ch'i-ch'ao pass.

Liang Ch'i-ch'ao was one of the literati. He wrote for them and his intellectual need was theirs, the need to establish the fact of China's equivalence with the West. This being so, he was absolutely committed, as the class was generally, to a concept of China as a monolithic structure. When the great contest was seen as cultural, China against the West, not as economic, peasantry against gentry, China had to be whole, and the fission of Chinese society could not be acknowledged. Chinese cultural standards had always been created by the possessing class. In this time of transition, its defense of those standards—even Liang's attacks, we have seen, were a sort of defense—was thoroughly entwined with its defense of possessions.

In his apologia for China in the modern world, Liang came to the same conclusion about tradition as the revolutionaries did: the Chinese nation, not the traditional Chinese culture, should be the focus of loyalty of the new people. But, because different impulses set them on the road from culturalism to nationalism, their roads were different. A revolutionary, feeling himself disinherited by the traditional culture, might cast it off easily, hatred smoothing the way to rejection. Liang, however, was not disinherited. He was one of the heirs to a culture that was dying, and only with slow and careful steps could he pick his way down the tortuous path to a new loyalty. Today, the two brands of nationalism current in China show the marks of their separate origins.

Reabsorbing into itself much of the traditionalism against which it had to fight in order to be born, the conservatives' nationalism is meant as a bar to the West and a check on Chinese rebels. Cultural equivalence in the world is its aim, and social stability at home. This nationalism, then, takes class-consciousness as its feared and hated opposite, a wedge in Chinese culture, a knife to social peace. To the Communists, on the other hand, what nationalism precludes is not the subjective state, class-consciousness, but its objective cause, class-domination. This evil, they allege, and the rending weakness it visits on the nation, are fruits of the old system and the old tradition; the latter, then, have no call on the loyalty of a nationalistic Chinese.

When we trace back Chinese nationalism to the desperate social crisis which was one of its sources, we can see why it is that Communism has an appeal in modern China. But when we trace it back, as we have in the writings of Liang Ch'i-ch'ao, to the cultural crisis, to the conflict not of class with class but of China with the West, we can see why that appeal is limited. Liang, no matter how ready he became to liquidate the traditional Chinese culture, could never simply denounce it unilaterally and throw himself on the mercy of the West. By one rationalization or another, the autonomy and dignity of China had to be preserved. No man whose intellectual situation was the product of Chinese history could choose to see that history end.

In the last analysis, revolutionaries in China must face this same compulsion, the drive to perpetuate Chinese history. Impassioned with class hostility, they may denounce as a plot and a fraud the vaunted civilization of the old China; they may consider Confucius not a prophet, as the complete traditionalists did, not a hero, as Liang did, but a class-enemy. Nevertheless, though they are ready to make innovations from the West and change Chinese culture beyond all recognition, they are no more able than Liang was to snap the thread of history and surrender to Europe. That is why, in order to overcome the limitation set on their efforts by blank hostility to the past, so natural in the circumstances which nurtured them, they have been forced to create a Chinese tradition even as they rejected The Chinese Tradition. Ever since the days of the T'ai-p'ings, stories of that rebellion have been turning into folk-legend, increasingly as the social chasm widened. And Chinese tradition is ransacked for popular-revolutionary precedents, in such manner as this: Communist bands in Yunnan Province in 1948 were known as the *Liang-shan,* after dissidents, haters of officialdom, who took to Liang Mountain as bandits in the latter days of the Northern Sung.[173]

Now, too, we may find a new meaning in the Communist attempt to fit Chinese history into a Marxist time-scale, which is supposed to be also the time-scale of the rest of the world. It is the exact counterpart of the Confucian syncretic effort, as represented in Liang Ch'i-ch'ao's works, to use a Confucian time-scale for world history, to protect China from an inner sense of failure by interpreting its history as part of a universal pattern. A terrible doubt has haunted every Chinese generation since westernization began, a doubt that China could ever again feel thus protected. The industrial revolution has upset more than China's economy. Minds have been staggered, traditions shattered, and in the life and writings of Liang Ch'i-ch'ao, we can see how he and deduce how others rallied their forces, strained to regroup, and played out the drama of a hopeless battle.

---

[173] *The Christian Science Monitor,* June 3, 1948, 10. The original *Liang-shan* are celebrated in the famous Ming novel, *Shui hu chuan.*

PART THREE

1912-1929: REMEMBRANCE OF THINGS PAST

CHAPTER V

FROM POLITICS TO SCHOLARSHIP

Politics

BY THE TIME Liang Ch'i-ch'ao finally came back to China, in October 1912, Sun Yat-sen had retired from his presidency at Nanking and Yüan Shih-k'ai was the single legal chief-executive of the nation. Elections for the parliament were near at hand; among the few politically conscious Chinese, alliances and alignments had begun to take shape. "Parties"—cliques, groupings—emerged out of the revolution's confusion, and Liang became one of the leaders in this creation of a republican politics.

Sun and Yüan were the natural rivals for power. Both factions had sought in the beginning to win Liang over, but for a time he remained uncommitted. When Yüan, as premier of the doomed "constitutional monarchy," formed his first cabinet on November 16, 1911, Liang refused the proferred post of Vice-Minister of Justice.[1] And Yüan's enemies, the *Kuo-min tang* or Nationalist Party, which had evolved out of the revolutionary society *T'ung-meng hui,* decided at first not to attack Liang, though he had been a cherished target in the old days. A group in the *Kuo-min tang* had frankly no use for him still, but Huang Hsing, Sun's military aide, wished to know Liang's plans and tried for several days to meet him at Taku, the port of entry for Liang on his return to China. Huang tried in vain. Finally he sent Liang a bitter letter, charging that he was hostile to the Republic and that he hoped and plotted for its destruction.[2]

In late October, when Liang proceeded to Peking from his new

[1] Stanley K. Hornbeck, *Contemporary Politics in the Far East* (New York, 1928), 409; Ferdinand Valentin, *L'avènement d'une république* (Paris, 1926), 96.
[2] Ch'ien Chi-po, *Hsien-tai Chung-kuo wen-hsüeh shih* [History of contemporary Chinese literature] (Shanghai, 1933), 312.

173

home in Tientsin, rumors to such effect were spreading in the capital. It was said, among other things, that he planned to organize a monarchical party consisting mainly of Manchus, or that he intended to proclaim the necessity of enthroning Yüan Shih-k'ai.[3] Nevertheless, in spite of these allegations, he was given a series of tumultuous receptions. When he arrived at Peking on the twentieth, several hundred people were gathered at the Cheng-yang railroad station to greet him, among them a representative of the president, ministers and vice-ministers, members of the National Council and of all political parties, old associates of Liang, and reporters from every newspaper.[4] On this day and on succeeding ones, Liang was publicly hailed and feted by a whole army of organizations, political and religious, commercial and educational, provincial and generally fraternal. Even representatives of the Mongol nobility, a group rather far from Liang's main concerns, found their way to the great, climactic reception for him, on the last day of the month, just prior to his return to Tientsin.[5]

But Liang was already busy with more than festivities. As soon as he came back from Japan, he began the delicate task of consolidating political particles into a visible, influential party. The party was the *Chin-pu tang* or Progressive Party, formally organized in May 1913, in order to confront the *Kuo-min tang* with an effective opposition in the forthcoming session of Parliament. Chiefly under Liang's aegis, three minor parties had been amalgamated to form the *Chin-pu tang,* and these three, each with ties of some sort with Liang, were themselves composites; they were aggregates of earlier little groups, called into being, some of them before the Revolution, by Liang's constitutional ideas.[6] Although

---

[3] NR XII, 18 (November 2, 1912), 356.

[4] Liang, "Ch'u kuei-kuo yen-shuo-tz'u," 13b.

[5] *Ibid.,* 15-43b.

[6] The three parties which merged to form the *Chin-pu tang* were the *Min-chu tang* (Democratic Party), *Kung-ho tang* (Republican Party), and *T'ung-i tang* (United Party). The *Min-chu tang* was formed, under Liang's direction, in October 1912 by the amalgamation of the *Kung-ho chien-she t'ao-lun hui* (Association for

Li Yüan-hung was the nominal chief, it was Liang who formulated *Chin-pu tang* policy and drafted for the party its suggestions for a permanent Chinese constitution.

The *Chin-pu tang* proposed freedom of religion, compulsory military service, and a bicameral legislature. There was to be no legislation by presidential decree; all laws would have to be ratified by the legislative assembly. The president could veto, but a two-thirds vote in both houses would overrule him. The party stood for nationalism, a strong central government, and an open-minded awareness of world trends. It would encourage education on a mass basis and develop universities in the interior of the country. Suffrage, it felt, should be limited by certain educational and property standards. The government should conduct civil-service examinations and reform the monetary and tax systems.[7]

On immediate political issues, Liang set the party squarely in

---

Discussion of the Establishment of a Republic), *Kung-ho t'ung-i tang* (United Republican Party), *Kung-ho chü-chin hui* (Association for Utmost Advancement of the Republic), *Kung-ho ts'u-chin hui* (Association for Promoting the Republic), *Kuo-min hsin-cheng she* (Society for a New National Government), and *Min-hsieh hui* (People's Association). The first two of these groups had evolved from the pre-Revolutionary *Hsien-yu hui* (Friends of the Constitution), whose theology had been near Liang's and fed by his writings. See Li, 255, 256: Ma Chen-tung, *Yüan-shih tang-kuo shih* [History of Yüan's regime] (Shanghai, 1930), 174, 193; Chia I-chün, *Chung-hua min-kuo shih* [History of the Chinese Republic] (Peiping, 1930), 19.

The *Kung-ho tang* was formed in May 1912 by the fusion of the *Min-she* (People's Society) with several smaller groups. Yüan Shih-k'ai fostered this. Liang took part in at least one policy meeting of the party (he urged amalgamation with parties near it in principle), while the *Kung-ho tang* hailed him publicly as the architect of the new China, announced that the party followed his precepts, and claimed to recognize that he was at one with them in spirit (see Liang, "Ch'u kuei-kuo yen-shuo-tz'u," 5, 9, 23). The *T'ung-i tang* was very similar to the *Min-chu tang* (see Ma Chen-tung, 174).

[7] Liang, "Chin-pu tang ni Chung-hua-min-kuo hsien-fa ts'ao-an," YPSWC 51.31b-44b [Draft constitution proposed for the Chinese Republic by the *Chin-pu tang*]; Ma Chen-tung, 194; Hay Tsou Chai, *La Situation économique et politique de la Chine et ses perspectives d'avenir* (Louvain, 1921), 111-112. For a more detailed expression of Liang's opinion at this time on the respective roles of executive and legislature, see Liang, "Shih-shih tsa-lun," YPSWC 58.3b-7 [Miscellaneous discussions of current events].

opposition to the *Kuo-min tang*. On March 21 Sung Chiao-jen, one of the top *Kuo-min tang* leaders, had been shot and killed as he was taking the train at Shanghai for Peking. Liang announced that the *Chin-pu tang* did not consider the government (i.e., Yüan) responsible for the murder as the *Kuo-min tang* charged. His party, said Liang, favored Yüan for the presidency and supported Yüan's policy, which was hated by the *Kuo-min tang*, of soliciting a huge "Reorganization Loan" from the foreign powers. The *Chin-pu tang's* only concern was to see that the borrowed money was properly expended.[8]

Liang in Office

The *Kuo-min tang*, however, was convinced that the borrowed money was a personal fund for Yüan Shih-k'ai, and Sun, in the summer of 1913, led a Second Revolution in the south, failed completely, and fled to Japan. This outbreak brought the *Chin-pu tang* closer than ever to Yüan: in September, Liang accepted a post in the cabinet of Yüan's appointee, Hsiung Hsi-ling. The premier wanted Liang as his Minister of Finance, but Yüan disapproved of him for this position. Liang, in his turn, firmly refused the Education portfolio. Finally, although the *Chin-pu tang* did not fully endorse his decision, Liang was persuaded to become Minister of Justice. By a very large majority, Parliament voted its approval.[9]

This tour of duty in the cabinet, however, was unproductive, for cabinet government, parliamentary government, was doomed. Yüan Shih-k'ai, who had hitherto acted as the provisional president of China, was elected president in October. One month later, in order to prevent adoption of a constitution which would have curtailed his powers, he purged the parliament of its *Kuo-min tang* members, and in January 1914 he dissolved it altogether. Centralized personal government had emerged. The cabinet, even

[8] Ma Chen-tung, 194; Hornbeck, 80. For Liang's complete statement on the murder of Sung Chiao-jen, see Liang, "Shih-shih tsa-lun," 8b-11.

[9] Li, 298-299; NR XIV, 11 (September 13, 1913), 263.

this vaunted "cabinet of talents," had no role left. In February the premier and Liang resigned in succession.[10]

In a very short time, Liang took on a new responsibility. He had already served on the National Monetary Commission, which had existed from autumn 1912 to autumn a year later, and now, in March 1914, he became the first director of a newly established Monetary Bureau. He sought to give China a standard unit of silver money. His aim was to get rid of the hopelessly indeterminate *tael* and to require the use exclusively of the silver dollar in tax payments, government expenditures, and budget estimates. Liang had no success in this. Resistance of the Chinese Maritime Customs Service and opposition in foreign diplomatic circles, he said later, thwarted his plans.[11] He hoped also, in the interests of economy and better supervision, to reduce the number of mints from sixteen to three, one each to be located in Tientsin, Shanghai, and Canton. This idea fared no better than the last.[12] And his plan to stabilize the currency with a foreign loan was ruled out by the advent of the First World War. Before the year ended, Liang had resigned.[13]

He was not completely dissociated from the government, however. In June 1914 he had become a member of a new institution, the *Ts'an-cheng yüan,* or Council of State.[14] It failed to act on two important proposals which he brought before it in October, one for compulsory military service and one for compulsory education,[15] but his service in this office was still worth his while. It was as a member of the *Ts'an-cheng yüan* that he was able to learn about in detail and to fight with some measure of success the Japanese maneuvers in connection with the Twenty-one Demands.

[10] Li, 309.

[11] Liang, "Min-kuo ch'u-nien chih pi-chih kai-ko," YPSHC-WC 15:43.11-12 [Monetary reforms in the first years of the Republic].

[12] *Ibid.,* 13-14.

[13] Chin Kuo-pao, *Chung-kuo pi-chih wen-t'i* [The monetary problem in China] (Shanghai, 1928), 6.

[14] Ma Chen-tung, 378.

[15] NR XVI, 13 (October 24, 1914). 229.

Liang had written, in 1899, that Japan and China should co-operate to protect the independence of the yellow race.[16] But he was educable. After January 18, 1915, when Japan, with her political and economic demands, threatened the independence of China, Liang was unequivocally anti-Japanese. On May 8 Japan settled for only a modified acceptance of her conditions; and Liang's brilliant press campaign, which fired Chinese opinion that winter and spring, and stiffened the resistance of Yüan Shih-k'ai, and harrassed and embarrassed the Japanese negotiators, was in large part responsible for this modification. Very soon after his return to China in 1912 Liang had become a journalist again, writing first for his short-lived *Yung-yen* (subtitled in English "The Justice") and later, most frequently, for *Ta Chung-hua,* but not until now had his writings carried their old impact.

Japanese newspapers charged him with ingratitude. Liang freely acknowledged having received Japanese protection for more than ten years, but should he for that reason, he asked, abdicate his responsibility to his country? He fiercely resented insinuations that he must have been bought, and he made it abundantly clear that he acted from his own free convictions.[17] Besides riddling Japan's pretexts and pointing out the obstacles which would lie in her path, he issued a warning to the West. In 1907, he said, the great powers had permitted Austria-Hungary, with German support, to annex Bosnia and Herzegovina. A general war had soon followed. Exactly that was in store for the world if Japan's ambitions were left unchecked.[18]

This was 1915. But this statement has the ring of many others, of 1931.

[16] Liang, "Lun hsüeh Jih-pen wen chih i," YPSWC 29.19b [On the advantages of studying Japanese culture].

[17] Liang, "Chung-Jih chiao-she hui-p'ing," YPSWC 58.27b [Collected comments on the Sino-Japanese negotiations]. Collected under this title, YPSWC 58.22-42b, is the bulk of Liang's anti-Japanese writing during the period of negotiations. For an English translation of some of this material, see Liang, "China's Case Against Japanese Demands," CSM X, 7 (April 1915), 414-420.

[18] Liang, "Chung-Jih chiao-she hui-p'ing," 38-38b.

The Monarchical Plans of Yüan Shih-k'ai

Liang remained a member of the *Ts'an-cheng yüan* throughout the crisis of the Twenty-one Demands and into the summer, until he finally realized something that appalled him: Yüan was determined to be Emperor of China. He had heard a hint of this design in January 1915, when Yüan invited him to a banquet. Yang Tu, one of Yüan's followers, was present. He discussed at length the flaws in the republic and sought Liang's help in effecting a change in the form of state, but Liang, pointing out domestic and foreign dangers in such a course, gave him no encouragement. Some time later Liang traveled in the south, for the most part shuttling between Shanghai and Canton. Feng Kuo-chang, the governor of Kiangsu, troubled by the persistent rumors that Yüan Shih-k'ai meant to enthrone himself, told his fears to Liang, and the latter returned to Peking, to challenge Yüan to a plain statement of intentions. Did he wish to become emperor? Yüan swore he did not.[19]

This was in June. Dr. Frank J. Goodnow, an American professor who had been adviser to Yüan once before, was brought to Peking, in June, to advise him again. Goodnow stirred the boiling pot. He issued a memorandum recommending monarchy for China, and in very short order his arguments were reproduced in a pamphlet by Yang Tu and spread abroad by the *Ch'ou-an hui,* or Peace Promotion League, organized in August and dedicated to the greater glory of Yüan Shih-k'ai. Then Liang spoke out.

In "I-tsai so-wei kuo-t'i wen-t'i che" [How strange the so-called question of the form of state!], he killed any lingering suspicion that, as one who had been a monarchist in the past, he might still be one. The conduct of a government, he maintained, had no necessary connection with its form. Whatever was wrong with the Chinese Republic would be just as wrong with an Empire, if the political structure were all that were changed; and by the same

[19] Liang, "Kuo-t'i chan-cheng kung-li t'an," YPSWC 56.14b [Remarks on my experiences during the war over the form of state].

N

token, if Chinese ills were remediable, the Republic just as well as an empire could find the remedies. He scouted the idea that monarchy means stability while a republic, with its discontinuity in executive power, means chaos. Persia, Turkey, Russia were monarchies, he pointed out, and they were no beautiful examples of peace and order.[20]

This seems to be the old monarchist rhetoric turned inside out. Before 1911, Liang had tirelessly belabored unhappy republics. However, as Liang now emphasized, here was no inconsistency. Then and now he had fought revolution; and to wreck an established republic, he felt, would be just as revolutionary an act as the overthrow of monarchy had been. Progress was what he stood for, under the monarchy, under the Republic, and revolutions always retard progress. If revolution was bad in 1911, revolution in 1915 would compound, not cancel, the damage.[21]

This article, a package of intellectual attacks on Goodnow and *ad hominem* attacks on the *Ch'ou-an hui,* had a stunning effect. Everyone now knew that the leader of the *Chin-pu tang* stood with the anti-monarchists, and it helped to make up minds. A flurry of resignations from office ensued, along with defections from Yüan's own following.[22] Yüan had anticipated some such reaction when, before its publication, he had learned that the article existed. Liang later recounted, in a rather self-appreciative tone, that Yüan had tried, with an offer of a huge bribe, to make him suppress it. Liang, the story goes, pleasantly thanked him and sent him in reply a copy of the article. Then came threats. But the fearless author expressed his willingness to risk once more the plight of the exile.[23]

[20] Liang, "Hu-kuo chih i tien-wen chi lun-wen," YPSWC 55.18b-22b [Texts of telegrams and essays connected with the war for protection of the nation]; see also an English translation, "The Strange Monarchical Movement," NR XVIII, 11 (September 11, 1915), 204-206.

[21] Liang, "Hu-kuo chih i tien-wen chi lun-wen," 16b-17, 25b; NR XVIII, 203, 206.

[22] Li, 340; T'ang Leang-li, *The Inner History of the Chinese Revolution* (London, 1930), 127-128.

[23] Liang, "Kuo-t'i chan-cheng kung-li t'an," 15.

With respect to Yüan Shih-k'ai personally, Liang assumed in his article a pose of trustful simplicity. He gave wide advertisement to Yüan's protestations of republicanism and affected to believe that a great gulf existed between Yüan and the *Ch'ou-an hui*.[24] Without losing face, the would-be emperor could still have drawn back. He chose to go ahead with his plans. Hand-picked "citizens' representatives," winners in a preposterous election, gave him their practically unanimous endorsement, and the *Hung-hsien* reign, Yüan Shih-k'ai emperor, was set to begin on January 1, 1916.[25]

The Yunnan Revolt

In 1913, Ts'ai Ao, Liang's old Changsha student, had left his post as military governor of Yunnan and come to Peking. There he became one of Liang's constant companions. In the summer of 1915, when monarchist propaganda began to be insistent, Liang, for safety's sake, moved from Peking to the foreign-concession area in Tientsin, and Ts'ai paid him a special visit there on August 15, the day after the *Ch'ou-an hui* announced its existence and its purpose. Ts'ai, as something of a figure in the military world, could not help but interest Yüan Shih-k'ai, and Liang advised his friend to lie low for a while, to appear inactive and un-

---

[24] Liang, "Hu-kuo chih i tien-wen chi lun-wen," 23; NR XVIII, 206.

[25] The procedure by which Yüan generated this allegedly formal and legal public endorsement was exposed by Liang in a propaganda blast in the spring of 1916. Liang acquired and published the texts of secret telegrams which had been sent by the Peking government to the military and civil governors and the military commandants of the provinces. Military and civil governors were to select from among the residents of the provincial capital one person to represent each district. These persons were to be nominally elected in formal "elections" conducted by well-indoctrinated district magistrates. Then petitions concocted in Peking were to be sent from the provinces by these "representatives" and by the governors. See Liang, "Hu-kuo chih i tien-wen chi lun-wen," 27b-28; see also an English translation of this particular essay, published with Chinese text as *The So-called People's Will (A Comment on the Secret Telegrams of the Yüan Government)* (Shanghai, 1916), 1-2. In another exposé of fraud in the monarchist movement, Liang remarked that more opposition was recorded even in Napoleon I's plebiscite than in this provincial balloting. See Liang, "Yüan Shih-k'ai chih chiai-p'ou," YPSHC-WC 12: 34.5 [Analysis of Yüan Shih-k'ai].

committed, to allay suspicion, and to plot. The younger man acted on this suggestion. Back in Peking, he played at being a profoundly unserious person. With a two-months' show of heroic dissipation, he shook off Yüan's attention, but while he lived this masquerade he set up contact with friends of his, army men and others, in Kweichow and Yunnan.

Tai K'an, one of these friends, who had recently resigned his post as civil governor of Kweichow, came to Peking in October, and in Liang's Tientsin lodgings the three men hatched a conspiracy. Then, separately and secretly, Ts'ai and Tai embarked for Hong Kong, with Yunnan as their ultimate objective. Liang went surreptitiously to Shanghai. He arrived on December 18, the day before his colleagues reached Yunnan.[26]

The Yunnan troops, under T'ang Chi-yao, were committed to the anti-monarchist cause. According to the plan formulated in Tientsin, these troops were to be moved secretly to the Szechuan border. On the twenty-first, Ts'ai sent Liang a telegram saying that forward elements would march on the twenty-third and that, twenty days later, Yunnan would make a public declaration of independence. This was exactly in accordance with the Tientsin decisions, but Liang felt now that continued secrecy was impossible, and in his answering telegram he urged immediate action. This was agreed upon. On the twenty-third, T'ang Chi-yao and the civil governor of Yunnan, Jen K'o-ch'eng, telegraphed the Peking government that they meant to protect the Republic. December 25, at ten o'clock in the morning, was the deadline they set for a grand renunciation on the part of Yüan. No answer came, and when the ultimatum expired Yunnan declared her independence. Next day, Yunnan troops clashed with northern troops in Szechuan.[27]

Liang, in Shanghai, kept in communication with all important centers. Late in February 1916 the Kwangsi military governor, Lu Yung-t'ing, sent emissaries to invite Liang to his province; when

[26] Liang, "Kuo-t'i chan-cheng kung-li t'an," 15-15b.
[27] *Ibid.*, 15b; Chia, 34-35; Li, 349.

Liang would arrive, Kwangsi would join the revolt. A few provinces had already thrown in with Yunnan, but the adherence of Kwangsi was considered the key to success, at least in the south, and Liang had every interest in winning her over. Skirting Kwangtung, which was still loyal to Peking, he made his way to Haiphong, in Indo-China. The railroad from Haiphong would have brought Liang north into Kwangsi, but his movements had been observed and he knew that Yüan's agents were set to intercept him. Avoiding the railroad, he struck out through the mountains, crossed the Chinese border into eastern Yunnan, and was finally welcomed by Lu Yung-t'ing in the Kwangsi city of Nanning. On March 15 Liang, Lu, and a few others telegraphed a new ultimatum to Yüan Shih-k'ai; when the latter ignored it, Kwangsi joined the seceders.[28]

Yüan was ready now to trim his sails. On March 22, he reconverted himself from *Hung-hsien* emperor to simple, democratic, old President Yüan. This magic, unfortunately, made him no more attractive to his critics in the south. Liang and four other leaders rejected a direct appeal for negotiations, and the war went on.[29] After some dangerous and futile diplomatic efforts by Liang, Kwangtung succumbed to military pressure and joined the rebel bloc. Liang then drafted plans for a *Chün-wu yüan,* or Department of Military Affairs, to coördinate the activities of the anti-Peking provinces. The *Chün-wu yüan* was set up with a roster which included a commander-in-chief (T'ang Chi-yao), vice-chief, chief of secretariat, special commissioner for foreign affairs, and six army commanders, one of whom was Ts'ai Ao and one of whom, at least technically holding the rank, was Liang. The latter acted concurrently as chief of the political committee, that is, head of civil affairs in the rebellion.[30]

[28] Liang, "Kuo-t'i chan-cheng kung-li t'an," 16; Ch'en Kung-fu, *Chung-kuo ko-ming shih* [History of the Chinese Revolution] (Shanghai, 1930), 83. For a detailed account of Liang's journey from Shanghai to Kwangsi, see Liang, "Ts'ung-chün jih-chi," YPSWC 56.1-6 [Service diary].

[29] Li, 357.

[30] Liang, "Kuo-t'i chan-cheng kung-li t'an," 16-16b; Chia, 35-36.

Ultimately, eight provinces in all had cut their ties with Peking. Although Yüan was unacceptable in any shape or form, Liang's object was neither to split China nor to obliterate the whole central government, for his own purposes or for any one else's. Sun Yat-sen put out feelers to his fellow-foes of Yüan Shih-k'ai, but he was not encouraged.[31] Li Yüan-hung was the legally constituted vice-president of China, and Liang, presuming Yüan to be discredited and disqualified, was ready to recognize Li as president and to heal the breach between north and south. It seemed, in the spring of 1916, that such a resolution of the civil war would be difficult to bring about. But all at once it became possible, for suddenly, on June 6, Yüan died.

Return to the Peking Political Arena

Without let or hindrance, Li Yüan-hung succeeded to the presidency. He appointed as premier an Anhui military man, Tuan Ch'i-jui, and convoked the original parliament of 1913, the one which Yüan had first decimated and then dissolved. The southern government, in its turn, promised for July 14 the dissolution of the *Chün-wu yüan*. But certain leaders in the south were unwilling to liquidate the rebellion so soon; they preferred to wait until cabinet government had been finally restored, with cabinet members chosen from the members of Parliament. This would mean a delay in unification at least until August 1, when Parliament was scheduled to begin its session. Liang was opposed to this recalcitrance, for he urgently wanted a rapprochement with Tuan. After trying by himself to hold the key generals in line, he induced T'ang Ch'i-yao, the commander-in-chief, to telegraph from Yunnan the order for dissolution of the *Chün-wu yüan*. Now, once again, Peking could speak for all China. And now

---

[31] On May 15, Sun issued a declaration from "The Intelligence Department of the Republican Government of China," Shanghai. He expressed his gratification at learning from the Yunnan Revolt that "we are not the only men who are zealously striving for liberty." See Bernard Martin, *Strange Vigour, a Biography of Sun Yat Sen* (London, 1944), 180.

Liang, with a bond already established between himself and the premier, was ready again for Peking.[32]

When Parliament met, there was some fairly purposeless tampering with the chemistry of the old *Chin-pu tang*. Two separate blocs were derived from it, and then, when no one could quite identify the grounds for separation, they came together in a new synthesis, the *Hsien-fa yen-chiu hui* (Association for Constitutional Research). The *"Yen-chiu* Clique," as it was known, led by Liang, specialized in work behind the scenes; it made no attempt to gain a mass following and had no organization outside Peking. The clique supported Premier Tuan from 1916 to 1918, when he became able to lean on a clique of his own.[33]

The First World War provided the setting for the collaboration of Liang and Tuan. Both labored, against considerable domestic opposition, to bring China into the war on the side of the Allies. Whatever patriotic motives may have animated Tuan, they were certainly supplemented, or perhaps dwarfed, by an appetite for the foreign arms and money which he, as wartime premier of China, might expect to receive. Liang, on the other hand, saw himself simply as a Cavour, winning for his weak country a place at a crucial peace conference. He maintained that the peace of the Far East had been broken by the German occupation of Kiaochow in 1897; Germany was a national enemy, he stated, and China should war against her in the interests of humanity and international law.[34]

[32] Li, 389.

[33] Chia, 50-51; Ch'ien Tuan-sheng, *The Government and Politics of China* (Cambridge, 1950), 72; Jermyn Chi-hung Lynn, *Political Parties in China* (Peking, 1930), 29. The two blocs which united to form the *Yen-chiu* Clique were the *Hsien-fa t'ao-lun hui* (Constitutional Discussion Association), led by T'ang Hua-lung, and the *Hsien-fa yen-chiu t'ung-chih hui* (Constitutional Research Comrades' Association) led by Liang.

[34] NCH 122 (March 31, 1917), 672-673; Liang, "Wai-chiao fang-chen chih yen (ts'an-chan wen-t'i)," YPSHC-WC 12:35.6 [Plain talk about tendencies in foreign relations—the question of participation in the war]. For Liang's answers to commonly voiced objections to China's participation in the war, see this article in its entirety, YPSHC-WC 12:35.4-14.

In March, Liang wrote the text of a telegram designed to be sent to each allied government. He proposed that China, as her part in the war, should supply laborers and raw materials. In return, China would expect concessions from the Allies—arms, confiscation of the German portion of the Boxer Indemnity, postponement of the other Indemnity payments for ten years, increase of the Chinese tariff to an effective 12 per cent, and general modification of the treaties in the direction of equality in status for China. The telegram was not sent, however. President Li Yüan-hung insisted that this was a commitment to war, which only Parliament had the right to declare, and he refused to stamp it with his official seal.[35]

Since Li, supported by the predominantly *Kuo-min tang* Parliament, was so unmilitant, Tuan attempted to force his hand. In late April, the premier convened in Peking a conference of *tuchuns,* military governors of the provinces, who declared for war. When Parliament hesitated, Tuan organized a mob demonstration, representing "public opinion," to threaten the members. The cabinet resigned in protest against this bald effrontery. Resisting a storm of demands that he, too, resign, Tuan had to be dismissed by the President on May 23. Then *tuchuns* of the northern (*Pei-yang*) military party expressed support of Tuan by declaring the independence of seven provinces, and Li, in a timid effort to placate them, dismissed their great enemy and Tuan's, the Parliament.

Suddenly a new player pushed into the game. Shortly after the dissolution of Parliament, which took place on June 12, Chang Hsün, a general who had fought for the Manchus against the Revolution, arrived in Peking. Li had summoned him from Kiangsu to mediate, but Chang, who loved neither republican presidents nor republican premiers, was bored with the contest between them and simply cut the Gordion knot. On July 1, he announced the restoration of the *Hsüan-t'ung* emperor, last of the Ch'ing, to the throne of China. (None other than K'ang

[35] Robert T. Pollard, *China's Foreign Relations* (New York, 1933), 11.

Yu-wei directed this futile project.) Within two weeks, for the second time in his manipulated life, the last of the Ch'ing had his throne abstracted from under him, for troops of the *tuchuns* captured Peking, and Tuan Ch'i-jui, with his parliamentary foes dispersed for him, came back to be premier of the Chinese Republic.

But China was split again. Sun Yat-sen and the *Kuo-min tang* had refused to accept as legal the dissolution of Parliament by Li Yüan-hung. By August 1917 they had succeeded in reconvening the Parliament, or a sufficiently large part of it to constitute a quorum, in Canton. A "provisional military government" was set up, claiming jurisdiction over all China. In his capacity as generalissimo of this government, Sun issued orders for the arrest of Tuan Ch'i-jui and other northern leaders, among them Liang Ch'i-ch'ao; for the latter had joined Tuan's new cabinet, and moreover, the *Kuo-min tang* considered that the recent disastrous train of events had been set in motion by Liang and his *Yen-chiu* Clique.[36]

Orders from Sun Yat-sen, of course, were most ludicrously dead letters in Peking, and Liang, at least until capital politics undid him, remained undisturbed as Minister of Finance. In September, he tried to revive his 1914 plan for stabilization of the currency by a foreign loan. Turning to English, French, Russian, and Japanese banking combines, he proposed a loan of £20,000,000, but he failed to get it.[37] While he was Minister, however, one project important for Chinese finance was actually executed. On November 21, with Liang's approval, the charter of the Bank of China was revised to increase the power of the body of shareholders and to recognize it as the highest authority in the bank's administration. The governor and vice-governor were to be appointed by the national government, but they were to be chosen only from the Bank's directors, who were to be elected by a general meeting of the large shareholders (owners of more than 100 shares). Under this arrangement, the policies of the bank became

[36] Anatol M. Kotenev, *New Lamps for Old* (Shanghai, 1931), 116; Lynn, 28.
[37] Chin, 6-7.

independent of changes in the political texture of the government.[38]

Liang's stay in office, the last in his life, was not a long one. After the monarchical interlude in July 1917, Feng Kuo-chang, hitherto vice-president of the republic, had supplanted Li Yüanhung as president. He had taken up with Tuan the contest for power, and in late November, in one of the vicissitudes of the struggle, Tuan went out of office. Liang, and other members of the *Yen-chiu* Clique, followed him. Eventually, in the next year, Tuan regained his position,, but he worked then with a new group, the so-called *"An-fu* Clique," and Liang was permanently politically dispossessed.

Liang had misjudged the Chinese situation badly. The terrible inadequacies of the first republican parliament had made him pin his hopes on strong personal control by the executive. Thus, he cut himself off from the parliamentary interest, which eventually became identified with the *Kuo-min tang* in the south. On the other hand, Liang, an honest man, seriously interested in good government, had been a dreamer to think China would get it from his strong men in Peking. Their interest was plunder, their methods were violent, and they could hardly consider the sincere, intellectual reformer as anything but a blister on the proceedings. From 1918 on, isolated from the warlords of the north and the nationalists of the south, Liang had no voice in the domestic political settlement.[39]

[38] Hsü Ch'i-ch'ing, *Tseng-kai tsui-chin Shang-hai chin-jung shih* [History of the Shanghai money market in recent times], (Shanghai, 1932), I, 25; S. H. Chafkin, "Modern Business in China: The Bank of China before 1935," *Papers on China,* vol. 2 (mimeograph) (Committee on International and Regional Studies, Harvard University, 1948), 112-113. See also, on this episode, Liang, "Min-kuo ch'u-nien pi-chih kai-ko," 15.

[39] In 1919 the press carried a report that the *Chin-pu tang,* "a political party which recently has not done much," would be reorganized. Liang would be leader of the reorganized party, which was to be called the *Hsin-hsüeh tang* (Newstudy Party). See MR (September 13,·1919), 72. This project came to nothing. Although Liang played no political role in the 'twenties, his influence as a political leader was never entirely dissipated and lived on atter his death. At the end of the war with Japan, a weak political party was organized and led by

The Last Decade

Liang still had some slight role to play in the conduct of foreign relations. China had finally declared war on the Entente and could claim a seat at the Paris Peace Conference. Toward the end of 1918, Liang sailed for Europe to be an unofficial delegate to the conference, an adviser to the Chinese ambassadors to France, England, and the United States, who comprised the official Chinese delegation. Before his departure, he made a speech in Shanghai about the Chinese right to tariff autonomy. He appealed to the principle of national independence, for which, ostensibly, he said, the war had been fought. Once in Europe, he expressed himself in similar fashion, in statements which were reported by European newspapers. Foreign interference he held responsible for China's hopeless situation, and he stigmatized Japan above all as a "robber neighbor." He demanded the return to China of foreign leaseholds, shelving of the Boxer Indemnity obligation, abolition of extraterritoriality and other forms of privilege for foreigners, unification of railroads, and abrogation of agreements made under conditions of duress or collusion.[40]

Liang improved the time during his European journey seeing the sights of England, France, the Rhineland, and Belgium and thinking long thoughts about the nature and destiny of Western civilization—but he won no political concessions for China. She carried her grievances into the twenties, and Liang continued to plead her case in the public press. When, in 1921, the Washington Conference was convened to define the power situation in the Pacific area, he argued strongly for Chinese territorial integrity

Carsun Chang (Chang Chün-mai), a disciple of Liang's. This party, the *Chung-kuo min-chu she-hui tang* (Chinese National Socialist Party, or, as it is better known in the West, the Social Democratic Party) was formed by the amalgamation of two parties dating from the thirties; one of the latter, composed of Chinese living in North America, was the lineal descendant of the *Pao-huang hui,* and the leaders of the other had all been associated with the *Yen-chiu* Clique. See Ch'ien Tuan-sheng, 354.

[40] CA VII 24, 75-77, 143-144.

and administrative autonomy.[41] And in 1925, when the "May 30th Incident" in Shanghai and the subsequent "Shameen Massacre" in Canton fired Chinese nationalism with a new intensity, Liang wrote a long series of articles, eloquent but basically temperate in tone, which called for gradual revision of the "unequal treaties."[42] After the first of these incidents, he was one of seven signers of the "Tientsin Manifesto," issued June 7, which warned that China's rights could not be set aside with impunity nor her sensibilities flouted, but which urged a fair and free investigation and a settlement by conciliation.[43]

In the twenties, however, Liang's activities were centered more in university and intellectual circles than in the world of affairs. He taught successively at Tung-nan University, in Shanghai, and at the Tsinghua Research Institute, in Peking.[44] He was one of the founders, in 1920, of the *Chiang-hsüeh she* (Chinese Lecture Association), which brought to China such figures as Dewey, Russell, Driesch, and Tagore.[45] He had close ties with the magazine *Che-hsüeh* [Philosophia], published in Peking by the *Che-hsüeh she* (Philosophical Association) in 1921 and for some time thereafter, at irregular intervals. Most of its articles dealt with

---

[41] Liang, "Shih-shih tsa-lun," YPSWC 76.10-16b.

[42] Nine articles written on this subject in 1925 may be found in YPSHC-WC 14:41.106-114 and 15:42.1-38. They embody an interesting form of criticism of Western society and will be discussed in this connection in the next chapter. In the two incidents mentioned, British troops fired into Chinese demonstrations against foreign actions in the concessions.

[43] H. G. W. Woodhead (ed.), *China Year Book, 1926-1927* (Tientsin, 1927), 932.

[44] Ch'ien Chi-po, 349. *China Journal of Science and Arts*, V, 1 (July 1926), 16, gives a list of fifteen courses and research projects which Liang directed in 1925-1926. They include investigations in the fields of Chinese painting, literature, history, sociology, and philosophy.

[45] Richard Wilhelm, "Intellectual Movements in China," CSPSR VIII, 2 (April, 1924), 122-123. Of these figures, Russell made perhaps the greatest impression on Chinese intellectuals. Liang's address of welcome to Russell, November 9, 1920, may be found in *Lo-su yüeh-k'an* [The Russell Monthly], published by the *Chiang-hsüeh she* (Shanghai, 1921), I, appendix, 1-7. Hostility to Tagore, and to Liang as one of his main sponsors, was intense in radical student circles; see Wieger, V ("Nationalisme"), 66-83.

Western philosophy, but Liang, among others, contributed several studies of ancient Chinese philosophy.[46] In sum, although by the time of his death Liang had, to a large extent, lost the allegiance of youth, he was widely regarded as a sort of dean of intellectuals, a figure of commanding prestige, one of the Chinese most fitted to mingle with the international society of the learned.[47]

Liang's scholarly production in the last decade of his life was prodigious. History was his main concern, and he wrote prolifically on topics in Chinese cultural history, Chinese literary history, and historiography.[48] He made sociological interpretations as well as historical criticisms of many ancient texts. His interest in Buddhism, which had stubbornly persisted throughout his youthful Confucian-reformist phase and the years of western-oriented nationalism which succeeded it, survived and flowered in Liang's last period. He spoke publicly in Peking against the "Anti-religious movement."[49] In the summer of 1923, although he was not able to attend, he gave his backing to the Abbot T'ai Hsü's World Conference of Buddhists, held in Ku-ling.[50] He wrote many articles on the history, philosophy, and influence of Buddhism in China. A Buddhist ceremony was performed for him when he died.[51].

[46] J. K. Fairbank, and K. C. Liu, *Bibliographical Guide to Modern China* (Cambridge, 1950), 472.

[47] For example, on October 26, 1926, when the Crown Prince of Sweden, a distinguished archaeologist, was welcomed to Peking by The Geological Society of China, The Peking Society of Natural History, and Peking Union Medical College, it was Liang who gave the keynote address. See Liang, "Archaeology in China," *Smithsonian Report for 1927* (Washington, 1928), 453-466.

[48] For a severe criticism of Liang in this role, see Kuwabara Sadamasa, "Liang Ch'i-ch'ao shi no 'Chung-kuo li-shih yen-chiu fa' wo yomu," [On reading Mr. Liang Ch'i-ch'ao's *A Method of Studying Chinese History*] SG II, 12 (August 1922), 1-18. He charges Liang with errors of fact and with carelessness and lack of thoroughness in the use of materials.

[49] Y. Y. Tsu, "Spiritual Tendencies of the Chinese People As Shown Outside of the Christian Church Today," CR LVI, 12 (December 1925), 777.

[50] Karl Ludwig Reichalt, "A Conference of Chinese Buddhist Leaders," CR LIV, 11 (November 1923), 667.

[51] *The Week in China* XII, 200 (January 26, 1929), 84.

Liang died when still comparatively young, but he lived long enough to see Sun Yat-sen and K'ang Yu-wei pass before him. Sun died on March 12, 1925, and Liang called at his home the next day to extend sympathy to the bereaved.[52] When K'ang died two years later, Liang made the funeral oration. He described his old teacher and colleague as the great pioneer of reform, who had seen earlier and more clearly than anyone else that China must choose either progress along modern lines or hopeless decay and ruin. Liang regretted, however, K'ang's effort in 1917 to restore the monarch.[53]

Liang died on January 19, 1929. He had seen in his fifty-six years tremendous political happenings—the fall of the Chinese Empire, the triumph of the Nationalists, the birth of Chinese Communism and the beginning of its ordeal by fire. And he had seen something else, one of those great intangibles and undatables of history, the change of an ethos. For approximately half his adult life, his writings did much to effect this change; they never ceased to reflect it. Liang was never as important in the Republic as he had been in the dying Empire, but he was just as significant in the Republic as he had always been.

[52] Lynn, 70.
[53] Liang, "Kung-chi K'ang Nan-hai hsien-sheng wen," YPSHC-WC 15:44.30 [Funeral Address for K'ang Yu-wei].

CHAPTER VI

BACK TO CHINA—THE LAST DEFENSE

The Confucian colleges are crumbling amongst thorns and thistles; their drums and gongs are thrown aside, amid rank grass and weeds. Thus the reverence paid for thousands of years to Confucius has declined, and none seeks to repair it.[1]

By 1912, Liang had made his journey from culturalism to nationalism, and now he had a new nation to capture his attention. The old way of life was crumbling, as Liang had half-wished. By reasoning the nation into the culture's place as the proper object of loyalty, he had managed, however imperfectly, to make this breakdown bearable. Out of concern for his culture, Liang had, to a large extent, banished the culture from his concerns, and from 1912 to 1919 he busied himself more with problems of the nation than with the problem of the destiny of Chinese civilization. In these seven years, he wrote less about this subject; there were no new directions. Old ideas recurred, and almost the whole network of logic and illogic described in Part Two of this study can be reconstructed, in miniature, from scraps of Liang's works in the first few years of the Republic.[2]

[1] From a presidential mandate of Yüan Shih-k'ai. NR XVII, 21 (May 22, 1915), 370.

[2] Perhaps one qualitative change, closely related to the quantitative change, can be noticed in an essay written in 1915, after the episode of the Twenty-one Demands. Liang declared that if the Chinese were unpatriotic, this was a sign of execrable government. For patriotism comes easy; the difficult thing is to blot it out. When people feel that they have nothing to lose from foreign incursions, they will not be outstandingly patriotic. See Liang, "T'ung-ting tsui-yen," YPSWC 48.39-41 [Recriminations after the agony]; see also translation under the title, "Afterthoughts," NR XVIII, 4 (July 24, 1915), 67-68. What may be noted here is a shift away from Liang's old nationalism-culturalism dichotomy. The assumption now is that nationalism is a completely natural feeling, for the Chinese as well as for others. The alternative to nationalism, as Liang sees it here, is not loyalty to the culture but only apathy, stemming from disaffection, toward the nation.

Liang's Recapitulation

We hear again the old insistence that China must move. In the West there had always been change, each historical period having its own special character, but in China, from the founding of the Ch'in dynasty down to 1898, there had been just fixity.[3] Now China is in a period of transition. All ideas of restoring the old are hopeless. China is sick, from inherited poisons and from blindness to the progress of world civilization.[4] The Western countries are the pioneers of progress.[5]

Thus speaks Liang, in the second decade of the century as in the first. But if this seems to be a cruel blow struck at China's self-esteem, we should remember the palliative which Liang has prepared. The nation, he has said, and says again, is the basic unit in the modern world. And in that world only the great power can exist.[6] Will China be weeded out in the struggle for existence? This can be avoided, Liang thinks.[7]

If China is a nation and its duty is survival, it may with a clear conscience abandon its old teachers, its prophets. It does not have to pretend that Chinese tradition has provided everything which China needs. If innovations are valuable to the nation, they are acceptable to it; it is no concern of the nationalist's whether the sages had allegedly approved them or not. But a nation needs historic heroes to inspire it, and a refurbished prophet may do

[3] Liang, "Ch'u kuei-kuo yen-shuo-tz'u," 57.14.

[4] Liang, "Wu nien lai chih chiao-hsün," YPSWC 56.18-18b [Lessons of the last five years].

[5] Liang, "Ch'u kuei-kuo yen-shuo-tz'u," 42.

[6] Liang, "Chung-kuo li-kuo ta fang-chen," YPSWC 49.2-3 [Broad policy for the establishment of the Chinese state].

[7] Liang, "Chung-kuo tao-te chih ta yüan." YPSWC 47.4 [The great source of Chinese morality]. Liang's pre-1919 reliance on Social-Darwinist ideas is probably nowhere so clearly and so curiously demonstrated as in one of his attacks on Yüan Shih-k'ai, "Hu-kuo chi i tien-wen chi lun-wen," 35, and translation of one section, The So-called People's Will, 12: "Just think what would be the result if this man, wielding absolute power, were to arbitrarily introduce his own process of artificial selection and mould society accordingly? . . . the good elements of society would gradually become extinct, the degenerates alone would survive. . ."

very well. And so Liang, who no longer wants Confucius to dominate Chinese history, holds that, if one thinks of Chinese history
without Confucius, it is darkness and eclipse; it is impossible to
know, he says, whether the people could have been drawn together into one body, if Confucius had not lived. When Confucianism was fundamentally revered, he adds, it did not, like
other creeds, mold proud dogmatists who sought to stamp out
heteredoxy.[8] We have heard this note from Liang before and have
realized its implication: Confucius was great, but a new word
must be spoken.

Yet Liang, as a nationalist, is ever ready to announce that some
valuable words had been spoken first in China, only later in the
West. Buddhist and Confucianist philosophers of the Six Dynasties
and T'ang periods had the scientific spirit, says Liang, for they
based their inquiries on fixed principles. Pushing this questionable
claim, he feels that China may condescend to Europe and America, where scientific principles had begun to be generally followed
only in the last two or three centuries. And socialistic economic
principles, which the West thinks are so "advanced," were foreshadowed by the *ching-t'ien* system, the "well-field" system of
Confucian economic theory.[9]

But Liang, as we have seen, felt that he could assert China's
equivalence with the West even when there was no Chinese precedent for things which China needed and the West possessed.
These were not implicit in Western culture; Europe had lacked
them only yesterday. A century ago the economic situation in the
various European countries was just like that in contemporary
China.[10] A century ago the governments of all nations were autocratic, just like China's for thousands of years.[11]

[8] Liang, "Fu-ku ssu-hu p'ing-i," YPSWC 52.19-20 [A balanced discussion of
the "revive-the-old" thought-tide].

[9] Liang, "Lun Chung-kuo ts'ai-cheng-hsüeh pu fa-ta chih yüan-yin chi ku-tai
ts'ai-cheng hsüeh-shuo chih i-pan," YPSHC-WC 12:33.92-93 (On the reason for
the lack of progress in Chinese study of finance, and a miscellany of ancient
financial theories); see also translation under the title, "Economic Science in
China," NR XIX, 12 (March 18, 1916), 230-231.

[10] Liang, "Ch'u kuei-kuo yen-shuo-tz'u," 28.

[11] *Ibid.*, 24b; Liang, "Cheng-chih shang chih tui-k'ang li," YPSWC 47.15b
[Conflicting forces in politics].

o

When Liang speaks like this, he means to free China from the specter of debt. The West, in moving into its modern period, had not "westernized" but had modernized itself. China should do the same and can do it without shame. Space is partitioned, but time belongs to everyone.

Thus, with these ideas, slightly stale, Liang comes to 1919, still busy deserting culturalism, still introducing its substitute, nationalism; and with him, indestructible, is the old inner confusion. Which shall he cherish, history or value? As a nationalist, anxious to strengthen the nation, he is ready to call Chinese errors as he sees them and to advocate corrective measures developed and demonstrated outside of China. But, too, as a nationalist, he must believe in and wish to preserve a Chinese national spirit, which inspired the Chinese past and may be deduced from it. Is Chinese tradition sacrosanct or is it not? Liang is clearly on all sides of this question. That is why the almost inconceivable happens: after all his express opposition to this very idea, he turns up in 1913 as one of the founders of the General Confucian Association, dedicated to the proposition that Confucianism, which is at the heart of the national character, should be made the state religion. As one of the signers of a petition to Parliament, he associates himself with that weary old piece of special pleading—he himself had discredited it—the reference to Yao and Shun, abdicating their thrones and refusing the succession to their sons, and acting thereby "out of regard for the democratic principle."[12] The traditionalist espouses what the practical man dismisses.

Thus, pride in the Chinese past and impatience with it were still compounded in Liang's nationalism. The failures of the young republic had made this paradox, if anything, more perplexing. Liang had fought so long for liberal parliamentary government along Western lines; what was he to make of the sorry record of the Chinese Parliament? On the one hand, he might, and he did, blame China for not transcending tradition and really

[12] Hu Shih, "The Confucianist Movement in China," CSM IX, 7, (May 12, 1914), 535; NR XIV, 15 (October 11, 1913), 392.

trying to make a new institution work.[13] On the other hand, and he did this too, he could explain the fact of its not working by pointing out that the National Assembly had no traditional authority and was therefore not the center of confidence.[14] In other words, tradition should be dispensed with, and it cannot be dispensed with.

And it is not only difficult, it is disastrous, he feels, to break with the past. A nation must act in keeping with its national character, which is manifested in language, literature, religion, customs, ceremonies, and laws; for a nation dies when its national character is obliterated. This happened, said Liang, to Annam and Korea. So many Chinese elements entered their cultures that their national characters could never be more than half-developed. Hence, they fell to aliens.[15]

In this post-mortem of Annam and Korea, Liang is making a simple, important statement: Chinese civilization is not good for foreigners. Because he means by this that a nation must cherish what its history gives it, the statement has a corollary: foreign civilizations are not good for China. The idea of history transcends the idea of value.

This is what Liang's nationalism made him believe, because nationalism is emotionally powered by pride in the uniqueness of the nation's people. But nationalism, we have already seen, meant also something else to Liang, and something quite different. Nationalism was his escape from history, his abandonment of the

[13] See Liang, "Tsui-yen," YPSWC 48.30-31 [Antagonizing words], where he observes that in England "the old is name and the new is fact" (he approves of this), while in China "the old is fact and the new is name." He ridicules the belief which he ascribes to China that by calling itself a constitutional government it really is one.

[14] Liang, "Shih-shih tsa-lun," 58.13; see also translation under the title, "The Suicide of the National Assembly," NR XIV, 14 (October 4, 1913), 361.

[15] Liang, "Ta Chung-hua fa-k'an-tz'u," YPSHC-WC 12:33.83-84 [Foreword to the publication of *Ta Chung-hua*]; see also translation under the title, "The Future of China," NR XVII, 9 (February 27, 1915), 146; and Liang, "Kuo-hsing p'ien," YPSWC 47.1b [Essay on national character], where he says that a national character preserves a nation (e.g., Poland) even when it is politically submerged.

tradition and society which had come down to him and which, in the face of Western progress and confidence, he could not value intellectually. As a nationalist, with culturalism left behind him, he could bring ideas from the outside world into China on the pretext that the nation needed them. The idea of value transcends the idea of history.

In short, from the Reform Movement to the end of the War, Liang's nationalism posed a difficult question: would an infusion of Western civilization cure China or kill it? And both possible answers, logically incompatible with each other, were implied in Liang's thought.

This conflict between history and value had been impossible in the great ages of the Chinese Empire. Then, Chinese loved their civilization not only because they had inherited it from their fathers but because they were convinced that it was good. It had been a basic assumption of Chinese civilization that if Annam and Korea, for example, adopted a certain amount of it, to that degree did Annam and Korea become civilized. Liang would have liked to contemplate such a harmony of history and value. After 1919, he felt that he was able to do so.

The disharmony in his thinking before that time stemmed simply from the fact that he still admired Western civilization. As in his Japanese years, he threw a few glancing shots at the West. He spoke slightingly, for example, of Western "immediate hedonism."[16] Nevertheless, he made nothing at all like the joyous, fierce attacks which were soon to come. Europe came up to and into the First World War with as yet unchallengeable prestige, and not the war itself but the postwar reflections on it marked the turning point.

From 1919 on, he brought value back to Chinese history, for the West could be revalued. Preservation of the Chinese spirit was no longer simply a blind charge on the Chinese. When the Western spirit was not good, but bad, the Chinese spirit was not just Chinese, but good.

[16] Liang, "Chung-kuo tao-te chih ta yüan," 9b.

The Decline of the West

"Progress," that old European discovery and Chinese need, became "material progress" in 1919, and the beauty sifted out of it. The sum total of material progress in the last hundred years, noted Liang, had been many times that of the previous three thousand; yet mankind had not only not attained happiness but had met with abundant disasters.[17] Technological advances aside, was there really, he asked himself, such a thing as inevitable progress? He answered with an explicit disavowal of his earlier fancies. Years before, in the *Hsin-min ts'ung-pao,* he had deplored a sentence in Mencius, a statement implying the doctrine of the "eternal return."[18] He had attacked Mencius then but he praised him now for suggesting that progress was an illusion. Had Mencius not been vindicated by the course of Chinese history? Was present-day India better than the India of the Upanishads and of Sakyamuni? Did the condition of modern Egypt represent progress from the days of the Thirtieth Dynasty? Liang ticked off a list of Chinese dynasties, great names in Eastern and Western literature, conquerors, and defied anyone to call the chronological sequence progressive.[19]

Defending the study of ideas of many centuries ago, he insisted that Confucius and Mencius had something to say to the moderns. He explicitly quoted and then discounted the opinion that the law of progress made ideas of the past outdated.[20] "New" does not necessarily mean "true."[21]

[17] Liang, "Ou yu hsin-ying lu chieh-lu," YPSWC 72.10 [Reflections on my European travels]. An important part of this work has been summarized in Kiang Wen-han, *The Chinese Student Movement* (New York, 1948), 40-42.

For exactly the same point, made in different words, see Liang, "Yen-chiu wen-hua shih ti i-ko chung-yao wen-t'i," YPSWC 69.33b [Some important questions in the study of cultural history].

[18] The sentence, in the Legge translation, is as follows: "A long time has elapsed since this world of men received its being, and there has been along its history now a period of good order, and now a period of confusion" (Legge, II, 279).

[19] Liang, "Yen-chiu wen-hua shih ti i-ko chung-yao wen-t'i," 33-33b.

[20] Liang, "Tai Tung-yüan che-hsüeh," YPSWC 65.16b-17 [Tai Chen's philosophy].

[21] Liang, "Ou yu hsin-ying lu chieh-lu," 22b.

Mere passage of time, then, was no guarantee of improvement in the quality of human civilization. If men thought that it was (and Liang had thought so), they must be identifying the advancement of science, which had certainly taken place in time and was clearly going to continue, with advancement toward the ultimate ends of life. In page after page the new Liang insisted that this identification was false. And it was not simply that naked science was not enough. When science was idolized for its successes and considered to be all-sufficient for man, it did not just bring him half-way to happiness; it set him on the wrong way.

What civilization but the modern Western civilization could possibly be charged with this error? And so Liang wrote:

Men are like travellers in the desert and have lost their direction. At a distance they saw a big black shadow and tried hard to catch up with it, thinking it might be depended upon as a guide. How were they to know that, after they had caught up a little, the shadow would suddenly disappear? They were thus in utter despair. What is this shadow? It is this Mr. Science. The European people have had a big dream about the omnipotence of science. Now they are talking about its bankruptcy. This is then a great turning point in the change of modern thought.[22]

And Liang, too, talked of its bankruptcy. He dwelt lovingly on European confusion and pessimism. Science, he wrote, had triumphed absolutely in modern European civilization, and now people were characterized by impersonality, a sense of insecurity, anxiety, fatigue, loss of leisure, and the dread combination of expanding desires and constricting opportunities.[23] For desires increase with the increase of material things, and satisfaction always recedes in the distance, and the West, Liang testified, mechanical, materialistic, withered and dry, was sick.[24]

[22] *Ibid.*, 10-10b, and Kiang, 41. I have altered one sentence of Kiang's translation.

"Mr. Science" (k'o-hsüeh hsien-sheng) is a phrase popularized by Ch'en Tu-hsiu in the pages of the culturally pro-Western periodical, *Hsin ch'ing-nien* (La Jeunesse).

[23] Liang, *ibid.*, 8-12b, and Kiang, 40-42.

[24] Liang, "Tung-nan Ta-hsüeh k'o-pi kao pieh-tz'u," YPSWC 70.3b-4 [Leave-

The sickness was spiritual famine.

Of the methods of relieving spiritual famine, I recognize the Eastern —Chinese and Indian—to be, in comparison, the best. Eastern learning has spirit as its point of departure; Western learning has matter as its point of departure. . .

Slavery to the body—that had been the Western fate, but Eastern philosophies teach release.[25] China had learned from India the Buddhist idea of absolute freedom.[26] Buddhism, the highest achievement of world culture, had been developed jointly by China and India.[27]

Bertrand Russell, Liang was proud to note, had paid beautiful tribute to Chinese culture and had publicly hoped that the Chinese people would escape Americanization. Liang believed that the American way of life was superior to the militaristic German or Japanese, but spiritual famine had blighted it like the rest. Its nature was anxious haste, its end was death. In bitter and sardonic phrases he listed the American stages of life's way, and the death he found in the last stage was not just physical death but death the mocker of man's enterprise, destroyer of illusions. "I runne to death, and death meets me as fast," we seem to read in this Chinese prose, and here, too, is an echo of Macbeth, his brief candle, strutting player, sound and fury, nothing. But Donne and Shakespeare had written of the human condition, while Liang means to write of the Western condition. He heaps on the West the universal vanity, and the matter of art becomes a matter of ideology.[28]

---

taking after teaching at Tung-nan University]; Liang, "Chih-kuo-hsüeh ti liang t'iao ta-lu," YPSWC 69.21b [The two main roads of political philosophy].

[25] Liang, "Tung-nan Ta-hsüeh k'o-pi kao pieh-tz'u," 4b.

[26] Liang, "Yin-tu yü Chung-kuo wen-hua chih ch'in-shu ti kuan-hsi," 45b. The paraphrase of this essay (which was a lecture welcoming Rabindranath Tagore) in Tseng, 130-131, is in serious error on this point. Tseng has Liang affirm what the Chinese text explicitly denies, that "liberation" through Buddhism, besides being the emancipation of the individual from slavery to material existence, includes the aspect of liberation from outward (i e., social) oppression.

[27] Liang, "Chih-kuo-hsüeh ti liang t'iao ta-lu," 23b-24.

[28] Liang, "Tung-nan Ta-hsüeh k'o-pi kao pieh-tz'u," 2b-3.

If life in the West was a failure, then knowledge, which had certainly been accumulating in the West, must be of little worth. "Spirit" has connotations of immediacy, intuitive comprehension, illumination; and for Liang, the antitheses of China, spirit, and illumination were West, matter, and learning. He played at being an anti-intellectual. "The more knowledge increases, the more bitter is man's despair," he wrote. Adding the qualifying phrase, "if there be no spiritual life," he reiterated this idea twice in the same article, and he illustrated it with a piece of sentimentality of a very familiar type: the rickshaw coolie, with meager knowledge, never has the melancholy of the young intellectual.[29]

High among the categories of learning which Liang was thus ready to disparage were Darwinian biology and the inferences for society which some men, himself included, had drawn from it. Once, Liang had accepted Social Darwinism as an abstract scientific principle, one which established at least the potential equivalence of China with the West. It had made it possible for Liang to avoid a seemingly hopeless battle to justify Chinese civilization by value. But now World War I and Western pessimism had made such a battle seem far from hopeless, and Darwinian, or pseudo-Darwinian, theory had a new role to play in Liang's apologetics. No longer was it pure science, which Liang invoked to save China from embarrassment; now, when evil might conceivably be traced to it, it was a cultural exhibit, submitted by Liang to embarrass the West.

He discussed Nietzsche, and quoted him on the principle that love for others is a slave morality, that it is the duty of the strong to exterminate the weak, and that this is the condition of progress. This weird theory, said Liang, was derived from Darwinian biology. It governed men's minds, led to the worship of power and money, became a fixed principle. Militarism and imperialism stemmed from it. Here, in this doctrine, was the seed of the Great War, and here was the origin of the internal class-wars of the future.[30]

[29] *Ibid.*, 3-4.
[30] Liang, "Ou yu hsin-ying lu chieh-lu," 8.

He discussed Lao-tzu—the banishment of consciousness of self, merging of the ego with the cosmos, abolition of the distinction between subjective and objective, with the concomitant quietism, inactivity, and death to contention. Anyone who finds this thought in Lao-tzu, wrote Liang, must call to mind another, modern, school of thought:

Since Darwin's discovery of the principle of the evolution of species, a great revolution has occurred in intellectual circles of the whole world. His service to learning must be acknowledged. But afterwards his theory of struggle for existence and survival of the fittest was applied to the study of human society and became the core of thought, with many evil consequences. This great European war nearly wiped out human civilization; although its causes were very many, it must be said that the Darwinian theory had a very great influence. Even in China in recent years, where throughout the whole country men struggle for power, grasp for gain, and seem to have gone crazy, although they understand nothing of scholarship, yet the things they say to screen themselves from condemnation are regularly drawn from Yen Fu's translation of "The Principles of Evolution." One can see that the influence of theory on men's minds is enormous. No wonder that Mencius said, "These evils, growing in the mind, do injury to government, and, displayed in the government, are hurtful to the conduct of affairs."[31] Perhaps the European's current fondness for the study of Lao-tzu is in reaction to this theory.[32]

Sometimes Darwinism, with, as he saw it, its corrosive effects, seemed to represent science in general in Liang's thought. After the rise of science, he said, religion was the first to get a death-blow, for where is the personal relationship of man with Creator when man is relegated to the company of the lower species?

[31] Legge, II, 191-192.
[32] Liang, "Lao-tzu che-hsüeh," YPSWC 63.14-14b [The philosophy of Lao-tzu]. For other suggestions that Darwinism was at the root of the First World War, see Liang, "Sheng-wu-hsüeh shu-chieh chih wei-chih," YPSWC 68.8b-9 [The place of biology in the intellectual world], and Liang, "Ou yu hsin-ying lu chieh-lu," 10. For an indication of modern European interest in Lao-tzu, see Adolf Reichwein, China and Europe (New York, 1925), 5, where it is said that in the first quarter of the twentieth century no less than eight translations of Lao-tzu's Tao te ching [The way and its power] had appeared in Germany.

Hitherto, in times of indescribable bitterness, there could still be hope of heaven, but now this sort of religious narcotic could not exist; science had deprived men of the bases of belief. When all phenomena in the universe are only material, there is no room left for "heaven" and "the soul." "The Origin of Species" had dealt a crushing blow to the idealist philosophy. Now all inner and outer life is thought to be ruled by unchangeable laws, and with "free will" gone, where lies the responsibility for good and evil? Dualism between matter and spirit has vanished: all is matter.[33]

All is matter. . . . When Liang could believe that the West said that, he had a new way to take the sting away from the westernization of China.

The New Syncretism

Liang was willing to let China use the Western conquest of matter. Even when he attacked the West, Liang never believed that China might preserve, or recover, the authentic Chinese civilization. He never meant to bar the West, but, meant, rather, to explain its invasion away. Let us recall his three successive explanations: (a) Western successes can be construed as Chinese successes too. (b) "Western" successes are not basically Western, but belong to anyone who will achieve them. (c) Western "successes" are not really such; Chinese culture is entitled to every bit as much respect as the West's. Any one of these statements lets the West into China, but with the third, China condescends. In Liang's last writings, China's acceptance of a rival civilization becomes a testimony of faith in its own.

Charging that the West believes that everything is matter, Liang calls the West materialistic. Behind this adjective, used pejoratively, as Liang uses it, is the idea that not everything is matter *but something is* and that this plus spirit is totality. The

---

[33] Liang, "Ou yu hsin-ying lu chieh-lu," 9-9b, and Kiang, 41; Liang, "Tung-nan Ta-hsüeh k'o-pi kao pieh-tz'u," 3-3b; Liang, "Chih-kuo-hsüeh ti liang t'iao ta-lu," 21.

Western heresy, thinks Liang, is the doctrine that matter is all-inclusive, but Liang, for his part, is no absolute idealist; existence, he will acknowledge, includes matter. Matter exists, he cheerfully admits, and scientific method is the only valid method whereby man may organize his perception of it.

But what if science, the proper mistress of a part of reality (matter), rests on a claim of universality, a claim which the spokesman for spirit cannot admit? This spokesman sees behind science a premise which he calls false, twin metaphysical assumptions: first, that all phenomena are subject to empirically verifiable inflexible laws; second, that all reality is phenomenal. Unless science reigns over all existence, the existence of science itself is incomprehensible. Values, then, are illusions (or so the critics of science understand it to say), and these illusions are as phenomenal, as completely subject to scientific law, as any solid, liquid, or gas. Materialistic, deterministic science, to find out the secrets of dead, caused matter, expels from the universe freedom and life.

Thus science—and for Liang, this is the West, which developed it—in order to tell the truth about matter, tells a lie about reality. When China, to learn that truth, borrows science from the West, the very borrowing, the need of it, proclaim that China has been too spiritual to tell the lie. China has clearly never (and Europe clearly has) gambled for the world at the risk of its soul. Indeed, the dualism of matter and spirit becomes a wonderful all-purpose instrument for China. First, using it, China can disparage science and the West as materialistic; which means simply that, accepted as a postulate, the dualism smothers the Western attempt to do away with it. And second, under its sanction, China can take science and put it in its place; for science deals with matter, and matter, as any dualist can plainly see, exists and must be dealt with.

That is why we find Liang acknowledging the value of science and carefully delimiting its sphere. Emphasizing the impossibility of a mechanistic view of life, he nevertheless rejects extreme idealism as well as extreme materialism.[34] His own philosophical view-point, he says, derives rather from certain mystical phrases of Confucius and Lao-tzu than from the pragmatism of the modern West, which asks the purpose of every contemplated action and the result of every completed one; yet, he explicitly states that his two Chinese attitudes, although they have an absolute value for man's spiritual life, may well have obstructed the progress of China's material civilization, and he does not intend to deny the validity of pragmatism.[35] Thinking men in China, he says, all know the importance and value of science.[36] But scientific method belongs solely to that sphere of existence which reason may contemplate, and emotion, which combines with reason to make up human nature, governs the realms of love and beauty and that sublimity which transcends the "reasonable."[37] Liang speaks here

[34] Liang, "Fei *wei,*" YPSWC 68.15b-18 [Anti-monism].

[35] Liang, "*Chih pu k'o erh wei* chu-i yü *wei erh pu yu* chu-i," YPSWC 68.21 [The principle of *chih pu k'o erh wei* and the principle of *wei erh pu yu*]. The first of these phrases, which is cited more completely in the body of the article, is found in the following passage from the *Lun-yü* [Analects of Confucius], Legge, I, 290: " 'It is he—is it not—', said the other, 'who knows the impracticable nature of the times and yet will be doing in them.' " In the second phrase, Liang appears to have kaleidoscoped two successive phrases of the *Tao te ching,* "sheng erh pu yu, wei erh pu shih," which appear twice, in chapters 10 and 51, respectively. They are translated as follows in Arthur Waley, *The Way and Its Power* (Boston and New York, 1942), 153 and 205: "Rear them, but do not lay claim to them." "Control them, but never lean upon them."

In this connection, see also Liang, "Hsien-Ch'in cheng-chih ssu-hsiang shih," YPSHC-CC 13:50.125 [A history of pre-Ch'in political thought] and a translation of this work under the mistranslated title, *History of Chinese Political Thought During the Early Tsin Period* (London, 1930), 104-105: "Real happiness comes in life from doing a thing for the mere doing of it. . . In such matters as food and clothing it is possible to answer the question 'why?'. For things in the spiritual realm it is impossible to answer the question 'why?' "

[36] Liang, "Mei-shu yü k'o-hsüeh," YPSHC-WC 13:38.11 [Art and science].

[37] Liang, "Jen-sheng-kuan yü k'o-hsüeh," YPSWC 68.4b-5 [The philosophy of life and science]. For the same distinction, see also Liang, "Kuan-yü hsüan-hsüeh k'o-hsüeh lun-chan chih 'chan-shih kuo-chi kung-fa'," YPSWC 68.5b-6b ['Rules of war' for the polemical battle between metaphysics and science]. For a criticism of Liang for making this distinction, see Ya-tung t'u-shu-kuan (publ.), *K'o-hsüeh yü jen-sheng-kuan* [Science and the philosophy of life] (Shanghai, 1923), 7-8. Here, in his preface to this symposium, Ch'en Tu-hsiu flatly disputes

of man, but he means the world. Reason and emotion, combination and transcendence—Europe and China.

Matter and spirit:

How can we harmonize the spiritual and material life? . . . Material life is merely a means for the maintenance of spiritual life; it should never be taken as substitute for the object which it serves. . . Yet there is no denial of the fact that men are now subject to the oppression of material forces to a degree unparalleled in history. The progress of scientific knowledge we cannot obstruct and should not obstruct; but it has resulted in excessive material development, thus increasing the power of materialism far beyond reasonable proportions. It is of course foolish to dilate on spiritual value and ignore the present state of material development. It is equally wrong to think that materialism is the key to everything. . . In European nations today, the tendency is to regard life solely as material development, with the result that, no matter how plausible the contrivances, the malady only becomes worse. . . Our problem is, under the conditions of this unprecedented scientific progress, how can the Confucian ideal of equilibrium be applied so that every man may live a balanced life. . .[38]

Here, then, is the new syncretism. China's responsibility is to accept an infusion of Western culture and to contribute its own to the West.[39] Admittedly, this program does not seem particularly new; it was explicit in the "inflationary distortion" of Confucianism which we found in Liang's earliest writings. But there is a difference, below the surface. Now, instead of thinking that the

Liang's claim that reason (science) is barred from any realm of existence. Emotion, he says, is stimulated by the external material world. Ideas have a material foundation and therefore are subject to law. For the social scientist there must be only considerations of fact, not considerations of value. In the same symposium, T'ang Yüeh, "I-ko ch'ih-jen ti shuo-meng" [An idiot's dream] also takes issue with these essays of Liang's. The title of T'ang's essay is derived from Liang's epithet for the effort to explain the emotions by scientific method.

[38] Liang, "Hsien-Ch'in cheng-chih ssu-hsiang shih," 182-183, and its translation, *History of Chinese Political Thought During the Early Tsin Period*, 139-140.

[39] Liang, "Li-shih shang Chung-hua kuo-min shih-yeh chih ch'eng-pai chi chin-hou ko-chin chih chi-yün," YPSWC 67.16b [Successes and failures in the historic task of the Chinese people and the chance of advances in the future]; Liang, "Ou yu hsin-ying lu chieh-lu," 29 and 30b.

Western contribution was of so high an order that sanction for it must be found in Chinese tradition, Liang could believe that what the West brought to China was of a lower order than what China had inherited from itself. Yet syncretism is still necessary. Matter needs spirit, spirit needs matter. And China needs Europe, not only to make itself whole, but to make itself look grand in comparison.

Persistence of Earlier Rationalizations

Since Liang had found this way to justify to China its irresistible invasion by the modern West, he never carried his deprecation of science and materialism to the point of rehabilitating the Western Middle Ages. Europeans who shared his disillusionment with the idea of progress might become medievalists, but Liang still talked of the "dark ages," when culture was at a standstill and political disturbances were endemic.[40] This is a perfectly understandable point of view. When Chinese civilization can be deemed superior to modern Western civilization, then China's position in relation to the West is secure all along the line, if only the modern West's superiority over the earlier West be reaffirmed. One way of implicitly reaffirming it was a familiar way for Liang: Chinese history up to the present, he said in 1921, corresponds to the European dark ages; now China moves into its own Renaissance.[41]

What have we here? Can Liang, the spokesman for spiritual China, so lightly dismiss the old China, the unwesternized China which must have created the spirituality? He can, because he knows that he can always call it back. When Western-style innovations must be accepted, Liang makes them acceptable, on the one hand, by questioning their value; in that case, the dichotomy of matter and spirit being invoked, the comparison is always between China and the West. But insofar as acceptance of the innovations implies a certain acknowledgment of their value,

[40] Liang, "Li-shih shang Chung-hua kuo-min shih-yeh chih ch'eng-pai chi chin-hou ko-chin chih chi yün," 9.
[41] *Ibid.*, 11.

Liang is ready with another trick, a new comparison (an old comparison): medieval versus modern. The existence or nonexistence of the scientific spirit, he says, when he wants to commend the scientific spirit to China, is a criterion of distinction only between new and old, not between West and East.[42] Europe takes the blame for the modern world. History takes the credit.

Thus, China becomes at least equivalent to Europe either because it is different or because it is the same. What one rationalization leaves out, the other supplies, and Liang, who spent much of his time in his last decade denouncing Western ideas, spent much of the rest of it searching for Chinese parallels and precedents. He found some for the ideas of Smith, Russell, Luther, Kant, Rousseau, James, Dewey, Hobbes, Locke, Jesus; for democracy, internationalism, socialism, and the scientific spirit itself.[43] Occasionally he made his old warning against this, his old practice. It was a strained analogy, he said, to relate the abdications of Yao and Shun to democracy.[44] The *ching-t'ien* system was a dead issue, pertaining to the time of the Chou Dynasty, not to modern times.[45] We know from Liang's earlier history that such refusals

[42] Liang, "K'o-hsüeh ching-shen yü tung-hsi wen-hua," YPSWC 68.15 [The scientific spirit and eastern and western cultures].

[43] Liang, "Hsien-Ch'in cheng-shih ssu-hsiang," YPSWC 40b [Pre-Ch'in political thought]; Liang, "Lao-tzu che-hsüeh," 12b; Liang, "Ming Ch'ing chih chiao Chung-kuo ssu-hsiang-chieh chi ch'i tai-piao jen wu," YPSWC 64.20b-22 [The Chinese thought-world and its representatives during the period of transition from Ming to Ch'ing], and translation under the title, "An Outline of the Chinese Cultural History of the Last Three Centuries," CSPSR VIII, 3 (July 1924), 39-42; Liang, "Yen-Li hsüeh-p'ai yü hsien-tai chiao-yü ssu-hu," 24b; Liang, "Hsien-Ch'in cheng-chih ssu hsiang shih" and trans., *History of Chinese Political Thought During the Early Tsin Period, passim;* Liang, "Shih-shih tsa-lun," 76.1b; Liang, "Li-shih shang Chung-hua kuo-min shih-yeh chih ch'eng-pai chin-hou ko-chin chih chi-yün," 11-12; Liang, "Ou yu hsin-ying lu chieh-lu," 74.18b and 72.26b; Liang, "Ju-chia che-hsüeh," YPSHC-CC 24:103.10 [The Confucian philosophy]; Liang, "Tai Tung-yüan sheng-jih erh-pai nien chi-nien hui yüan-ch'i," YPSWC 65.1b [The origin of the meeting commemorating the two hundredth anniversary of the birth of Tai Chen]; Liang, "Mo-ching chiao-shih," YPSHC-CC 10:38.1 [Revised commentary on the Mo-tzu book].

[44] Liang, "Chung-kuo li-shih yen-chiu fa pu-pien," YPSHC-CC 23:99.15 [Methods of studying Chinese history—a supplement].

[45] Liang, "Hsü-lun shih-min yü yin-hsing," YPSHC-WC 13; 37.40 [Supplementary discussion of citizens and banks].

to exploit the Chinese past do not preclude a nationalistic assertion of Chinese equivalence with the West. But Liang was ready
to defend again the reputation of Chinese culture, as he had always
wished to do, and for the most part now it was a cultural equivalence which he openly proclaimed, with new rationalizations and
with old, enabling China to look down on the West and to climb
to its place on the Western pedestal.

Liang's Hostility to Communism

Another old attitude which Liang retained was hostility to
revolution. As in the past, his protest against social evils was exclusively reformist. During the early years of the Republic, he
savagely excoriated the gentry-literati-official class, but he chastised
only to improve, not to replace these "natural leaders of society."[46]
After the Bolshevik triumph in Russia, when Marxism and the
Communist Party came to China, he was still unsympathetic with
revolutionary ideas.

It was not only that he distrusted the Soviet Union;[47] he felt
that, by any Marxist criteria, China was far from being in a revolutionary situation. For one thing, the class system had disappeared
long ago in China, so that at present no class struggle could exist.[48]
The West, preaching equality, had never known it—witness
Athenian slavery, Christian intolerance, American lynching, British oppression of the Irish, Russian class-domination. But China,

[46] Liang, "Tso-kuan yü mou-sheng," YPSWC 48.21-26 [Being an official and
planning to make a living]; Liang, "T'ung-ting tsui-yen," 41b-42, and its translation, "Afterthoughts," NR XVIII, 5, 91; Liang, "Ta Chung-hua fa-k'an-tz'u," 81,
and its translation, "The Future of China," NR XVII, 8, 131.

[47] See Liang, "Ju-chia che-hsüeh," 8, where he states that in Russia, allegedly
the land of "workers and peasants," everything is controlled by a small group,
and Liang, "Fu Liu Mien-i shu lun tui O-men t'i," YPSHC-WC 15:42.66-67
[Reply to Liu Mien-i's book on the Soviet question], where he calls the Soviet
Union imperialistic. Russia is trying, he says, to supplant private capitalism by
tate capitalism, which has many times the power of the former system to invade
ind to exert pressure abroad.

[48] Liang, "Hsien-Ch'in cheng-chih ssu-hsiang shih," 3, and its translation,
History of Chinese Political Thought During the Early Tsin Period, 9.

ever since the period of the Warring States (ending 221 B.C.), had been a country of genuine, manifest equality. Class distinctions elsewhere had arisen out of pride of blood and zeal for religious oppression; since these points of view were alien to the Chinese, a Chinese class-system had not been constituted.[49]

Nevertheless, although he argued in this fashion that China had missed the poison of class in the past, he acknowledged that a change was at hand. Modern class-systems were based not on racial or religious but on economic grounds, and China would have to face up to the problem sometime.[50] But it was to be sometime in the future. The life-or-death issue for China now was not between the unpropertied class and the propertied but between the unarmed (China) and the armed.[51] Chinese society was pre-industrial, pre-capitalist; socialistic theories did not apply, because no proletariat existed. For China to concern itself with a labor movement now would be like studying marriage problems in primary school.[52]

With this piquant analogy, Liang underscored an old conviction of his, reiterated now, that increased production, not better distribution, was China's most pressing concern. Both a capitalist class and a laboring class had yet to be created, and China, with the sad example of the industrialization of Europe before it, should work for a spirit of mutual aid between them. There was nothing intrinsically good about revolution; it was only the consequence of failure to achieve equity by other means.[53]

And, in the last analysis, could China ever live under socialism? Chinese historical experience, said Liang, has been one of negative regulation, not of positive assistance by government to any process

[49] Liang, "Li-shih shang Chung-hua kuo-min shih-yeh chih ch'eng-pai chi chin-hou ko-chin chih chi-yün," 12-12b.

[50] *Ibid.*, 13.

[51] Liang, "Shih-shih tsa-lun," 76.17b-18.

[52] Liang, "Ou yu hsin-ying lu chieh-lu," 72.26b-27; Liang, "Shih-shih tsa-lun," 75.36b and 76.35.

[53] Liang, "Ou yu hsin-ying lu chieh-lu," 72.27-27b; Liang, "Shih-shih tsa-lun," 75.41 and 75.37b-38.

P

of development. The character of the Chinese people is such that it resists government intervention. The new political life of China must be founded on this fact.

Therefore, the dream of the last few decades, that of fostering a policy on the German and Japanese model, has already failed completely, because it ran counter to the national character. From now on, if we desire to transplant to China the centralized socialism conceived of by Marx and put into practice by Lenin, then it, too, I venture to say, because it runs counter to the national character, must fail in the end.[54]

The Area of Agreement between Liang and the Communists

Yet, for all the difference in their views on China, Liang and the Communists had some strikingly similar ideas about Europe.[55] Liang admitted freely that movements of social protest were warranted in the West, and he implicated capitalism in the war. Capitalists stir up war, he said, when their interests demand it. They try always to keep the workers' wages at the lowest possible level and their hours at the highest.[56]

The most pressing problem in the West, he felt, was the betterment of the lot of the proletariat.[57] There, class warfare was rife, a hopeless disease; indeed the whole of Western history could be summed up as a history of class warfare.[58] Under cover of extraterritoriality, foreign nations were bringing to China the horrors of their capitalistic system.[59]

[54] Liang, "Li-shih shang Chung-hua kuo-min shih-yeh chih ch'eng-pai chi chin-hou ko-chin chih chi-yün," 13b-14.

[55] About China, too, there was some agreement, in regard to means if not to ends. The Communists, during their period of collaboration with the Kuo-min tang (1924-1927), believed, officially, that imperialism was their first enemy. They, like Liang, saw the primary issue as that between "the armed and the unarmed."

[56] Liang, "Ou yu hsin-ying lu chieh-lu," 72.5b-7.

[57] Liang, "Shih-shih tsa-lun," 75.32b.

[58] Liang, "Chung-kuo li-shih yen-chiu fa pu-pien," 126; Liang, "Wei kai-yüeh wen-t'i ching-kao yu-pang," YPSHC-WC 14:41.110 [A respectful warning to friendly powers on the treaty-revision question]; Liang, "Shih-shih tsa-lun," 76.17.

[59] Liang, "Wei Hu-an ching-kao Ou-Mei p'eng-yu," YPSHC-WC 15:42.6 [A re-

Liang, then, was just as ready as the Communists to consign the West to revolution. Western society was sick, and something had to be done for it. But if that something was revolution, and both Liang and the Communists agreed that it could be, how was this revolution to be understood? To Communists, it was a cure for disease. Liang saw it in a different light. Where the materialistic, mechanistic view of life prevails, he wrote (and we recognize here the "diseased West"), a revolutionary proletariat, gaining power, would live just as the modern financial and military titans do, by the same disastrous rule: *Jo jou ch'iang shih,* "the weak are meat, the strong eat."[60] To Liang, Western revolution was not a cure but only a treatment, interesting and welcome, to him, not because it was effective but because it was symbolic. Social protest in the West was a proof that Western civilization was in distress. Revolution on the European model was not a prescription for China, but a sign that China, once thought to be ailing because not westernized, was perhaps not so sick at all.

Thus, just as the European war could be used by Liang to rehabilitate the reputation of Chinese culture, so could he use the Russian Revolution and the other European revolutions which threatened. They enabled him to claim with a new justification the equivalence of China and the West. Western revolution helped Liang to contemplate Chinese westernization. Chinese Communism, as our Introduction has suggested, got similar help. The Communist criticism of Western civilization made it intellectually easier for traditionalists to defend old China and psychologically easier for iconoclasts to desert it.

Liang appreciated the symbolic in Communism—the indication that the West, which developed it, was in distress. Chinese Communists appreciated both symbol and substance—the doctrines which, they felt, would renovate China. But Liang and the

---

spectful warning to our European and American friends concerning the Shanghai affair]; Liang, "Tui Ou-Mei yu-pang chih hsüan-yen," YPSHC-WC 15:42.10 [Statement to the friendly powers of Europe and America].

[60] Liang, "Ou yu hsin-ying lu chieh-lu," 72.10.

Communists, with different answers, met the same Chinese question. Liang and the Communists, contemporaries, stood simultaneously on the same Chinese ground.

Liang and the Pro-Western Liberals

A third group stood with them, a group which, without benefit of the comforts of Communism, rejected Chinese civilization. Liang, in the 1920's, made his adjustment to inevitable westernization by disparaging the West. The Communists made theirs by disparaging the nonrevolutionary West and traditional China. But non-Communist liberals, like Hu Shih, who had been one of the principal contributors to the avant-garde magazine, *Hsin Ch'ingnien,* took refuge in neither "Chinese spirituality" nor "capitalistic decay." They disparaged only China. What kind of a Chinese adjustment could that be?

"My Attitude toward Modern Western Civilization," a postwar essay by Hu Shih, begins:

Today the most baseless and, moreover, the most poisonous legend is the deprecation of western civilization as merely "materialistic" and the honoring of eastern civilization as "spiritual." This is fundamentally a very old view, but today it seems to be having a new vogue...

And Hu then mentions the effect of the First World War on the Chinese mind.[61] As Hu describes it, it is precisely the effect which we have seen the war have on Liang.

Elsewhere in Hu's writings, Liang was expressly named as the villain in the piece. He condemned Liang's account of his European travels for its strictures on science and its report of European disillusionment with science. Ever since the publication of this work, said Hu, Chinese respect for science had been greatly diminished. Old-fashioned traditionalists, who had kept their interests strictly and parochially Chinese, now cried out gleefully,

---

[61] Hu Shih, *Hu Shih wen-ts'un san-chi* [Collected essays of Hu Shih, third collection] (Shanghai, 1930), I, 3.

"Science is bankrupt! Liang Ch'i-ch'ao has said so!" Had Liang
said so? The latter had protested that this extreme conclusion was
not his, that he meant merely that science was not all-powerful.
But Hu refused to accept this disavowal. The damage had been
done. Liang, it must be said, had given the aid of his awe-inspir-
ing reputation to the forces opposed to science in China.[62]

Hu Shih's faith in Western civilization, his challenge to Liang,
was expressed simply: the civilization which substitutes the machine for human labor is infinitely more spiritual than civilizations which still use men as beasts of burden.[63] Though his words
would have been different, the prewar Liang could have agreed
with this. Indeed, in 1912, remarking on Watt's invention of the
steam engine, he had noted with obvious approval the substitu-
tion of machine power for human power.[64] But Liang had
changed, and Hu Shih had not followed him.

Yet, Hu had changed, too. We have seen, in the Introduction,
that an idea changes when its alternatives change. For not only
what he says but what he leaves unsaid defines a man's position.
Hu, living as a contemporary of Liang, is not only Hu; he is
not-Liang. His idea is given a certain particular quality by virtue
of the fact that some other idea is demonstrably an alternative.
And when Liang changes, not-Liang changes. Hu need not
budge; as in a Taoist parable, he proceeds without moving. A new
meaning pervades his old thought in the postwar period, for he
thinks now in a new world of possibilities.

In order to feel that they were not deserting China, the prewar
Liang and his prewar fellow westernizers, whatever their generation and however they had come to their beliefs, had held one
simple, uneasy conviction. The conviction was that their choice
lay not between two concretenesses, Europe and China, but between two abstractions, the new and the old. Why should China
not modernize with as little embarrassment as anyone else? Un-

---

[62] *K'o-hsüeh yü jen-sheng-kuan*, 3-7.
[63] Wang Chi-chen (tr.), xix-xx.
[64] Liang, "Ch'u kuei-kuo yen-shuo-tz'u," 28.

fortunately, however, modernization was faintly embarrassing for China, because no amount of verbiage could smother the fact that "the new" was an extension of European history and a break with the Chinese. Hence, Liang returned, after the war, to a frank choice between China and Europe.

Just because he did this, the unwavering westernizers found their alternatives shifting too—not, it is true, like Liang's, but to another pair of abstractions: the false and the true. If the China which the Chinese must not desert was the spiritual China of Liang's late works, then Hu could feel that he was not deserting China at all, but a dream. a fantasy, a lie. When the traditionalist can be accused of speaking cant (and Liang could be accused out of his own mouth),[65] the clear-eyed, unsentimental critic is asserting primarily not the failure of China but the integrity of his own mind, not the dependence of China but the independence of himself. A westernizer who fails to prize China over the West may see himself prizing not the West over China but *Wahrheit über Alles*. One Chinese gains self-respect by believing a questionable doctrine; but the Chinese who denies this doctrine is not thereby consigned to humiliation. For intellectual honesty is itself an avenue to self-respect.

[65] In 1915, before the time came when others might write similarly of him, he wrote: "If one wishes to fight the blaze of the new learning and the new polity, it is difficult to do so with plain talk; frequently, then, one borrows the 'moral question' in order to stamp them out. One links, for this purpose, the 'moral question' with the 'revive-the-old' question." See Liang, "Fu-ku ssu-hu p'ing-i," 20.

The fact that the later Liang had reversed his earlier position and was himself injecting the "moral question" into the controversy about the respective values of the Chinese and Western civilizations was noted by Yang Ming-chai, a contemporary critic who felt that Liang's postwar polemics were not intellectually respectable. In a detailed criticism of Liang's *History of Chinese Political Thought in the Pre-Ch'in Period*, he observed that Liang was no longer the thinker who, in his prewar concern for national success, had been moved to discover a Chinese "bushido"; now, the war and his postwar European travels and impressions had impelled him to rediscover the nonmilitaristic Chinese way. Yang paid special attention to Liang's errors of fact and of interpretation of Chinese and European history and to his use of verbal jugglery. See Yang Ming-chai, *P'ing Chung-Hsi wen-hua kuan* [A critique of views on Chinese and Western civilization] (Peiping, 1924), 107-191, esp. 110-111.

But an idea, we have said, depends for its significance as much upon what it denies as upon what it affirms. No man can take a special satisfaction in speaking what he thinks is true unless he thinks he hears the false spoken. Someone must man the shaky defenses so that someone else, whose stake in victory is just as high, may be above the battle. Liang's position, a possible postwar Chinese position, simply by existing as a target to be riddled made Hu's position possible, Chinese, and contemporaneous.

As it was, however, the non-Communist westernizers were riding a tight wire. The Communists could criticize Liang as well as they;[66] and the Communists, while enjoying, like Hu, the satisfaction of fancying that they were telling the truth no matter what it cost, had the further satisfaction of knowing that it cost them little. The communistic theory which led them to deal so coldly with Chinese civilization was no respecter of non-Communist Western civilization. Liang's theory, too, contriving to let China swallow industrialism and science, was able to sweeten the pill. Only he who rejected both these theories took his Westernism plain and not glossed over. He might call himself, proudly, a man; but such men could not be numerous. When one civilization is losing ground to another, adherents of the first, for the most part, will cling to their individuality as they feel it passing from them. Universality is not enough. A modern Chinese will find some way to call himself, proudly, Chinese.

Therefore, with its own old civilization in full process of dissolution, postwar China, rather than aver that light came from the West, preferred to believe that Western civilization was damned for its materialism or doomed for its capitalism. Of these two positions, Liang's, the first, was stranger than Communism to the youth that had passed through the May Fourth Movement. Liang had once found for them pastures new, outside Chinese tradition, and they had been so cleanly delivered from that tradition as to stir up openly the most untraditional of Chinese conflicts, the conflict of generations. New youth was not to be ruled

[66] See, for example, Ch'en Tu-hsiu in *K'o-hsüeh yü jen-sheng-kuan*, 7-9.

by old age. And while Liang looked back, the Communists looked forward.

Some two decades earlier, with great difficulty, Liang had begun to loose himself from the bonds of tradition. Others had taken from him their intellectual independence. But these others, the young students of this new generation, having missed his early pain at wrenching the self away from tradition, missed his postwar compulsion to reconstitute the tie. Traditional China had lost them. And Hu's position, as we have indicated, a possible rival to Communism in the radical criticism of traditional China, was cursed with psychological inadequacy. That is why the coming general triumph of Communism in China was foreshadowed in the 1920's; for in that decade, the desertion of the intellectuals to Communism became assured, and it began.

Conclusion

When the movement began, Liang's last ideas and Chinese Communism, formally distinct, had their brief moment of historical union. They were truly contemporaneous then, equally vital, drawing their common life from a real and common problem. But as time passed, and the distintegration of traditional Chinese society became ever more irreversible, Liang's ideas proceeded towards anachronism. The wheel had come full circle for Liang; for his first syncretism, which had set him on the road to his last, had been an effort to make Confucianism relevant to the actual world of which China was a part rather than to a by-gone world which was China alone.

When orthodox Confucianists of the nineties saw the Reform Movement simply as a new phase of a traditional battle between the Confucian "rule of virtue" and the Legalist "rule of law," when they identified Western invasions with the earlier, "traditional," barbarian invasions, their wisdom was but the knowledge of dead secrets. A new civilization was flooding into China, and Liang had known, in his early years, that Confucius must either preside over the process or be drowned in it.

But the Jesuits had known that, as for their intrusion, Confucius would either preside over it or block it. Somewhere, then, in the course of the years between Matteo Ricci and Liang Ch'i-ch'ao, Confucianism had lost the initiative. The orthodox Confucianists, standing still, had been moving towards oblivion. In the beginning, their idea was a force, the product and the intellectual prop of a living society. In the end it was a shade, living only in the minds of many, treasured in the mind for its own sake after the society which had produced it and which needed it had begun to dissolve away.

Liang's was one of the minds which treasured it. Confucianism, like any idea, although it originated in a social situation, defied change in the situation and persisted on the strength of some nonutilitarian appeal of its own. Yet, an idea's independence of the objective reality which it purports to mirror is never complete and always uneasy. Facts strain against loyalties, mind is drawn back to nature. The young Liang Ch'i-ch'ao knew this strain and this pull, and these are what made him as we introduced him— intellectually alienated and emotionally tied to his tradition.

The tie, though sometimes hidden, was never lost. But the tradition dies of his alienation, his and so many others'.

THE CONTROVERSY OVER THE AUTHENTICITY OF THE CONFUCIAN CLASSICS

THE CLASSICS CONTROVERSY had begun with a dispute over the authenticity of the *Shu-ching*, the Book of History. Traditional opinion on the *Shu-ching* had been stated definitively in a seventh-century work, the *Shang-shu cheng-i* of K'ung Ying-ta (574-648): Confucius compiled the *Shu-ching* in one hundred sections. It disappeared in the burning of the books (213 B.C.). Under the Emperor Wen of the Han (179-157) an old man named Fu-sheng recited from memory twenty-nine sections of the *Shu-ching*, which were transcribed with the characters used at that time. This was the *chin-wen* (modern character) version.

In the last years of the second century or the first years of the first century B.C., K'ung An-kuo worked on another *Shu-ching*, written in archaic characters and reputedly discovered in a wall of Confucius' house. There were serious discrepancies between the two texts. K'ung's recension is known as the *ku-wen* (ancient character) version.

The history of the *Shu-ching* is difficult to follow in the troubles of the third century. Finally, under Emperor Yüan of the Eastern Chin (317-323), a scholar named Mei Tse presented to the throne a *Shu-ching* with preface and commentary which he certified to be the *ku-wen Shu-ching* with the authentic preface and commentary of K'ung An-kuo. This text, with this preface and commentary, has been transmitted, with but few alterations in detail, down to the present.

The question arises of the source of K'ung An-kuo's text. The Han historian Ssu-ma Ch'ien says only that "the K'ung family possessed it." The most ancient text which tells the story of its discovery in the wall (and the unearthing there of other *ku-wen*

221

texts) is a letter of Liu Hsin, written just before the beginning of the Christian era and inserted in Pan Ku's *Ch'ien-Han shu*. At the time of the writing of this letter, in the reign of the Emperor Ai (6-1), Liu Hsin had just succeeded his father as imperial librarian. Liu Hsin's letter and his catalogue of the Han imperial library, both given in résumé by Pan Ku, show that in the Han archives, among the *ku-wen*, was also preserved a manuscript of the *Ch'un-ch'iu* with a commentary to which the *Tso-chuan* corresponds.[1]

At the beginning of the Eastern Han dynasty (A.D. 25-220), believers in the authenticity of the *ku-wen* classics were very few. However, by the end of the dynasty, the great scholars Ma Yung (79-166), Cheng Hsüan (127-200), Chia K'uei (30-101), and Fu Ch'ien, partisans of the *ku-wen*, had won the field. Ho Hsiu (129-182), who upheld the authenticity of the *Kung-yang chuan* against the *Tso-chuan*, was the strongest *chin-wen* champion. But with Cheng Hsüan's counterblasts, followed by those of Tu Yü (222-284) and Wang Su (195-256), the *chin-wen* school was routed. The T'ang commentators Lu Te-ming and K'ung Ying-ta followed Cheng and Wang. With the Sung dynasty, the classics were reëdited by Cheng I (1033-1107), Chu Hsi (1130-1200), and others, and the Han and T'ang commentaries fell into desuetude.[2]

With the beginning of the Ch'ing dynasty there was an increasing tendency to search the past. A group of scholars known as the *P'u-hsüeh* (school of unadorned learning), the first of the *Han-hsüeh* literati, advocated textual research in preference to literary elegance or philosophical speculation. Troubled by China's weakness in the late Ming period, they felt that the dead hand of Sung neo-Confucianism must be shaken off. They preferred to probe further into the past and interpret the classics with the commentaries of the Han *ku-wen* scholars.

---

[1] This discussion of the textual problem is drawn from P. Pelliot, "Le Chou King en caractères anciens et le Chang Chou Che Wen," *Mémoires concernant l'Asie Orientale* (1916), 123-177.

[2] Liang, "Ch'ing-tai hsüeh-shu kai-lun," 52-53.

This does not sound like a promising beginning for a movement to break the crust of orthodoxy. But the new research in
Han scholarship served to revive the controversy which had died
centuries before. Before long, revolt began against the rule of the
P'u-hsüeh. Yen Jo-chü (1636-1704) launched classical scholarship
on its last great phase with his epoch-making *Shang-shu ku-wen
shu-ching* [Inquiry into the authenticity of the Book of History in
ancient characters] which proved the extant *Shu-ching* a forgery
by Wang Su. He was without a successor in the field for many
decades. Finally Chuang Ts'un-yü (1719-1788) stressed the importance of the *Kung-yang* commentary, and the way was paved
for the revival of the *chin-wen* school of criticism.

His pupil and grandson, Liu Feng-lu (1776-1829) studied Ho
Hsiu's work on the *Kung-yang chuan.* In his great work on the
Tso-chuan, the *Tso-shih ch'un-ch'iu k'ao-cheng,* he presented evidence that Liu Hsin had had a hand in its rearrangement, to
make it follow the chronological order of the *Ch'un-ch'iu.* Wei
Yüan (1794-1856), in his *Shih ku-wei,* attacked the traditional
Mao commentary on the *Shih-ching;* his *Shu ku-wei* refuted the
views of Ma Yung and Cheng Hsüan on the *Shu-ching.* And
Shao I-ch'en (1810-1861), in the *Li-ching t'ung-lun,* maintained
that the *ku-wen Li-chi* (Book of Rites) in the *I* recension was another Liu Hsin forgery.[3]

Liang, in his summary of Ch'ing scholarship, pointed out that
the *chin-wen* school, in its first phase, was concerned only with the
Kung-yang commentary. Through works on individual classics,
the family relationships between the disputed texts became clear,
and the authenticity of one determined the authenticity of all.

[3] Su-ch'ih, "Chin-tai Chung-kuo hsüeh-shu-shih shang chih Liang Jen-kung
hsien-sheng," HH 67 (January, 1929), 2-3 [Mr. Liang Ch'i-ch'ao's role in the
intellectual history of modern China]; Hummel, *passim.*

BIBLIOGRAPHY

1. *Chinese and Japanese*

Chao Erh-hsün *et al.* (eds.), *Ch'ing-shih kao* [Draft history of the Ch'ing dynasty], 536 chüan, Peiping, 1924-1928.

Chao Feng-t'ien, "K'ang Ch'ang-su hsien-sheng nien-p'u kao" [A draft chronological sketch of the life of K'ang Yu-wei], SHNP II, 1 (September 1934), 173-240.

Ch'en Ch'iu, "Wu-hsü cheng-pien shih fan-pien-fa jen-wu chih cheng-chih ssu-hsiang" [The political thought of the anti-reformists during the 'Hundred Days of Reform'], YCHP 25 (June, 1939), 59-106.

Ch'en Kung-fu, *Chung-kuo ko-ming shih* [History of the Chinese Revolution], Shanghai, 1930.

Ch'en Tuan-chih, *Wu-ssu yün-tung shih ti p'ing-chia* [An appraisal of the history of the May Fourth Movement], 2nd ed., Shanghai, 1936.

Ch'en T'ung-sheng (ed.), *Kuang-hsü cheng-yao* [Important documents of the Kuang-hsü reign], 34 chüan, Shanghai, 1908.

Chia I-chün, *Chung-hua min-kuo shih* [History of the Chinese Republic], Peiping, 1930.

Chiang Fu-lin, "Chang T'ai-yen yü Liang Jen-kung" [Chang Ping-lin and Liang Ch'i-ch'ao], TF 79 (1940), 2561-2562.

Ch'ien Chi-po, *Hsien-tai Chung-kuo wen-hsüeh shih* [History of contemporary Chinese literature], Shanghai, 1933.

Ch'ien Mu, "Liu Hsiang Hsin fu-tzu nien-p'u" [Chronological lives of Liu Hsiang and Liu Hsin, father and son], YCHP 7 (June 1930), 1189-1318.

Chin Kuo-pao, *Chung-kuo pi-chih wen-t'i* [The monetary problem in China], Shanghai, 1928.

Chu Ch'i-hua, *Chung-kuo chin-tai she-hui-shih chieh-p'ou* [Anatomy of modern Chinese social history], Shanghai, 1933.

Chu Shou-p'eng (ed.), *Kuang-hsü tung-hua hsü-lu* [Kuang-hsü supplement to the archival records], 64 ts'e, Shanghai, 1908.

Feng Tzu-yu, *Chung-hua min-kuo k'ai-kuo-ch'ien ko-ming shih* [History of the revolution prior to the establishment of the Chinese Republic], 2 vols., 2nd ed., Chungking, 1944.

Feng Tzu-yu, *Ko-ming i-shih* [Historical reminiscences of the revolution], 3 vols., Chungking, 1943.

Hsü Ch'i-ch'ing, *Tseng-k̲ai tsui-chin Shang-hai chin-jung shih* [History of the Shanghai money market in recent times], revised ed., 3rd printing, 1932.

Hu Shih, *Hu Shih wen-ts'un san-chi* [Collected essays of Hu Shih, third collection], 4 vols., Shanghai, 1930.

―――― *Ssu-shih tzu-shu* [Autobiography at the age of forty], Shanghai, 1935.

Kao I-han, "Tu Liang Jen-kung ko-ming hsiang-ssu chih yüan li-lun" [On reading Liang Ch'i-ch'ao's basic theory of the propensity of revolution to perpetuate itself], *Hsin ch'ing-nien* I, 4 (December 15, 1915).

Ko Kung-chen, *Chung-k̲uo pao-hsüeh shih* [History of Chinese journalism], Shanghai, 1928.

Kuo Chan-po, *Chin wu-shih-nien Chung-k̲uo ssu-hsiang shih* [History of Chinese thought in the last fifty years], Peking, 1926.

Kuwabara Sadamasa, "Liang Ch'i-ch'ao Shi no *Chung-k̲uo li-shih yen-chiu fa* wo yomu" [On reading Mr. Liang Ch'i-ch'ao's *A Method of Studying Chinese History*], SG II, 12 (August 1922), 1-18.

Kuzū Yoshihisa, *Tōa senk̲aku shishi k̲iden* [Historical records of East Asian pioneer adventurers], 3 vols., Tokyo, 1933-1936.

Li Chien-nung, *Tsui-chin san-shih nien Chung-k̲uo cheng-chih-shih* [Political history of China in the last thirty years], Shanghai, 1930.

Liang Ch'i-ch'ao, *Yin-ping-shih ho-chi* [Collected works and essays of the Ice-Drinkers' Studio], 40 vols., Shanghai, 1936.

―――― *Yin-ping shih wen-chi* [Collected essays of the Ice-Drinkers' Studio], 80 chüan, 2nd ed., Shanghai, 1925.

Liu Hsi-sui, "Liang Jen-kung hsien-sheng chuan" [Liang Ch'i-ch'ao, a biographical sketch], TSKHCK IV, 1-2 (June 1929), 135-138.

Lo-su yüeh-k̲'an [The Russell monthly], I, Shanghai, 1921.

Ma Chen-tung, *Yüan-shih tang-k̲uo shih* [History of Yüan's regime], Shanghai, 1930.

Mai Chung-hua (ed.), *Nan-hai hsien-sheng wu-hsü tsou-k̲ao* [K'ang Yu-wei's memorials in 1898], place of publication not indicated (probably Shanghai), 1911.

Min Erh-ch'ang (ed.), *Pei-chuan chi-pu* [Supplement to the *Pei-chuan chi*], 60 chüan, Peiping, 1932.

Miyazaki Torazō (Tōten), *San-ju-san nen no yume* [Thirty-three years' dream], 2nd ed., Tokyo, 1926.

Ōkuma Kō hachi-ju-go nen shi hensan-kai [Collected papers for the life of Marquis Ōkuma], 3 vols., Tokyo, 1926.

Shumbō kō tsuijō kai (Prince Shumbō eulogy society), *Itō Hirobumi den* [Biography of Itō Hirobumi], 3 vols., 2nd ed., Tokyo, 1942.

Su-ch'ih (Chang Yin-lin), "Chin-tai Chung-kuo hsüeh-shu-shih shang chih Liang Jen-kung hsien-sheng" [Liang Ch'i-ch'ao's role in the intellectual history of modern China], HH 67 (January 1929), 1-8.

Sun Yat-sen, *Chung-shan ch'üan-shu* [Collected works of Sun Yat-sen], 4 vols., Shanghai, 1926.

Tsou Lu, *Chung-kuo Kuo-min tang shih-kao* [Draft history of the Kuomintang], 2 vols., Shanghai, 1929.

Wang Feng-yüan, *Chung-kuo hsin-wen-hsüeh yün-tung shu-p'ing* [Critical account of the new-literature movement in China], Peiping, 1935.

Wu Ch'i-ch'ang, *Liang Ch'i-ch'ao*, Chungking, 1945.

Ya-tung t'u-shu-kuan (publ.), *K'o-hsüeh yü jen-sheng-kuan* [Science and the philosophy of life], 2 vols., Shanghai, 1923.

Yang Ming-chai, *P'ing Chung-Hsi wen-hua kuan* [A critique of views on Chinese and Western civilizations], Peking, 1924.

Yano Jinichi, "Bojutsu no hempō oyobi seihen" [The reform and political change of 1898], SR 8 (1923), 54-67, 212-226, 443-462.

Yeh Ch'ang-ch'ih, *Yüan-tu lu jih-chi* [Yüan-tu lu diary], 16 chüan, Shanghai, 1933.

Yeh Te-hui (ed.), *I-chiao ts'ung-pien* [Compilation of miscellaneous papers in support of orthodox doctrine], 6 chüan, place of publication not indicated, 1898.

2. Western

Britton, Roswell S., *The Chinese Periodical Press 1800-1912*, Shanghai, 1933.

Cameron, Meribeth E., *The Reform Movement in China, 1898-1912*, Palo Alto, California, 1931.

Chafkin, S. H., "Modern Business in China: The Bank of China before 1935," *Papers on China* (mimeograph), II, Committee on International and Regional Studies, Harvard University, 1948.

Chapin, Frederic L. and Kates, Charles O., "Homer Lea and the Chinese Revolution" (manuscript).

Chen, Stephen and Robert Payne, *Sun Yat-sen, a Portrait,* New York, 1946.

Chiang Monlin, *Tides from the West,* New Haven, 1947.

Ch'ien Tuan-sheng, *The Government and Politics of China,* Cambridge, 1950.

China Journal of Science and Arts, V, 1, (July, 1926).

Darroch, J., "Current Events as Seen Through the Medium of the Chinese Newspaper," CR XLIII, 1 (January 1912), 23-33.

d'Elia, Pascal M., "Un Maître de la jeune Chine: Liang K'i Tch'ao," TP XVIII (1917), 249-294.

Fairbank, J. K. and K. C. Liu, *Modern China, a Bibliographical Guide to Chinese Works, 1898-1937,* Cambridge, Massachusetts, 1950.

Forke, Alfred, "Ein chinesischer Kantverehrer," MSOS XII (1909), 210-219.

—— *Geschichte der Neuern Chinesischen Philosophie,* Hamburg, 1938.

Franke, O., "Die wichtigsten chinesischen Reformschriften vom Ende des neunzehnten Jahrhunderts," *Bulletin de l'Académie Impériale des Sciences de St-Pétersbourg,* fifth series, XVII (1902), 047-059.

—— *Ostasiatische Neubildungen,* Hamburg, 1911.

Glick, Carl, *Double Ten,* New York, 1945.

Glick, Carl, and Hong Sheng-hwa, *Swords of Silence,* New York, 1947.

Hay Tsou Chai, *La situation économique et politique de la Chine et ses perspectives d'avenir,* Louvain, 1921.

Hornbeck, Stanley K., *Contemporary Politics in the Far East,* New York, 1928.

Hu, H. H., "Ch'en San-li, the Poet," THM VI, 2 (February 1938), 134-143.

Hu Shih, "The Confucianist Movement in China," CSM IX, 7 (May 12, 1914), 533-536.

Hummel, Arthur W. (ed.), *Eminent Chinese of the Ch'ing Period,* 2 vols., Washington, 1943-1944.

Japan Chronicle, Kobe, 1905-1911.

Japan Weekly Chronicle, Kobe, 1902-1941.

Kiang Wen-han, *The Chinese Student Movement,* New York, 1948.

Kobe Chronicle, Kobe, 1898-1901.

Kotenev, Anatol M., *New Lamps for Old,* Shanghai, 1931.

Levy, Marion J., *The Family Revolution in Modern China,* Cambridge, Massachusetts, 1949.

Liang Ch'i-ch'ao, "Archaeology in China," *Smithsonian Report for 1927,* Washington, 1928, 453-466.

Liang Chi-chao, *Chinese Political Thought During the Early Tsin Period,* London, 1930.

Liang Ch'i-ch'ao, *"The So-called People's Will"* (*A Comment on the Secret Telegrams of the Yüan Government*), Shanghai, 1916 (English and Chinese texts).

Lin Yutang, *A History of the Press and Public Opinion in China,* Chicago, 1936.

Lynn, Jermyn Chi-Hung, *Political Parties in China,* Peking, 1930.

Ma Te-chih, *Le Mouvement réformiste et les événements de la cour de Pékin en 1898,* Lyon, 1934.

Macnair, Harley Farnsworth, *China in Revolution,* Chicago, 1931.

Martin, Bernard, *Strange Vigour: A Biography of Sun Yat Sen,* London, 1944.

Maybon, Albert, *La Politique chinoise,* Paris, 1908.

Morgan, Evan, *Wenli Styles and Chinese Ideals,* Shanghai, 1916.

National Review, Shanghai, 1910-1916.

North-China Herald and Supreme Court and Consular Gazette, Shanghai, 1870- .

Peking Gazette (published by *North-China Herald*), Shanghai, 1872-1899.

Pelliot, Paul, "Le Chou King en caractères anciens et le Chang Chou Che Wen," *Mémoires concernant l'Asie Orientale,* II (1916), 123-177.

Pollard, Robert T., *China's Foreign Relations,* New York, 1933.

Reichelt, Karl Ludwig, "A Conference of Chinese Buddhist Leaders," CR LIV, 11 (November 1923), 667-669.

Reichwein, Adolf, *China and Europe,* New York, 1925.

Richard, Timothy, *Forty-five Years in China,* New York, 1916.

Sharman, Lyon, *Sun Yat-sen, His Life and Its Meaning,* New York, 1934.

Soothill, William E., *Timothy Richard of China,* London, 1924.

T'ang Leang-li, *The Inner History of the Chinese Revolution,* London, 1930.

The Week in China, Peking, 1926-1932.

Tseng Yu-hao, *Modern Chinese Legal and Political Philosophy,* Shanghai, 1930.

Tsu, Y. Y., "Spiritual Tendencies of the Chinese People as Shown Outside of the Christian Church Today," CR LVI, 12 (December 1925), 777-782.

Tsung Hyui-puh (Hui-po), "Chinese Translations of Western Literature," CSPSR XII, 3 (July 1928), 369-378.

Valentin, Ferdinand, *L'Avénement d'une republique,* Paris, 1926.

Wen Ching, *The Chinese Crisis from Within,* London, 1901.

Wieger, Leon, *La Chine moderne* (Vol. I: "Prodromes"; Vol. V: "Nationalisme"), Hsien-hsien, 1931.

Wilhelm, Richard, "Intellectual Movements in Modern China," CSPSR VIII, 2 (April 1924), 110-124.

Woodbridge, Samuel I., *China's Only Hope* (Chang Chih-tung: *Ch'üan-hsüeh p'ien*), New York, 1900.

Woodhead, H. G. W. (ed.), *The China Year Book, 1926-1927,* Tientsin, 1927.

A-li-shih-to-te chih cheng-chih hsüeh-shuo 亞里士多德之政治學說

Ai 哀

Ai-kuo lun 愛國論

Aisin Gioro 愛新覺羅

An Hsiao-feng 安曉峯

Anhui 安徽

Anking 安慶

Baka 馬鹿

Bojutsu no hempō oyobi seihen 戊戌の變法及び政變

bushidō 武士道

Canton 廣東

Ch'a-k'an chü-tsou 查看具奏

Chang Chi 張繼

Chang Ch'ien 張騫

Chang Chih-tung 張之洞

Chang Chün-mai 張君邁

Chang Hsün 張勳

Chang T'ai-yen yü Liang Jen-kung 章太炎與梁任公

Chang Wen-hsiang kung ch'üan-chi 張文襄公全集

Chang Yin-huan 張蔭桓

Chang Yin-lin 張蔭麟

Chang Yüan-chi 張元濟

Changsha 長沙

Ch'ang she nü-hsüeh-t'ang ch'i 倡設女學堂啟

Ch'ang-hsing li 長興里

Ch'ang-yen pao 昌言報

Ch'angteh 常德

Chao Erh-hsün 趙爾巽

Chao Feng-t'ien 趙豐田

Ch'ao-hsien mieh-wang chih yüan-yin 朝鮮滅亡之原因

Che-hsüeh 哲學

Ch'en Ch'iu 陳螯

Ch'en Kung-fu 陳功甫

Ch'en Pao-chen 陳寶箴

Ch'en San-li 陳三立

Ch'en Shao-pai 陳少白
Ch'en Tu-hsiu 陳獨秀
Ch'en Tuan-chih 陳端志
Ch'en T'ung-fu 陳通甫
Cheng Ho 鄭和
Cheng Hsüan 奠玄
Cheng I 程頤
Cheng-ch'i hui 正氣會
Cheng-chih shang chih tui k'ang-li 政治上之對抗力
Cheng-chih yü jen-min 政治與人民
Cheng-chih-hsüeh hsüeh-li chih-yen 政治學學理摭
Cheng-chih-hsüeh ta-chia Po-lun-chih-li chih hsüeh-shuo
政治學大家伯倫知理之學說
Cheng-lun 政論
Cheng-p'ien yüan-yin ta k'e-nan 政變原因答客難
Cheng-wen she 政聞社
Cheng-wen she hsüan-yen 政聞社宣言
Cheng-yang 正陽
Ch'i Tiao-tzu 漆雕子
Chia I-chün 賈逸君
Chia K'uei 賈逵
Chia-jen ch'i-yü chi 佳人奇遇記
Chiang Fu-lin 姜馥森
Chiang K'ai-shek 蔣介石
Chiang-hsüeh she 講學社
Ch'iang hsüeh-hui 強學會
Ch'iang hsüeh-hui shu-chü 強學會書局
Ch'iang hsüeh-pao 強學報
Chieh ch'an-tsu hui hsü 戒纏足會敘
Chieh-jen 接人
Ch'ien Chi-po 錢基博
Ch'ien Mu 錢穆
Ch'ien-Han shu 前漢書
Chih pu k'o erh wei chu-i yü *wei erh pu yu* chu-i 「知不可
而為」主義與「為而不有」主義
Chih-kuo-hsüeh ti liang tiao ta-lu 治國學的兩條大路
Chihli 直隸
Chih-shen 治身
Chih-shih 執事
chih-shun 治順
Chih-tsao chü 製造局
Chih-tu chü 制度局
Chin 晉

231

Chin 金

Chin Kuo-pao 金國寶

Chin ti-li che 盡地立者

Chin wu-shih nien Chung-kuo ssu-hsiang shih 近五千年
中國思想史

Chin-hua lun ko-ming che Hsieh-te chih hsüeh-shuo 進化
論革命者頡德之學說

Chin-pu tang 進步黨

Chin-shih 進士

Chin-shih ti-i nü-chieh Lo-lan fu-jen chuan 近世第一女
傑羅蘭夫人傳

Chin-shih ti-i ta che K'ang-te chih hsüeh-shuo 近世第一
大哲康德之學說

Chin-shih wen-ming ch'u-tsu erh ta-chia chih hsüeh-shuo
近世文明初祖二大家之學說

Chin-wen 今文

Ch'in Shih Huang-ti 秦始皇帝

Ching Pao 京報

Ch'ing 清

Ch'ing-i pao 清議報

Ch'ing-nien 青年

Ch'ing-shih kao 清史稿

Ch'ing-tai hsüeh-shu kai-lun 清代學術概論

Ch'iung pien t'ung chiu 窮變通久

Ch'iung tse pien, pien tse t'ung 窮則變變則通

Chou 周

Chou Chan-shu 鄒展書

Ch'ou-an hui 籌安會

Chu 朱

Chu Ch'i-hua 朱其華

Chu Hsi 朱熹

Chu Shou-p'eng 朱壽朋

Ch'u kuei-kuo yen-shuo-tz'u 初歸國演說辭

Chuan wei wei an 轉危為安

Chuang Ts'un-yü 莊存與

Chuang-tzu 莊子

Ch'uang-pan Shih-wu pao yüan-wei chi 創辦時務報
原委記

Ch'un-ch'iu 春秋

Ch'un-ch'iu Chung-kuo i-ti pien-hsü 春秋中國彝狄辨序

Chung wei-hsin hui 中維新會

Chung-hua min-kuo 中華民國

Chung-hua min-kuo k'ai-kuo-ch'ien ko-ming shih 中華民國
開國前革命史

Chung-hua min-kuo shih 中華民國史

Chung-Jih chiao-she hui-p'ing 中日交涉彙評

Chung-kuo chi jo su-yüan lun 中國積弱溯源論

Chung-kuo ch'ien-t'u chih hsi-wang yü kuo-min tse-jen 中國
前途之希望與國民責任

Chung-kuo chih wu-shih-tao 中國之武士道

Chung-kuo chih-min pa ta-wei-jen chuan 中國殖民八大
偉人傳

Chung-kuo chin-tai she-hui-shih chieh-p'ou 中國近代社會
史解剖

Chung-kuo chuan-chih cheng-chih chin-hua shih lun 中國
專制政治進化史論

Chung-kuo fa-li-hsüeh fa-ta shih-lun 中國法理學發達
史論

Chung-kuo hsin-wen-hsüeh yün-tung shu-p'ing 中國新文學
運動述評

Chung-kuo hsüeh-shu ssu-hsiang pien-ch'ien chih ta-shih 中國
學術思想變遷之大勢

Chung-kuo ko-ming shih 中國革命史

Chung-kuo kuo-hui chih-tu ssu-i 中國國會制度私議

Chung-kuo li-kuo ta fang-chen 中國立國大方針

Chung-kuo li-shih yen-chiu fa pu-pien 中國歷史研究法
補編

Chung-kuo min-chu she-hui tang 中國民主社會黨

Chung-kuo pi-chih wen-t'i 中國幣制問題

Chung-kuo pao-hsüeh-shih 中國報學史

Chung-kuo pu-wang lun 中國不亡論

Chung-kuo tao-te chih ta yüan 中國道德之大原

Chung-kuo wan-pu-neng shih-hsing kung-ho lun 中國萬不能
實行共和論

Chung-kuo wei-hsin hui 中國維新會

Chung-shan ch'üan-shu 中山全書

Chung-wai chi-wen 中外記聞

Chung-wai kung-lun 中外公論

Chung-wai kung-pao 中外公報

Chung-wai shih-wen 中外時聞

chü-jen 舉人

Chü-luan shih 據亂世

Ch'üan-hsueh p'ien 勸學篇

Chün-wu yüan 軍務院

fa-chih 法治

Fa-li-hsueh ta-chia Meng-te-ssu-chiu 法理學大家孟德
斯鳩

233

Fei *wei* 非「唯」

Fei-sheng wu-fa 非聖無法

Feng Ching-ju 馮鏡如

Feng Kuo-chang 馮國璋

Feng Tzu-yu 馮自由

Fu Ch'ien 服虔

Fu Liu Ku-yu shan-ch'ang shu 復劉古愚山長書

Fu Liu Mien-i shu lun tui O-men t'i 復劉兔己書論對
　俄門題

Fu-ku ssu-hu p'ing-i 復古思潮平議

Fu-sheng 伏生 (或伏勝)

Fukuzawa Yukichi 福澤諭吉

Han 漢

Han-hsüeh 漢學

Hankow 漢口

Hanlin 翰林

Han-shu 漢書

hao i-p'ang 好依傍

Hirayama Shu 平山周

Ho Hsiu 何休

ho-chi 合集

Hong Kong 香港

Hong Kong Maru 香港丸

Hossō 法相

Hsi-hsüeh shu-mu-piao hou-hsü 西學書目表後序

Hsi-hsüeh shu-mu-piao hsü-li 西學書目表序例

Hsi-shu t'i-yao nung-hsüeh tsung-hsü 西書提要農學
　總序

Hsia-wei-i wei-hsin hui 夏威夷維新會

Hsia-wei-i yu-chi 夏威夷遊記

Hsiang 湘

Hsiang hsüeh hsin-pao 湘學新報

Hsiao-ching 孝經

Hsiao-k'ang 小康

Hsieh Tsan-t'ai 謝讚泰

Hsien-Ch'in cheng-chih ssu-hsiang 先秦政治思想

Hsien-Ch'in cheng-chih ssu-hsiang shih 先秦政治思
　想史

Hsien-fa t'ao-lun hui 憲法討論會

Hsien-fa yen-chiu hui 憲法研究會

Hsien-fa yen-chiu t'ung-chih hui 憲法研究同志會

Hsien-tai Chung-kuo wen-hsüeh shih 現代中國文學
　史

Hsin ch'ing-nien 新青年

Hsin Chung-kuo chien-she wen-t'i 新中國建設問題

Hsin Chung-kuo pao 新中國報

Hsin Chung-kuo wei-lai chi 新中國未來記

Hsin hsiao-shuo 新小說

Hsin hsiao-shuo pao 新小說報

Hsin shih-hsüeh 新史學

Hsin Ying-kuo chü-jen K'o-lin-wei-erh chuan 新英國巨人
克林威爾傳

Hsin-hsüeh tang 新學黨

Hsin-hsüeh wei-ching k'ao 新學偽經考

Hsin-min shuo 新民說

Hsin-min ts'ung-pao 新民叢報

Hsin-ta-lu yu-chi chieh-lu 新大陸游記節錄

Hsing-Chung hui 興中會

Hsinti 新堤

hsiu-ts'ai 秀才

Hsiung Hsi-ling 熊希齡

Hsiung-chia-li ai-kuo-che K'o-su-shih chuan 匃加利愛國者
嗒蘇士傳

Hsü Chi-yü 徐繼畬

Hsü Ch'i-ch'ing 徐寄顧

Hsü Chih-ching 徐致靖

Hsü Ch'in 徐勤

Hsü-lun shih-min yü yin-hsing 續論市民與銀行

Hsüan-t'ung 宣統

Hsüeh-chiao tu-ching wen-t'i 學校讀經問題

hsün-ku tz'u-chang 訓詁詞章

Hsün-tzu 荀子

Hu Shih 胡適

Hu Shih wen-ts'un san-chi 胡適文存三集

Hu Yen-hung 胡衍鴻

Hua-yen 華嚴

Huang Hsing 黃興

Huang Shao-chi 黃紹箕

Huang Tsun-hsien 黃遵憲

Huichow 惠州

Hunan 湖南

Hunan Shih-wu hsüeh-t'ang hsüeh-yüeh 湖南時務
學堂學約

Hunan shou-chiu tang 湖南守舊黨

Huo-pu-shih hsüeh-an 霍布士學案

huo-shih wu-min 惑世誣民

235

Hupei 湖北

I 逸
I-chiao ts'ung-pien 翼教叢編
I-ching 易經
I-ko ch'ih-jen ti shuo-meng 一個瘋人的説夢
I-ta-li chien-kuo san-chieh chuan 意大利建國三傑傳
I-tsai so-wei kuo-t'i wen-t'i che 異哉所謂國體題者
Inukai Takeshi 犬養毅
Itō Hirobumi 伊藤博文
Itō Hirobumi den 伊藤博文傳

Jen K'o-ch'eng 任可澄
Jen-sheng-kuan yü k'o-hsüeh 人生觀與科學
Jih-pen heng-pin Chung-kuo ta-t'ung hsüeh-hsiao yüan-chi
　　日本橫濱中國大同學校緣起
Jih-pen kuo chih hou-hsü 日本國志後序
Jo jou ch'iang shih 弱肉強食
Ju-chia che-hsüeh 儒家哲學
Jüan Yüan 阮元

Kai-yung t'ai-yang-li fa i 改用太陽曆法議
k'ai-ming chuan-chih 開明專制
K'ai-ming chuan-chih lun 開明專制論
Kang-chien i-chih lu 綱鑑易知錄
K'ang Ch'ang-su hsien-sheng nien-p'u kao 康長素先生
　　年譜稿
K'ang Kuang-jen 康廣仁
K'ang Yu-wei 康有為
Kansu 甘肅
Kao I-han 高一涵
Kao-teng ta-t'ung hsüeh-hsiao 高等大同學校
Kashiwara Buntarō 柏原文太郎
Kegon 華嚴
Kiangnan 江南
Kiangsu 江蘇
Kiaochow 膠州
Kinkikan 錦輝館
Ko Kung-chen 戈公振
Ko-kuo hsien-fa i-t'un lun 各國憲法異同論
Ko-ming i-shih 革命逸史
Ko-sheng lan-chu t'ung-yüan shao-shih 各省濫鑄
　　銅元小史

236

K'o-hsüeh ching-shen yü tung-hsi wen-hua 科學精神與東西文化

k'o-hsüeh hsien-sheng 科學先生

K'o-hsüeh yü jen-sheng-kuan 科學與人生觀

Kōbe 神戶

Kokuryūkai 黑龍會

Ku i-yuan k'ao 古議院考

Ku-ling 古嶺

ku-wen 古文

Ku-wen-tz'u lei-tsuan 古文辭類纂

kuan shih-pien che 觀時變者

Kuan-yü hsüan-hsüeh k'o-hsüeh lun-chan chih 'chan-shih kuo-chi kung-fa' 關於玄學科學論戰之「戰時國際公法」

Kuang Ju-p'an 鄺汝盤

Kuang-chih shu-chü 廣智書局

Kuang-hsü 光緒

Kuang-hsü cheng-yao 光緒政要

Kuang-hsü tung-hua hsü-lu 光緒東華續錄

Kuei hsüeh hui 桂學會

Kung-chi K'ang Nan-hai hsien-sheng wen 公祭康南海先生文

kung-chü 公車

Kung-ho chien-she t'ao-lun hui 共和建設討論會

Kung-ho chü-chin hui 共和俱進會

Kung-ho tang 共和黨

Kung-ho ts'u-chin hui 共和促進會

Kung-ho t'ung-i tang 共和統一黨

Kung-shang-hsüeh pao 工商學報

Kung-yang 公羊

K'ung An-kuo 孔安國

K'ung Ying-ta 孔穎達

K'ung-tzu chiang-sheng 孔子降生

K'ung-tzu kai-chih k'ao 孔子改制考

Kuo Chan-po 郭湛波

Kuo wen yü yüan chieh 國文語原解

kuo-chia 國家

Kuo-feng pao 國風報

Kuo-hsing p'ien 國性篇

Kuo-min hsin-cheng she 國民新政社

Kuo-min tang 國民黨

Kuo-nei ta-shih chi 國內大事記

Kuo-t'i chan-cheng kung-li t'an 國體戰爭躬歷談

Kuo-tu shih-tai lun 過渡時代論
Kuwabara Sadamasa 桑原隲藏
Kuzū Yoshihisa 葛生能久
Kwangtung 廣東
Kweichow 貴州

lang-pei 狼狽
Lao-tzu che-hsüeh 老子哲學
Li Chien-nung 李劍農
Li Han-chang 李瀚章
Li hsien-fa i 立憲法議
Li Hung-chang 李鴻章
Li Ping-huan 李炳寰
Li T'ai-po 李太白
Li Tuan-fen 李端棻
Li Yüan-hung 黎元洪
Li-chi 禮記
Li-ching t'ung-lun 禮經通論
Li-shih shang Chung-hua kuo-min shih-yeh chih ch'eng-pai
   chi chin-hou ko-chin chih chi-yün 歷史上中華國民
   事業之成敗及今後革進之機運
Liang Ch'i-ch'ao 梁啓超
Liang Ch'i-ch'ao Shi no *Chung-kuo li-shih yen-chiu fa* wo
   yomu 梁啓超の「中國歷史研究法」を
   讀む
Liang Jen-kung hsien-sheng chuan 梁任公先生傳
Liang Pao-ying 梁寶瑛
Liang T'ieh-chün 梁鐵君
Liang Ting-fen 梁鼎芬
Lieh-chuan 列傳
Lin 林
Lin Kuei 林圭
Liu Feng-lu 劉逢祿
Liu Hsi-sui 劉盼遂
Liu Hsiang Hsin fu-tzu nien-p'u 劉向歆父子年譜
Liu Hsin 劉歆
Liu Kuang-t'i chuan 劉光第傳
Liu K'un-i 劉坤一
Lo-li chu-i t'ai-tou Pien-shen chih hsüeh-shuo 樂利主義
   泰斗邊沁之學說
Lo-su yüeh-k'an 羅素月刊
Lu Hsün 魯迅
Lu Yung-t'ing 陸榮廷

238

Lun chia-shui 論加稅

Lun chiao-yü tang-ting tsung-chih 論教育當定宗旨

Lun Chih-na tsung-chiao kai-ko 論支那宗教改革

Lun Chih-na tu-li chih shih-li yü Jih-pen tung-fang cheng-ts'e
論支那獨立之實力與日本東方政策

Lun chuan-chih cheng-t'i yu pai-hai yü chün-chu erh wu i-li
論專制政體有百害於君主而無一利

Lun Chung-kuo chih chiang-ch'iang 論中國之將強

Lun Chung-kuo hsüeh-shu ssu-hsiang pien-ch'ien chih ta-shih
論中國學術思想變遷之大勢

Lun Chung-kuo jen-chung chih chiang-lai 論中國人動
之將來

Lun Chung-kuo kuo-min chih p'in-ko 論中國國民之
品格

Lun Chung-kuo ts'ai-cheng-hsüeh pu fa-ta chih yüan-yin chi
ku-tai ts'ai-cheng hsüeh-shuo chih i-pan 論中國財政
學不發達之原因及古代財政學說之一斑

Lun chün-cheng min-cheng hsiang-shan chih li 論君政民
政相嬗之理

Lun Fu-chiao yü ch'ün-chih chih kuan-hsi 論佛教與
群治之關係

Lun hsiao-shuo yü ch'ün-chih chih kuan-hsi 論小說與
群治之關係

Lun hsüeh Jih-pen wen chih i 論學日本文之益

Lun hsüeh-shu chih shih-li tso-yu shih-chieh 論學術之
勢力左右世界

Lun li-fa ch'üan 論立法權

Lun min-tsu ching-cheng chih ta-shih 論民族競爭之
大勢

Lun-yü 論語

Ma Ch'en-tung 馬震東

Ma Yung 馬融

Mai Chung-hua 麥仲華

Mai Meng-hua 麥孟華

Mao 毛

Matsukata 松方

Matsukuma 松隈

Mei Tse 梅賾

Mei-shu yü k'o-hsüeh 美術與科學

Meng 孟

Mi-tzu 宓子

Miao 苗

Mieh-kuo hsin-fa lun 滅國新法論
Min Erh-ch'ang 閔爾昌
Min-chu tang 民主黨
min-ch'üan 民權
Min-hsieh hui 民協會
Min-kuo ch'u-nien chih pi-chih kai-ko 民國初年之
　幣制改革
Min-li 民立
Min-pao 民報
Min-she 民社
Ming 明
ming shih hun-hsiao 名實混淆
Ming T'ai-tsu 明太祖
Ming-chi ti-i chung-yao jen-wu Yüan Ch'ung-huan chuan
　明季第一重要人物袁崇煥傳
Ming-Ch'ing chih chiao Chung-kuo ssu-hsiang-chieh chi ch'i
　tai-piao jen-wu 明清之交中國思想界及其
　代表人物
ming-yü 名譽
Miyajima 宮島
Miyazaki Torazō (Tōten) 宮崎寅藏 (滔天)
Mo-ching chiao-shih 墨經校釋
Mo-tzu 墨子
mou-ch'in tien 懋勤殿

Nan hsüeh-hui 南學會
Nan hsüeh-hui hsü 南學會敘
Nan-hai 南海
Nan-hai hsien-sheng wu-hsü tsou-kao 南海先生戊戌奏稿
Nan-hai K'ang hsien-sheng chuan 南海康先生傳
Nanking 南京
Nanning 南寧
Nei Ko 內閣
Nichirō sensō to sekai no heiwa 日露戰爭と世界の平和
Nung-hsüeh pao 農學報
Nurhaci 努爾哈赤

Ōkuma 大隈
Ōkuma Kō hachi-ju-go nen shi hensan kai 大隈侯八十五年
　史編纂會
Ōshima 大島
Ou yu hsin-ying lu chieh-lu 歐遊心影錄節錄
Ou-chou cheng-chih ko-chin chih yüan-yin 歐洲政治革進
　之原因

Ou-chou ti-li ta-shih lun 歐洲地理大勢論

pai-hua 白話
Pan Ch'ao 班超
Pan Ku 班固
Pao-chiao fei so-i tsun K'ung lun 保教非所以尊孔論
Pao-ch'ing 保靖
Pao-huang hui 保皇會
Pao-tung yü wai-kuo kan-she 暴動與外國干涉
Pei-chuan chi pu 碑傳集補
Peiping 北平
Peking 北京
Pen-chi 本紀
Pen-kuan ti-i-pai ts'e chu-tz'u ping lun pao-kuan chih tse-jen
　　chi pen-kuan chih ching-li 本館第一百册祝辭並
　論報館之責任及本館之經歷
Pi Yung-nien 畢永年
pien-fa 變法
Pien-fa t'ung-i 變法通議
P'ing Chung-hsi wen-hua kuan 評中西文化觀
Po-lan mieh-wang chi 波蘭滅亡序
Po-luan 撥亂
P'u-hsüeh 樸學

Saitō 齊藤
San-ju-san nen no yume 三十三年の夢
san-shih 三世
San-shih tzu-shu 三十自述
Shang Nan-p'i Chang-shang-shu shu 上南皮張尚書書
Shang-shu cheng-i 尚書正義
Shang-shu ku-wen shu-ching 尚書古文疏證
Shanghai 上海
Shao I-chen 邵懿辰
Shao-nien Chung-kuo shuo 少年中國說
Shen-lun chung-tsu ko-ming yü cheng-chih ko-ming chih
　　te-shih 申論種族革命與政治革命之得失
Shen-shih Yin-shu hsü 沈氏音書序
sheng erh pu yu, wei erh pu shih 生而不有,爲而不恃
Sheng Hsüan-huai 盛宣懷
Sheng-chi-hsüeh hsüeh-shuo yen-ko hsiao-shih 生計學
　學說沿革小史
sheng-p'ing shih 升平世
Sheng-wu-hsüeh tsai hsüeh-shuo-chieh chih wei-chih 生物學
　在學術界之位置

Shih ku-wei 詩古微

Shih-chi 史記

Shih-chi huo-chih lieh-chuan chin-i 史記貨殖列傳今義

Shih-ching 詩經

Shih-hsüeh nien-pao 史學年報

Shih-hsüeh pao 實學報

Shih-k'o-chai chi-yen chi-hsing hsü 適可齋記言記行序

shih-pien 時變

shih-shih 時事

Shih-shih tsa-lun 時事雜論

Shih-tzu 世子

Shih-wu hsüeh-t'ang 時務學堂

Shih-wu pao 時務報

Shih-wu pao kuan 時務報館

Shimonoseki 下關

Shimpotō 進步黨

Shinagaku 支那學

Shirin 史林

Shu ku-wei 書古微

Shu-ching 書經

Shui hu chuan 水滸傳

Shui-shih hsüeh-t'ang 水師學堂

Shumbō kō tsuijōkai 春畝公追頌會

Shun 舜

Shuo yu-chih 說幼樨

Shuo-ch'ün hsü 說羣序

Ssu-ma Ch'ien 司馬遷

Ssu-shih tzu-shu 四十自述

Su-ch'ih 素癡

Sun Chia-nai 孫家鼐

Sun Yat-sen 孫逸仙

Sung Chiao-jen 宋教仁

Sung Po-lu 宋伯魯

Szechuan 四川

Ta Chung-hua 大中華

Ta Chung-hua fa k'an-tz'u 大中華發刊辭

Ta Chung-hua min-tsu kuo 大中華民族國

Ta mou-pao ti-ssu-hao tui-yü pen-pao chih po-lun 答某報
第四號對於本報之駁論

Ta-feng 大風

Ta-t'ung (place-name) 大通

ta-t'ung 大同

Ta-t'ung hsüeh-hsiao 大同學校

Ta-t'ung i-shu-chü hsü-li 大同譯書局敘例

Ta-t'ung shu 大同書

Tai Chen 戴震

Tai K'an 戴戡

Tai Tung-yüan sheng-jih erh-pai nien chi-nien-hui yüan-ch'i
戴東原生日二百年紀念會緣起

T'ai Hsü 太虛

T'ai-p'ing shih 太平世

Takahashi Kichitarō 高橋橘太郎

T'an Ssu-t'ung 譚嗣同

T'an Ssu-t'ung chuan 譚嗣同傳

T'ang 唐

T'ang Chi-yao 唐繼堯

T'ang Chüeh-tun 唐覺頓

T'ang Hua-lung 湯化龍

T'ang Ts'ai-ch'ang 唐才常

T'ang Yüeh 唐鉞

Tao te ching 道得經

taotai 道台

te-chih 德治

Te-yü chien 德育鑑

Tendai 天台

Ti-li yü wen-ming chih kuan-hsi 地理與文明之關係

Tientsin 天津

t'ien-hsia 天下

Ting Jih-ch'ang 丁日昌

t'o-ku kai-chih 託古改制

Tōa senkaku shishi kiden 東亞先覺志士記傳

Tōkyō 東京

Tōyō no heiwa wo ronzu 東洋の平和を論ず

Tsa-ta mou-pao 雜答某報

Tsai po mou-pao chih t'u-ti kuo-yu lun 再駁某報之土地
國有論

Tsai-chen 戴振

Ts'ai Ao 蔡鍔

Ts'ai Chün 蔡鈞

Ts'an-cheng yüan 參政院

Tseng Kuo-fan 曾國藩

Tseng Lien 曾廉

Tseng-kai tsui-chin Shang-hai chin-jung shih 增改最近
上海金融史

Tso Tsung-t'ang 左宗棠

Tso-chuan 左傳

Tso-kuan yü mou-sheng 作官與謀生

Tso-shih ch'un-ch'iu k'ao-cheng 左氏春秋考證

Tsou Lu 鄒魯

Tsu-kuo ta hang-hai-chia Cheng Ho chuan 祖國大航海家
　　鄭和傳

Tsui-chin san-shih nien Chung-kuo cheng-chih shih 最近
　　三十年中國政治史

Tsui-yen 罪言

Tsungli-yamen 總理衙門

Ts'ung-chün jih-chi 從軍日記

Tu Jih-pen shu-mu-chih shu-hou 讀日本書目志書後

Tu Liang Jen-kung ko-ming hsiang-hsü chih yüan li-lun 讀梁
　　任公革命相續之原理論

Tu Meng-tzu chieh-shuo 讀孟子界說

Tu Yü 杜預

tu-shu 讀書

T'u-shu-kuan-hsüeh chi-k'an 圖書館學季刊

Tuan Ch'i-jui 段祺瑞

tuchun (tu-chün) 督軍

Tui Ou-Mei yu-pang chih hsüan-yen 對歐美友邦之宣言

Tung-nan 東南

Tung-nan Ta-hsüeh k'o-pi kao pieh-tz'u 東南大學課畢
　　告別辭

T'ung-hsüeh pao 通學報

T'ung-i tang 統一黨

T'ung-ting tsui-yen 痛定罪言

T'ung-wen kuan 同文館

Tzu Mo-tzu hsüeh-shuo 子墨子學說

tzu-ch'iang 自強

Tzu-li hui 自立會

Tzu-yu shu 自由書

wai-wu 外務

Wan-kuo kung-pao 萬國公報

Wan-mu-ts'ao t'ang 萬木草堂

Wang An-shih 王安石

Wang Chao 王照

Wang Ching-kung 王荊公

Wang Feng-yüan 王豐園

Wang K'ang-nien 汪康年

Wang Mang 王莽

Wang Su 王肅

Wang Wen-shao 王文韶

Wang Yang-ming 王陽明

Waseda 早稻田

Wei Hu-an ching-kao Ou-Mei p'eng-yu 爲滬案敬告歐美朋友

Wei kai yüeh wen-t'i ching-kao yu-pang 爲改約問題敬告友邦

Wei Yüan 魏源

Wen 文

Wen T'ing-shih 文廷式

wen-yen 文言

Weng T'ung-ho 翁同龢

Wu Chi-ch'ing 吳季青

Wu Ch'i-ch'ang 吳其昌

Wu nien lai chih chiao-hsün 五年來之教訓

Wu-hsü cheng-pien shih fan-pien-fa jen-wu chih cheng-chih ssu-hsiang 戊戌政變時反變法人物之政治思想

Wu-hsü chia-tzu chi-nien hui 戊戌庚子紀念會

Wu-ssu yün-tung shih ti p'ing-chia 五四運動史的評價

Wuchang 武昌

Ya-tien hsiao-shih 雅典小史

Ya-tung t'u-shu-kuan 亞東圖書館

Yamato-damashii 大和魂

Yang Ch'ung-i 楊崇伊

Yang Ch'ü-yün 揚衢雲

Yang Jui chuan 楊銳傳

Yang Ming-chai 楊明齋

Yang Shen-hsiu 楊深秀

Yang T'u 楊度

yang-hsin 養心

Yangtze 楊子

Yano Jinichi 矢野仁一

Yao 堯

Yao Shun wei Chung-kuo chung-yang chün-ch'üan lan-shang k'ao 堯舜爲中國中央君權濫觴考

Yeh Ch'ang-ch'ih 葉昌熾

Yeh Te-hui 葉德輝

Yen Fu 嚴復

Yen Jo-chü 閻若璩

Yen t'ieh lun 鹽鐵論

Yen Yüan 顏元

Yen-chiu 研究

245

Yen-chiu wen-hua shih ti i-ko chung-yao wen-t'i 研究文化史的幾個重要問題

Yen-Li hsüeh-p'ai yü hsien-tai chiao-yü ssu-hu 顏李學派與現代教育思潮

Yenching hsüeh-pao 燕京學報

Yin-ping shih ch'üan-chi 飲氷室全集

Yin-ping shih ho-chi 飲氷室合集

Yin-ping shih ts'ung-chu 飲氷室叢著

Yin-ping shih wen-chi 飲氷室文集

Yin-tu yü Chung-kuo wen-hua chih ch'in-shu ti kuan-hsi 印度與中國文化之親屬的關係

Ying-huan chih-lueh 瀛寰志略

Yokohama 横濱

Yoshida Shin 吉田晉

Yu T'ai-wan shu-tu 游臺灣書牘

Yung-yen 庸言

Yunnan 雲甫

Yü chih ssu-sheng kuan 余之死生觀

Yü Chin-san 余晉珊

Yü Lin Ti-ch'en t'ai-shou shu 與林迪臣太守書

Yü Yen Yu-ling hsien-sheng shu 與嚴幼陵先生書

Yü-pei li-hsien kung-hui 預備立憲公會

Yüan 元

Yüan Chung-huan 袁崇煥

Yüan Shih-k'ai 袁世凱

Yüan T'ai-tsu 元太祖

Yüan-shih tang-kuo shih 袁氏當國史

Yüan-tu-lu jih-chi 綠督廬日記

Yün-ch'ü shu-chü 雲衢書局

ADDENDUM

Chang Po-wang Pan Ting-yüan ho-chuan 張博望班定遠合傳

Ch'en T'ung-sheng 沈桐生

Chih-ch'ih hsüeh-hui hsü 知恥學會敍

Chin-pu tang ni Chung-hua-min-kuo hsien-fa ts'ao-an 近步黨擬中華民國憲法草案

Chin-tai Chung-kuo hsüeh-shu-shih shang chih Liang Jen-kung hsien-sheng 近代中國學術史上之梁任公先生

Chung-kuo Kuo-min tang shih-kao 中國國民黨史稿

Chung-kuo li-shih shang ko-ming chih yen-chiu 中國歷史上革命之研究

Hsin-min i 新民議
Hu-kuo chihi tien-wen chi lun-wen 護國之役電文及
論文

Kuan-tzu 管子
Kuan-tzu chuan 管子傳

Lun Chung-kuo yü Ou-chou kuo-t'i i t'ung 論中國與歐洲
國體異同
Shih chung te-hsing hsiang-fan hsiang-ch'eng i 十種德性相反
相成義
Tai Tung-yüan che-hsüeh 戴東原哲學

Wai-chiao fang-chen chih yen (ts'an-chan wen-t'i) 外交方針芻言
（參戰問題）
Yung Wing (Jung Hung) 容閎
Yüan Shih-k'ai chih chiai-p'ou 袁世凱之解剖

INDEX

Aisin Gioro, 161
Alexander the Great, 68
Allen, Young J., 21n
An Hsiao-fen, 37n
An-fu Clique, 188
Analects, see *Lun-yü*
Annam, 30, 86, 197, 198
Arabs, 126
Aristotle, 129, 158
Athens, Greece, 91, 210
Australia, 68
Austria, 161, 178

Bacon, Francis, 97, 98, 107, 129
Bank of China, 187, 188
Belgium, 189
Bentham, Jeremy, 130, 144, 150-152
Bismarck, Otto von, 118
Bluntschli, Johann, 107, 114n
Board of Ceremonies, 30
Bonaparte, Louis, 104
Bonaparte, Napoleon, 68, 181n
Bosnia and Herzegovina, 178
Boston Tea Party, 70
Bourbons, 159
Boxer movement, 66, 67, 75n, 186, 189
Brazil, 69
Buddhism, 18, 47, 47n, 81n, 94, 129,
    130, 130n, 131, 132, 191, 191n, 195,
    201
Burke, Edmund, 144, 145, 150-152

Canada, 69
Carlyle, Thomas, 105-107
Cavour, Camillo di, 110, 159, 185
Ceylon, 68
Chang, Carsun, *see* Chang Chün-mai
Chang Chi, 78
Chang Ch'ien, 123
Chang Chih-tung, 6-9, 20, 22n, 24, 25,
    59, 67
Chang Chün-mai, 189n
Chang Hsün, 186

Chang Yin-huan, 27, 56n
Chang Yüan-chi, 27
Ch'ang-yen pao, 29n
Che-hsüeh, 190, 191
Che-hsüeh she, 190
Ch'en Pao-chen, 24, 25
Ch'en San-li, 20, 24n
Ch'en Shao-pai, 59, 60
Ch'en Tu-hsiu, 200n, 206n, 207n, 217n
Ch'en T'ung-fu, 17, 18, 35n
Cheng Ho, 124
Cheng Hsüan, 224, 225
Cheng I, 224
Cheng-ch'i hui, 67
Cheng-lun, 78
Cheng-wen she, 77-79
Cheng-wen she hsüan-yen, 77
Ch'i T'iao-tzu, 38
Chia K'uei, 224
Chia-jen ch'i-yü chi, 59
Chiang K'ai-shek, 155
Chiang-hsüeh she, 190
Ch'iang hsüeh-hui, 20, 22, 23, 29n
Ch'iang hsüeh-hui shu-chü, 22n
Ch'iang hsüeh-pao, 22
Ch'ien-Han shu, 16, 138, 224
Chih-tsao chü, 27n
Chih-tu chü, 30
Chin Yüan-ti, 223
Chin-pu tang, 174, 175, 176, 180, 185,
    188n
Chin-wen, 99, 100, 223-225
Ch'in Dynasty, 35, 87, 88, 118, 122,
    124, 137, 194, 206n
Ch'in Shih Huang-ti, 45
China's Destiny, 155
Chinese Maritime Customs Service, 177
Ching-pao, 21, 33
Ching-t'ien system, 195, 209
Ch'ing Dynasty, viii, 36, 59, 80, 94,
    110, 161, 165, 186, 187, 209n, 224,
    225
Ch'ing-hua hsüeh-hsiao, 62, 63

249

Ch'ing-i pao, 60, 62, 63, 68
Chou Chang-shu, 29n
Chou Dynasty, 48n, 85n, 87, 139, 209
Ch'ou-an hui, 179-181
Christianity, 21, 28, 64, 81n, 84, 88, 95, 97, 98, 100, 101, 125n, 130, 150, 166, 210
Chu family, 161
Chu Hsi, 129n, 224
Chuang Ts'un-yü, 225
Chuang-tzu, 119n
Ch'un-ch'iu, 15, 35-37, 39, 46, 87, 118, 224, 225
Chung wei-hsin hui, 68
Chung-kuo hsüeh-shu ssu-hsiang pien-ch'ien chih ta-shih, 83
Chung-kuo min-chu she-hui tang, 189n
Chung-kuo wei-hsin hui, 61
Chung-wai chi-wen, 21
Chung-wai kung-lun, 21n
Chung-wai kung-pao, 21n
Chung-wai shih-wen, 21n
Chü-luan shih, 38-40, 42, 87, 91, 131
Chün-wu yüan, 183, 184
Colombia, 73
Columbus, Christopher, 121, 124
Communism, 5-7, 9, 11, 50, 156, 167-169, 192, 210-212, 213, 214, 217, 218
Condorcet, Marie de, 119
Confucian classics, 2, 7, 8n, 15, 16, 34-37, 38n, 40n, 42, 43, 45, 46, 48n, 51, 83, 84, 87-89, 92, 93, 119, 121, 223-225
Confucianism, 1, 2, 7, 9, 18, 34, 35, 37, 40, 41, 43-49, 50n, 81n, 84, 85, 86-91, 94-96, 98, 99, 100, 119n, 120-124, 129n, 131, 132, 163, 165, 166, 169, 191, 193, 195, 196, 207, 209n, 218, 219, 224
Confucius, 7n, 22n, 34, 35, 37, 38, 40n, 41, 43, 46, 48, 87-89, 94, 95, 98n, 100, 108, 119n, 120-122, 129, 132, 168, 195, 199, 206-218, 223
Copernicus, Nicolaus, 98
Council of State, *see* Ts'an-cheng yüan
Critique of Pure Reason, 129
Cromwell, Oliver, 104, 108

Culturalism, 2, 4, 10, 50, 108-120, 122-128, 131-133, 135, 142, 149, 150, 159, 161, 162, 167, 193, 196, 198

Da Gama, Vasco, 124
Danton, Georges Jacques, 104
Darwin, Charles, 44, 95, 96, 121, 130-132, 150, 203
Democracy, 2, 19, 25, 37, 40, 42, 43-45, 71, 78, 88, 92, 104, 105, 108, 126, 158, 196, 209
Descartes, René, 97, 98, 107, 129
Dewey, John, 190, 209
Donne, John, 201
Driesch, Hans, 190

Egypt, 73, 99, 199
Empress Dowager, *see* Tz'u Hsi
England, 23, 31, 32, 40, 48n, 62, 69, 72, 73, 90, 91, 104-108, 111, 124, 140, 147, 148, 151, 158, 160, 187, 189, 197n, 210
Examination system, 15, 15n, 16-19, 19n, 26, 141

Falkenberg, R. A., 74n, 75n
Feng Ching-ju, 58, 60
Feng Kuo-chang, 179, 188
Feng Tzu-yu, 56, 57, 61
Feudalism, 91, 150, 165
Four Books, 15, 83
France, 23, 28, 40, 48n, 62, 69, 104-07, 148, 151, 156-58, 164, 181n, 187, 189
Fu Ch'ien, 224
Fu-sheng, 223
Fukuzawa Yukichi, 107, 140

Gambetta, Léon, 77
Gandhi, Mohandas K., 3
Garibaldi, Guiseppe, 110, 159
Garnier, Monsignor, 28
General Confucian Association, 196
Geological Society of China, 191n
George, Henry, 77
Germany, 48n, 69, 105, 129, 148, 161, 178, 185, 189, 212
Gerontes, 91n

Gibbon, Edward, 112
Goethe, Johann Wolfgang von, 129
Goodnow, Frank J., 179, 180
Grand Secretariat, *see* Nei Ko
Great Harmony, the, *see* Ta-t'ung
Great Northern Railroad, 73
Great Peace, the, *see* T'ai-p'ing Shih
Greece, 42, 48n, 88, 91, 97, 99, 102, 104, 112, 121, 122, 158
Gustavus Adolphus, 68

Han Dynasty, viii, 16, 35, 36, 123, 223-225
Han Wen-ti, 223
Han Learning, *see* Han-hsüeh
Han-hsüeh, 2, 224, 225
Han-shu, *see* Ch'ien-Han shu
Hankow rising, 26, 66, 67
Hanlin Academy, 21, 27
Hapsburg, the, 159
Harvard University, 70
Hawaiian Islands, 61-67 *passim*
Hay, John, 72
Hegel, Georg Wilhelm Friedrich, 105, 129
Herbart, Johann Friedrich, 129
Hirayama Shū, 56, 57, 59, 66
History of Chinese Political Thought in the Pre-Ch'in Period, 216n
Hobbes, Thomas, 124, 125, 209
Ho Hsiu, 224, 225
Holland, 124
Hong Kong Maru, 64
Hossō sect, 130
Hsi-hsüeh shu-mu-piao i. -hsü, 41
Hsia-wei-i wei-hsin hui, 65n
Hsiang hsüeh hsin-pao, 24, 25
Hsiang hsüeh-pao, see *Hsiang hsüeh hsin-pao*
Hsiao-ching, 119n
Hsiao-k'ang, 38n
Hsieh Tsan-t'ai, 58-60
Hsien-fa t'ao-lun hui, 185n
Hsien-fa yen-chiu hui, *see* Yen-chiu clique
Hsien-fa yen-chiu t'ung-chih hui, 185n
Hsien-yu hui, 175n
Hsin ch'ing-nien, 9, 10, 200n, 214

Hsin Chung-kuo pao, 76
Hsin Chung-kuo wei-lai chi, 79
Hsin Dynasty, 36, 37
Hsin hsiao-shuo, 68
Hsin hsiao-shuo pao, 79
Hsin-hsüeh tang, 188n
Hsin-hsüeh wei-ching k'ao, 35, 36, 37n
Hsin-min shuo, 83, 87n, 88, 112, 116, 121, 148
Hsin-min ts'ung-pao, 68, 69, 77, 82, 136, 199
Hsing-Chung hui, 61, 65, 66
Hsiung Hsi-ling, 24, 176
Hsü Chih-ching, 27, 40n
Hsü Ch'in, 20, 23, 58-61
Hsüan-t'ung, 80, 94, 186, 187
Hsüeh-hai t'ang, 16, 17
Hsün-tzu, 35, 38, 88, 124, 125
Hu Shih, 82, 83, 214, 214n, 215-218
Hu Yen-hung, 77n
Hua-yen sutra, 130
Huang Hsing, 173
Huang Shao-chi, 20
Huang Tsun-hsien, 20, 23-25, 27, 29n, 50n
Hume, David, 129
Hunan Conservative Party, *see* Hunan shou-chiu tang
Hunan shih-wu hsüeh-t'ang, *see* Shih-wu hsüeh-t'ang
Hunan shou-chiu tang, 30, 31
Hungary, 110
Huns, 86
Huxley, Thomas, 82

I-ching, 40n, 43
I-tsai so-wei kuo-t'i wen-t'i che, 179
India, 7n, 8n, 30, 48n, 112, 130, 199, 201
Indo-China, 183
Industrialism, 8, 9, 39, 45, 155n, 165, 169, 211
International Settlement, 22n
Inukai Takeshi, 56, 57, 62, 78
Ireland, 150, 210
Islam, 81n, 161
Italy, 15, 110, 112, 127n, 159
Itō Hirobumi, 55, 56n, 114

James, William, 209

Japan, 10, 19, 23, 27, 28n, 30, 31n, 32, 36n, 40, 43n, 48n, 50, 55-64, 66-68, 73, 74, 76-81, 82, 87, 90, 94, 95, 108, 110, 117, 118, 128, 130, 138, 141, 160, 161n, 176-178, 187, 188n, 189, 198, 201, 212

Japan Chronicle, 81

Jen K'o-ch'eng, 182

Jesuits, 84, 219

Jesus, 100, 121, 125n, 133, 134, 209

Jews, 75, 150

Jung Lu, 62

Jüan Yüan, 16

Jüchen, 86

Kang-chien i-chih lu, 16

K'ang Kuang-jen, 58

K'ang Yu-wei, 2, 17-20, 22, 26, 27, 29, 30-33, 35, 36, 37, 38n, 43n, 55, 56, 57-61, 63, 65-67, 74n, 75n, 77, 79, 80, 82, 88, 93-97, 114, 186, 187, 192

Kant, Immanuel, 129, 129n, 132, 209

Kao-teng ta-t'ung hsüeh-hsiao, *see* Ta-t'ung hsüeh-hsiao

Kashiwara Buntaro, 62

Kegon sect, 130

Kiangnan Arsenal, 17

Kidd, Benjamin, 115

Kokuryūkai, 55n, 57

Korea, 86, 141, 197, 198

Kossuth, Louis, 110

Ku-wen, 35, 223-225

Ku-wen-tz'u lei-tsuan, 16

Kuan-tzu, 124

Kuang Ju-p'an, 58

Kuang-chi shu-chü, 68

Kuang-hsü, 22n, 31, 32, 57, 62, 63, 65, 113

Kuei hsüeh-hui, 20

Kung-chü memorial, 19

Kung-ho chien-she t'ao-lun hui, 174n, 175n

Kung-ho tang, 174n, 175n

Kung-ho ts'u-chin hui, 175n

Kung-ho t'ung-i tang, 175n

Kung-shang hsüeh-pao, 23n

Kung-yang chuan, 35-37, 38n, 40, 99, 224, 225

K'ung An-kuo, 223

K'ung Ying-ta, 223, 224

K'ung-tzu kai-chih k'ao, 35, 37

Kuo-feng pao, 79

Kuo-min hsin-cheng she, 175n

Kuo-min tang, 77n, 78, 165, 173, 174, 176, 186-188, 192, 212n

Lao-tzu, 203, 206

Lattimore, Owen, 157n

Lea, Homer, 74n, 75n

Legalism, 85, 86, 124, 218

Leibniz, Gottfried, 129

Lenin, Nikolai, 212

Li Han-chang, 37n

Li Hung-chang, 37, 56n

Li Ping-huan, 25

Li Po, 16

Li Tuan-fen, 30

Li Yüan-hung, 175, 184, 186-188

Liang-shan, 168, 169n

Li-chi, 38n, 225

Li-yün, 38n

Liang ch'i-ch'ao: as journalist, vii, 9n, 20-25, 29, 59, 60, 62, 68, 69, 77, 81-83, 156n, 178, 179-81, 189, 190; in political life, vii, 19, 20, 22, 26, 27, 30-33, 55-61, 63-73, 74n, 76-80, 85n, 173-190; pedagogy, 18, 20, 22-28 *passim*, 45, 48n, 62, 68, 81, 82, 83, 86, 190; scholarship, vii, 15-18, 34-51, 68, 81, 82, 84, 85n, 86n, 87-169, 190, 191, 193-219; summary of intellectual stages, vii-viii, 1-11, 204, 218

Liang Pao-ying, 15, 16

Liang T'ieh-chün, 59

Liang Ting-fen, 29n

Lin Kuei, 25, 66, 67

Lin Tse-hsü, 70

Liu Feng-lu, 225

Liu Hsiang, 36n

Liu Hsin, 35, 36, 224, 225

Liu K'un-i, 24

Liu Men-i, 210n

Locke, John, 125n, 209

Lu Hsün, 122n
Lu Te-ming, 224
Lu Yung-t'ing, 182, 183
Lun-yü, 46, 206n
Luther, Martin, 95, 97, 98, 107, 209

Ma Hsiang-pei (Father Joseph Ma), 28
Ma Yung, 224, 225
Macbeth, 201
Mackenzie, Robert, 18, 19n, 38
Magna Carta, 90
Mai Meng-hua, 23, 60-62
Malthusian theory, 69
Manchuria, 79, 80
Manchus, the, 19, 31, 56, 59, 80, 94, 110, 124, 158-161, 162, 174, 186
Marat, Jean Paul, 104
Marx, Karl, 212
Marxism, 82n, 169, 210
Matsukata Masayoshi, 56
May Fourth movement, 82, 217
May Thirtieth Incident, 190
Mazzini, Giuseppe, 110, 127n, 159
McKinley, William, 74
Mei Tse, 223
Meiji, 27, 30
Mencius, 7n, 38, 42, 44, 45, 48n, 87, 108, 117, 119n, 120, 139, 199
Miao, 161
Mi-tzu, 38
Michael, Franz, 157n
Middle Ages, 96, 97, 100, 208
Mill, John Stuart, 82, 89
Min-chu tang, 174n, 175n
Min-hsieh hui, 175n
Min-li pao, 80
Min pao, 77, 78, 158
Min-she, 175n
Ming Dynasty, 15, 124, 161, 169, 209n, 224
Ming T'ai-tsu, 45
Miyazaki, Torazō, 56, 57, 66
Mo-tzu, 82, 94, 99n, 125, 133, 134, 209n
Monetary Bureau, 177
Mongolia, 130n
Mongols, 87, 161, 174
Monroe Doctrine, 75, 76

Montesquieu, Charles, 87, 106, 107, 121, 133, 140
Morgan, J. Pierpont, 70
Moses, 121

Nan hsüeh-hui, 25
National Monetary Commission, 177
Nationalism, 2, 4, 65, 108-120, 122-125, 125n, 127-129, 131-137, 140, 142-145, 147-150, 154, 156, 158-163, 167, 168, 175, 190, 191, 193, 194-198, 210
Nationalists, *see* Kuo-min tang
Nei Ko, 29
Nietzsche, Friedrich, 202
Nineteenth Century—A History, 18
North China Herald, 21
Nung hsüeh-pao, 23n
Nurhaci, 161n

O'Connor, Nicholas, 20
Ōkuma Shigenobu, 56, 57, 63, 64
Opium War, 82, 110
Ōshima, 32, 55, 56

Pai-hua, 48n
Pan Ch'ao, 123
Pan Ku, 224
Panama, 73
Panama Canal, 73
Pao-huang hui, 65, 66, 72, 74, 75n, 77, 189n
Peking Gazette, see *Ching-pao*
Peking Society of National History, 191n
Peking Union Medical College, 191n
Peking University, 28n
Persia, 112, 180
Peru, 70
Peter the Great, 30
Philippines, 68, 140
Pi Yung-nien, 66, 67
Plato, 4, 129
Po-lan shih, 38n
Poland, 30, 47n, 48n, 197n
P'u-hsüeh, 224, 225

Reform Movement, 15, 17-33, 50, 51, 55, 57-63, 65-68, 70-74, 75n, 76-82, 84-86, 90-93, 100, 113, 156, 164, 191, 192, 198, 218
Renaissance, 97, 99, 208
Reorganization Loan, 176
Revolution of 1911, 26, 79, 80, 82, 112, 174, 175n, 180, 186
Ricardo, David, 89
Ricci, Mateo, 219
Richard, Timothy, 18-20, 32, 38, 40
Robespierre, Maximilian de, 104
Roland, Mme. Marie Jeanne, 102n, 156
Rome, 15, 42, 48n, 102, 104, 112, 113
Roosevelt, Theodore, 73-75
Rousseau, Jean-Jacques, 106, 107, 125n, 129, 150, 209
Russell, Bertrand, 190, 201, 209
Russia, 6, 23, 31, 40, 47n, 48n, 104, 107, 127, 150, 128, 180, 187, 210, 213

Saitō, 65
Sakyamuni, 199
San-shih, 37-42, 46, 88-91, 94, 100, 169
Science, 2, 3, 15, 18, 23, 37-40, 43, 44, 45, 48, 103, 130, 155, 195, 199, 202-209 passim, 214, 215, 217
Second Revolution, 176
Shakespeare, William, 201
Shameen Massacre, 190
Shang-shu cheng-i, 223
Shang-shu ku-wen shu-ching, 225
Shao I-ch'en, 225
Sheng Hsüan-huai, 24
Sheng-p'ing shih, 38, 39, 87, 91
Shih hsüeh-pao, 23n
Shih ku-wei, 225
Shih-chi, 16, 39n
Shih-ching, 15, 88, 225
Shih-tzu, 38
Shih-wu hsüeh-t'ang, 24, 25, 45, 62, 66
Shih-wu pao, 22-24, 29, 29n
Shih-wu pao kuan, 23, 29n
Shimpotō, 63
Shu Ku-wei, 225

Shu-ching, 43, 223, 225
Shubert, Sam S., 72
Shui hu chuan, 169n
Shui-shih hsüeh-t'ang, 27n
Sinkiang, 79
Six Boards, 30
Six Dynasties, 195
Slavs, 150, 161
Smith, Adam, 98, 106, 150, 209
Social Darwinism, 43n, 44n, 115-17, 119-121, 129, 137, 138, 142, 194, 194n, 202, 203, 203n
Socialist Party, 70
Socrates, 68, 129
Spain, 150
Sparta, 104
Spencer, Herbert, 130, 150
Spring and Autumn Annals, see Ch'un-ch'iu
Ssu-ma Ch'ien, 16, 223
Sun Chia-nai, 20, 28, 29, 30
Sun Te-chang, 61
Sun Yat-sen, 56, 57, 58-61, 65-67, 74n, 76, 77, 81, 156, 159-161, 163n, 173, 176, 184, 187, 192
Sung Chiao-jen, 176
Sung Dynasty, 15, 16, 129, 169, 224
Sung Po-lu, 29, 30
Sweden, 191n
Switzerland, 158

Ta Chung-hua, 178, 197n
Ta-hsüeh, 69n, 88, 89
Ta-li ssu, 24
Ta-t'ung, 38n, 50n, 91
Ta-t'ung hsüeh-hsiao, 62, 67, 68, 87n
Ta-t'ung shu, 37
Tagore, Rabindranath, 190, 201n
Tai Chen, 94, 199n, 209n
Tai K'an, 182
T'ai Hsü, 191
T'aip'ing Rebellion, 15, 110, 156, 164, 166, 168
T'ai-p'ing shih, 38-45 passim, 50n, 87, 91, 129, 138
Taiwan, 79, 80
Takahashi Kichitaro, 56
T'an Ssu-t'ung, 22, 24, 27, 31, 32, 66

T'ang Chi-yao, 182-184
T'ang Chüeh-tun, 20
T'ang Dynasty, 16, 195, 224
T'ang Hua-lung, 185n
T'ang Ts'ai-ch'ang, 25, 26, 66, 67
T'ang Yüeh, 207n
Tao te ching, 203n, 206n
Tendai sect, 130
The Adventures of Sherlock Holmes, 23
The Critique of Pure Reason, 129
The Origin of Species, 204
*The Romance of the Three Kingdoms
   (San-kuo chih yen-i)*, 141
Thebes, 103
Three ages, the, *see* San-shih
Tibet, 130n, 161
Tientsin Manifesto, 190
Ting Jih-ch'ang, 17n
Tolstoy, Leo, 107
Tsai-chen, 81
Ts'ai Ao, 25, 181-183
Ts'ai Chün, 63, 81
Ts'an-cheng yüan, 177, 179
Tseng Kuo-fan, 15, 17n, 49, 121
Tseng Lien, 30, 85n, 86
Tsinghua Research Institute, 190
Tso-chuan, 35, 36, 224, 225
Tso-shih ch'un-ch'iu k'ao-cheng, 225
Tsungli-Yamen, 27
Tu Meng-tzu chieh-shuo, 38, 94
Tu Yü, 224
Tuan Ch'i-jui, 184-188
Tung-nan University, 190, 200n, 201n
T'ung hsüeh-pao, 23n
T'ung-i tang, 174n, 175n
T'ung-meng hui, 77, 173
T'ung-wen kuan, 27n
Turkey, 104, 158, 180
Twenty-one Demands, 177, 178, 179,
   193n
Tzu-li hui, 67
Tz'u-hsi, 26, 31, 32, 55, 57, 62, 63, 72,
   75n, 81

United States, 27, 32, 40, 48n, 61, 64-
   66, 70-74, 75, 76, 107, 114, 127n,
   140, 155n, 158, 189, 195, 201, 210,
   213n

University of Chicago, 73, 157n
Upanishads, 199

Voltaire, François de, 107

Wan-kuo kung-pao, 21
Wan-mu-ts'ao t'ang, 17, 18
Wang An-shih, 82, 93n
Wang Chao, 56, 59
Wang K'ang-nien, 20, 23, 25, 29n
Wang Mang, 36
Wang Su, 224, 225
Wang Wen-shao, 24
Wang Yang-ming, 88, 129
Warring States, period of, 118, 211
Washington, George, 23
Washington Conference, 189, 190
Watt, James, 215
Wei Yuan, 225
Wen T'ing-shih, 20, 20n, 22
Weng T'ung-ho, 20n, 26
Wetenagemot, 69
Whitehead, Alfred North, 4
William of Egmont, 69
Wittfogel, Karl, 157n
World War I, 3, 10, 11, 150, 153, 177,
   185, 186, 189, 198, 202, 203, 212-
   214
Wu Chi-ch'ing, 29n
Wu-hsü chia-tzu chi-nien hui, 77n

Yale University, 70
Yang Ch'ung-i, 22
Yang Ch'ü-yün, 60
Yang Ming-chai, 216n
Yang Shen-hsiu, 30
Yang Tu, 179
Yao and Shun, 37, 92, 138, 196, 209
Yeh Te-hui, 85n
Yen Fu, 42n, 82, 203
Yen Jo-chü, 225
Yen Yüan, 7n, 94
Yen-chiu Clique, 185, 187, 188, 189n
Yen-Li school, 7n
Yen-t'ieh lun, 85, 86
Yin-ping shih ch'üan-chi, 68
Ying-huan chih-lüeh, 17

Yung Wing, 32
Yung-yen, 178
Yunnan Revolt, 25, 181-184
Yü Chin-san, 37n
Yü-pei li-hsien kung hui, 79

Yüan Ch'ung-huan, 124
Yüan Shih-k'ai, 20, 25, 62, 66, 173, 174, 175n, 176, 178-181, 182-184, 193n, 194n
Yüan T'ai-tsu, 45